Whether single or married, yo… vulnerability and biblical perspective, for those who suffer, is a breath of fresh air in a world full of trials and challenges.

— ***Cami Oetman,*** **Vice President, AWR**

My wife and I have known Melody for many years. She is a deeply spiritual person who loves God and serves Him faithfully. She is also our friend and prayer partner. In this new book, Melody makes herself vulnerable as she shares behind-the-scenes glimpses of her personal life, her struggles, and her joy. I encourage you to read this book. It will help you navigate through the tough challenges you might face and draw you closer to God.

— ***Pavel Goia,*** **editor, Ministry Magazine; author of *In the Spirit and in Power***

With compassion and authenticity, Melody Mason reaches to where we hurt. My Single Joy! exposes the storms of life, where we discover a God who loves us enough to walk beside us in the darkness, while leading us to the Light. Honest, biblical, and practical, this is a must-read for anyone who has experienced life. Truly transformational.

— ***Jill Morikone,*** **Vice President, Three Angels Broadcasting Network**

Thank you, Melody, for this book! To be honest, I thought it was going to be a powerful read just for single women. But I was wrong. As I have been reading page by page through My Single Joy!, I found myself amazed again and again at how it spoke to my own heart, as a child of God in need of answers. It has helped me gain fresh clarity with issues that I have been questioning God about. My Single Joy! also opened my eyes to many real and practical ways to be more intentional and intimate in my relationship with my Lord and Saviour. I highly recommend this book! Reading it will make your heart sing for joy.

— ***Gem Castor,*** **ASAP Ministries Prayer Missionary**

April and I witness the hand of God on Melody as she calls His people to pray. This is her holy passion and the cry of her soul. In My Single Joy!, Melody takes her readers to a new level as she shares her heart as a single. You will travel with her through her trauma and triumph, her pain and her peace. Through the pages of this powerful book Melody invites you to rest in Jesus as your complete Joy. This is not her theory. This is her life! No matter your life season, you will be inspired and encouraged to live each moment with the joy of Jesus, something that no one can ever take away from you!

— ***Don and April MacLafferty,* In Discipleship Ministries**

Reading Melody's book brought a flood of emotions to my heart. I absolutely loved it, and often found my eyes watering as I read. It's encouraging and relatable, meeting us right where we are in our journey. The Bible passages and thoughts shared are amazing, timely, and healing to the heart. I am thrilled to recommend this book.

— ***Luba Calculli,* Radio Faith FM, Australia**

Do you sometimes struggle, wondering why God doesn't always answer your heartfelt prayers in the way or timing you would want? Melody's new book, MY SINGLE JOY!, tackles this tough topic and much more. Filled with motivating stories, deep insights, and inspired teaching, this book is extremely practical and helpful for coping with life's difficult seasons. Read it, and not only will you grow in your trust relationship with Jesus, but we believe you will also experience peace and, best of all, beautiful joy.

— ***Jerry and Janet Page,* General Conference Ministerial Association, Retired**

Tears filled my heart and eyes while reading this book. It is so beautiful, so inspired, so real. It is obvious that God has placed His hand on the writing of this book. In MY SINGLE JOY!, Melody braves many of the beautiful and painful truths found in navigating love, relationships, heartbreak, and healing. Combined with many true stories and a rich abundance of Scripture, this book will not only show you God's design for true love, it will draw you to Him in a deeper way. I wish young adults everywhere would read this book.

— ***Kendra Miranda,* Graduate Student, Assistant, Central California Conference Youth and Young Adult Department**

My Single JOY!

Finding Peace and Purpose
in the Middle of Life's Difficult and Solitary Seasons

By Melody Mason

My Single JOY!

Finding Peace and Purpose
in the Middle of Life's Difficult and Solitary Seasons

By Melody Mason

Safeliz

Title: My Single Joy!
Subtitle: Finding Peace and Purpose in the Middle of Life's Difficult and Solitary Seasons
Author: Melody Mason

Project Design – Editorial Safeliz
CEO: Mario Paulo Martinelli
CFO: Sergio Mato Rhiner
Editing: Tompaul Wheeler and Melody Mason
Cover Design and Layout: Sara Calado
Cover photo: Scenic photos on front and back cover, taken by Raluca Ril, during a surprise hiking trip to Switzerland for Melody in 2023. Melody believes this trip was God's special gift to her for her 30th anniversary of waiting on Him! (Lam 3:25)

Editorial Safeliz, S. L. · Pradillo, 6 · Pol. Ind. La Mina
E-28770 · Colmenar Viejo, Madrid, Spain · Tel.: [+34] 91 845 98 77
contact@safeliz.com · www.safeliz.com

ISBN: 978-84-10361-10-2

August 2024

PRINTED IN CHINA
IMP23

All quotations from Ellen G. White are taken from the White Estate website at https://egwwritings.org

To My Best Friends

Valerie Crosier | Julia O'Carey | Season Smith

Vanessa Thiel | Gem Castor

Thank you for walking beside me through the ups and downs of life's changing seasons. Thank you for bringing me such joy in your friendship. Each one of you have also experienced your own personal journey with suffering and heartache, and yet you continue to radiate the love and joy of Jesus to all those around you. What a testimony! I love you, my precious friends. "How can [I] thank God for you! Because of you [I] have great joy as [I] enter God's presence" (1 Thess 3:9, NLT).

Secondly:
To all those who are searching for true love
To anyone walking through difficult and solitary seasons
To those who feel spiritually weak, but long to be strong

Don't give up! God is with you, and He loves you more than you can imagine!

"And He said to me, 'My grace is sufficient for you, for My strength is made perfect in weakness.' Therefore most gladly I will rather boast in my infirmities, that the power of Christ may rest upon me." (2 Cor 12:8-9)

Table of Contents

Acknowledgements and Gratitude!

"All the paths of the LORD are mercy." Psalm 25:10

Where do I even begin? As I complete the writing of this book, my heart overflows with gratitude and thanksgiving first for **my best friend Jesus**. Truly He is good, and He is my joy and song even in the midst of the difficult solitary seasons. Thank You Lord, for not always answering my prayers in the way I hoped and prayed. Thank You for instead giving me an amazing testimony of Your faithfulness to share. Truly, Your paths are mercy, and You know best! I can't wait for the day I get to run into Your arms and see You face to face. Thank You that You are coming soon to take us home!

Now to my family, friends, and ministry colleagues. First off: I'm so thankful for my precious parents, who continue to support me and stand by my side as I work and write for God's glory. **Mom and Dad**, thanks for loving me, for praying for me, for supporting me, for reading my rough drafts, and for enduring yet another writing marathon where I have often gone MIA (missing-in-action) from life on the farm. I couldn't do what I do in ministry without you! I love you!

I also must give a heartfelt thank you to my two adopted uncles, **John** and **Dick Graves**, who live with our family and are a great support to me personally behind the scenes. They have both walked their own silent journey with suffering, yet, despite their personal heartache and losses, at 84 and 81 years of age, they continue to joyfully serve. Not sure what we would do without them. The Bible says in Acts 20:35, "It is more blessed to give then to receive." They live this promise, and I am forever grateful.

Next, I'd like to give an extra special shout-out to my mentors **Jerry** and **Janet Page**, who continue to believe in me, encourage me, and who faithfully pray for me. Janet once told me, "Melody, I have found over and over that when we see hope, when we see a prayer that looks like it's going to be answered, there will be a death to the hope. But then God in His miraculous way brings the answer." How true those words are! Thank you, Janet, for this encouragement. Thank you both for inviting me to help with the General Conference Revival and Reformation prayer initiatives. Thanks for being a sounding board through many years of ministry, through heartbreaks, and also through the writing of three books—including this one. Although you have now retired, and I miss you so much, your friendship, mentorship, and prayers continue to make a huge difference in my life. I am forever grateful.

My friends and prayer partners, **Don** and **April MacLafferty**, also deserve a very special thank you. They have literally prayed me through the writing of *this book*, one chapter at a time. Thank you both for your many timely prayers on my behalf, for challenging me to a deeper walk with Jesus, and for encouraging me in my God-given mission. Thank you, April, for the meaningful Bible promises you text me each day. Thank you, Pastor Don, for taking time out of your very busy schedule to help me write "Thirty Days of Joy" in Appendix 7. I know your Holy Spirit-led inspiration will help many take this message deeper.

I'm also grateful to **Donnie** and **Connie Jones**, **Mike** and **Sherl Fenton**, **Vitalik Shablovsky**, **Mark Ringwelski** and **Susan Slikkers**, **Richard** and **Cynthia Spears**, **Scott Anderson**, **Susan Peña**, **Edith Kiggundu**, **Carlyle Verne**, **Naomi Dufrane**, **Barbara Wear**, **Lynne Macias**, **Danielle Beaudette**, as well as the many additional members of the ***In Discipleship*** team whom I have grown to love like family. Thank you for all your prayers for this book and for being such amazing ministry partners and encouragers.

Shiloh Howard, thanks for helping me make the final editing touches on this book. What a blessing. Thanks also for joining me on a journey of faith, as we serve Jesus together. You are an answer to prayer.

The following special people also deserve mention: **The Popcorn Girls—Marisa Ferreira**, **Rita Burjan**, **Nora Turner**, and **Daniela Popa**, who late one night in June of 2014, during a mutual friend's wedding weekend in Romania, allowed me to bare my soul about my single journey. I think *it was that night* when I first realized I needed to write a book about trusting God in the midst of quiet suffering. Now, ten years later, *My Single Joy!* is finally written. My thanks to **Rebecca Eller** and **Yvonne** and **James Hunt** who also encouraged me to start writing this book, while I was visiting their farm in Montana in the summer of 2022; **Teri Salvador** for her many prayers, spiritual encouragement, and partnership on our Africa adventures; **Adina Lupu** for her enthusiasm over every chapter, which kept me wanting to write more; **Frank Fournier** for praying for me through my challenging times; and **Valerie Crosier**, **Julia O'Carey**, **Season Smith**, **Cindy Magan**, **Gem Castor**, **Raluca Ril**, **Sarah Stefan**, **Pavel Goia**, **Rob Farinholt**, **Melissa Miranda**, **Karen Glassford**, **Kendra Miranda**, **Brian** and **Karen Holland**, **Jill Morikone**, **Luba Calculli**, **Cami Oetman**, and **Dawn Moffit** for their precious friendship, for reading different chapters, and for giving me honest input.

Thank you, **Ramon** and **Aurora Canals**, for trusting me and for your humble godly leadership at the General Conference. Thank you also for spearheading "Back to the Altar" for our world church. I'm excited for what God is doing all around the world as people are learning afresh what it means to be a daily disciple of Jesus. I'm excited to include some of the concepts of "Back to the Altar" in this book.

Mario Martinelli, thank you for your patience with me and for believing in me, and for helping make this book a reality with *Safeliz* Publishing house. Every step of this journey working with you and your team has been a blessing. I also loved the time I got to spend with you and your wife Liliam in Madrid. Hearing your testimonies of God's leading was so inspiring. Thank you for taking such good care of me.

Finally, last but not least, a heartfelt thank you to my many readers. While I may not know your names, remember I wrote this book for *you.* As you read this book, may Jesus truly become your strength, your joy, and your song.

INTRODUCTION

Summer Storms

"To everything there is a season, a time for every purpose under heaven... He has made everything beautiful in its time." Ecclesiastes 3:1, 11

As I write the introduction to this book, another summer is in full bloom here in the Ozark Mountains of Arkansas, and everything is vibrant green. I love summers on the farm with my family. Although I've traveled to many amazing and beautiful places around the world (54 countries and counting now), I've come to realize that there's just no place quite like *home.*

Besides being here with my family, I love many things about living on the farm. I love the beautiful music of the morning songbirds at dawn, and the steady buzz of the crickets and cicadas as they chirp their hearts out at dusk. I love the brilliant stars of the Milky Way galaxy that I can see in the night sky, without any light pollution to distract. I love eating home-cooked meals made with food grown in our own garden. I love hiking our trails or sitting down for quiet time with God beside our lake. Our home in the country has become my sanctuary. Here, hidden away from the chaotic bustle of a stressed-out, going-crazy world, I find a refuge. I find rest and peace.

However, today our peaceful sanctuary was rudely interrupted. A few hours ago two unexpected hailstorms hit our farm only fifteen minutes apart. I've never seen such large hail before. The hail came down so unexpectedly, so suddenly, and with such violent force, it almost felt *apocalyptic* in nature as it covered our ground like rocky snow.

"God, please save my mom's garden!" I began to pray earnestly. "Please stop the hail!"

The hail didn't stop falling, and I didn't stop praying. Just when I thought the storm was over, a second, more violent hailstorm hit. I knew that without a miracle everything in the garden would be destroyed.

Finally, after what seemed like *forever*, all was calm again. Quickly I ran to the garden to see the damage. Just as I feared, my mom's beautiful vegetable garden—the garden that was supposed to feed our family over the entire summer—lay in tattered ruins, nearly destroyed. I wanted to cry as I looked around at the massive devastation everywhere.

"God, why didn't you stop the hailstorm?" I asked silently as I surveyed the damage. Then a flicker of hope came into my heart.

"Well, the garden may be destroyed, but I know You have the power to bring a destroyed garden back to life!" I prayed. "You said in Psalm 107:20 that You sent Your Word and healed them and delivered them from their destructions. Thank You for healing and resurrecting our garden from this hailstorm!"

My friend, have you ever faced an unexpected and devastating storm? I'm not talking about a hailstorm. I'm talking about a life storm.

Perhaps you had dreams and plans for your life, and your garden of joy was growing strong, when *a sudden and unexpected storm* hit your life. Maybe the storm was so fierce and strong that all you could do was hold on and cry as you watched your dreams turn into tattered ruins.

Or maybe you haven't faced one big disastrous storm, but you've felt your joy slowly slipping away over the years, drained by life's many hurts, disappointments, and unanswered prayers. Maybe you are just overwhelmed with weariness from the daily spiritual battles, or discouraged by deep soul-loneliness that only gets worse with the passing of time.

I don't know your life story or your heart cry, *but God does.* I don't know where you are in your faith journey, *but He does.* I don't know your past or your future. I don't even know your name, *but He does.* He not only knows your name, but You are the apple of His eye! (See Zech 2:8.) And He wants to give you peace in the middle of your storm.

The Bible tells us, "For I know the thoughts that I think toward you, says the LORD, thoughts of peace and not of evil, to give you a future and a hope" (Jer 29:11).

Let me assure you, even if God seems silent, He is still with you. He has not forgotten or forsaken you. He never will. And He has a distinct and special purpose for your life *right now,* right in the middle of the life season wherever you are.

As I once read, "God sees more than your mistakes, more than your pain. He sees your possibility, the height to which you may attain." And He is still on the throne, even in the middle of the storm.

I don't have a perfect life story. There are times when I've been very broken, and times I haven't done very well weathering life's storms. I'm going to share some of those stories in this book. I've also walked through times where my life was nothing but a dry, desolate wilderness, and I wondered if there was any reason to hope. However, no person or situation is beyond hope. Perhaps that's why I love the promise of Ezekiel 36:35 so much.

> So they will say, "This land that was desolate has become like the Garden of Eden; and the wasted and desolate, and ruined cities are now fortified and inhabited."

God loves to work miracles in lives destroyed by sin. He loves to bring barren, dry desolate gardens into fruitful blossom. I want a "Garden of Eden" life story—a story that overflows with the goodness of God. How about you?

Time to Talk Heart to Heart

If you've read my previous books, this book isn't going to be quite like anything I've written before. While I'll talk about answered prayer, my main focus will be on how to trust God even when He doesn't answer our prayers in the way we might hope. While I will share fresh principles on how to live by God's Word, my greater emphasis will be on how to hold on to the Author of that Word—even in the middle of life's storms.

The Bible tells us, "To everything there is a season, a time for every purpose under heaven... He has made everything beautiful in its time" (Ecl 3:1, 11).

Have you had difficult seasons? Can you testify of God's goodness through those seasons?

If you long to sit down and talk heart-to-heart with someone about real life issues, about navigating tough disappointments, about dealing with loss, or about simply finding peace and purpose in the middle of life's difficult and solitary seasons, *My Single Joy!* is going to be a good book for you to read. While this book is not going to be an exhaustive work on the topic of joy, it is my story of how Jesus has faithfully led me through my own difficult seasons, and how He is leading me still.

A few years ago, God impressed me that it was *time* to be bold and share the story of the bitter-sweet solitary season I've walked through as a single for over four decades now. I have to be honest. I didn't really want to write this book! I still don't. My story, while not overly dramatic, is a story of finding peace and joy in the midst of silent suffering. The reality is, I still dream of finding true love. Because of this, I would prefer to wait to share my story until *after* I have found my miracle man. That's why I keep telling myself, "Just wait a little bit longer. Just wait until you have your godly prayed-for-husband by your side. Then you can tell the world more of your story."

Perhaps there is also a subtle fear in my heart that if I develop a ministry for those walking through solitary seasons, God will keep me single forever.

However, God has been convicting me to put all these thoughts and fears aside as He keeps urging me: "Melody, it's time to write! Don't worry about your current relationship status. Don't worry if everything in your life is in order. Don't think about the future. Just share about My faithfulness in the middle of your story, while you are still in the trenches, while you are still battling the storms. Don't write as one who has arrived or who has discovered all the answers. Write as one who has discovered My perfect peace and joy in the middle of those difficult and solitary seasons!"

So, that is what I'm going to do with this book!

While my goal will always be to lift your heart to Jesus and the abundant joy He alone can bring, let me assure you that I have no intention of spiritualizing away or downplaying the human longings, desires, frustrations, or difficulties we often experience in our solitary seasons. I will be candid and real. After all, life isn't always pretty, and holding on to one's faith and joy isn't always easy. But it is possible—with God all things are possible!

While I will be real about life's struggles, I will also be real about what it means to have an ongoing love story with Jesus. After all, Jesus is the One who gives me joy and purpose in my journey, even when life is messy. It is His love that gives me passion for living, for serving, and for opening my heart with honest, raw vulnerability in this book. My love story with Jesus has changed my life forever! I believe His love will change your life too.

Of course, behind every beautiful love story, there's always a backstory. And behind every triumphant mountaintop victory, there's always a steep climb filled with many prayers, tears, sweat, blisters, and often much passing of time. This book is my personal backstory. It's also my continuing faith story. While I will address a lot of issues that singles face, this book is not just for those who are single or alone. It's for anyone walking through the refiner's fire—and that pretty much includes all of us.

Walking in a love relationship with Jesus is not just a nice-sounding spiritual theory. Jesus wants to be our companion every day, and in every season, through both good times and bad. He loves to celebrate our joys with us. He also walks with us through life's sorrows.

But you know the times when I think Jesus is especially close? It's the times we are walking through the fire.

Truth be told, I don't relish the refiner's fire. You probably don't either. But it's a necessary part of the spiritual maturing process. As one author states, "We like to experience the benefits and blessings of suffering, without actually suffering. We admire other's stories of grace through the fire, but we want our own stories to be fireproof. But God loves us too much to let us have that kind of life."[1]

Maybe you are walking through some fiery trial right now. Maybe you are unsettled by the changing times in which we live, and you are feeling in need of fresh peace, a peace that will carry you through life's storms. No matter your circumstances, it is my prayer that this book will inspire you with fresh hope and revive your "garden of joy" once again.

Speaking of gardens—you want to know what happened to my mom's garden? It has been nearly seven months now since I wrote the first draft to the introduction of this book, and we are currently entering the winter season of snow and ice. My writing had to be put aside for many months, due to work and ministry responsibilities. So now, as I pick up this book again, I have to tell you about the goodness of God.

Would you believe that God heard our prayers and brought our tattered garden back to life? It didn't happen instantly, but with time, He fulfilled His promise in Psalm 107:20. He revived what had been destroyed. Our garden produced such a big harvest this past summer that we could hardly keep up with it: Tons of summer squash, cucumbers, peppers, potatoes, zucchini, boxes of butternut, and more than fifty watermelons. It's early December as I'm writing now, and we are still eating fresh tomatoes that have just finally ripened from this summer's garden. We've never had such a large crop. What an awesome God we serve!

My friend, God is in the business of rebuilding what has been destroyed by life's fiery storms. He is in the business of restoring the dreams that we thought were lost. And He can restore shattered hearts just like He can restore destroyed gardens. God's Word tells us, "For the LORD will comfort Zion, He will comfort all her waste places; He will make her wilderness like Eden, and her desert like the garden of the LORD; Joy and gladness will be found in it, Thanksgiving and the voice of melody" (Isa 51:3).

Whatever your wilderness or waste places, He wants to turn those places into gardens of abundant joy.

So, if you are hungry for more of Jesus and looking for a friend for your journey through life's fiery trials, then buckle up your seatbelt, and let's get started. I don't have all the answers to life's perplexities and sorrows, but I know the One who does. And He promises, "Weeping may endure for a night, but joy comes in the morning" (Ps 30:5).

And our morning is coming!

CHAPTER 1

Two Years, Ten Years, Twenty, Thirty

"I am weary with my groaning; All night I make my bed swim; I drench my couch with my tears." Psalm 6:6

"God, what are you doing?" I cried, as I struggled to keep my eyes on the road.

"You created me to be a wife, to work beside a godly man in ministry. You promised to grant the desires of my heart. But I've been waiting for years, *years now,* and still, there's no one! Every man I pray for walks away, almost as if I'm invisible. Is there something wrong with me?"

Tears poured down my face. I was alone, driving from Cheyenne, Wyoming, heading south on I-25 towards Denver, Colorado. But I was crying so hard, I could barely see the road.

My soul felt like a dry, destitute wilderness, matching the dry, desert prairie land flying by my windows. And yet, even in the midst of my sorrow, the Holy Spirit's gentle voice tugged quietly at my heart.

"Are you willing to surrender your hopes of love to Me? Are you willing to let Me choose the man in my own time and way, if I decide it's best?"

It wasn't the first time I'd had this conversation over surrender with the Lord. In fact, over the years I'd asked God many times to be the Author of my love story and to choose for me. I wanted Him to be my matchmaker, but for some reason, He never seemed in a big hurry to get the job done.

I pulled a tissue out of a box, that I'd conveniently tucked under the seat, and blew my nose loudly as I thought back over the many years I had waited and prayed.

My romantic dreams began quite young. I started dreaming about my Prince Charming when I was only five years old. I started planning my wedding not long after. By the time I was ten, I had my life all figured out. I would finish high school, marry my childhood best friend (just as my parents had done), and the two of us would go off into the sunset to serve the Lord together. We'd be so happy.

Well, as it turned out, life did not go according to my little girl plans. I experienced my first heartbreak at thirteen, when a guy I had a crush on failed to return my affections. I had a bigger disappointment a few years later with someone else. However, by the time I started my senior year in academy, a beautiful dream was beginning to take shape in my heart and mind. There was one young man whom my parents had been talking to me about for many years. *Maybe he will be the one,* I thought. I wasn't sure, but I started praying earnestly for my future husband, determined to wait and save myself for God's perfect plan.

One year of praying stretched into two. Two years stretched into five. I graduated from high school and then from college. I went to Bible school in Norway, and then to various mission fields. Adventures began to pile up as my parents and I continued to wait and pray.

Ten years into praying, I experienced the most devastating heartbreak of my young adulthood as I watched the "prayed for man" walk another way. While he chose to marry a beautiful, godly woman, whom I also loved and admired (she was a dear friend, and I even had the privilege of being a bridesmaid in their wedding), deep down I felt betrayed and abandoned by God.

"God, how could You let me hope and wait and pray all those long years, if he wasn't the one You had for me?" I cried again and again. "What's the point of praying and claiming all Your promises, if You're just going to do whatever You're going to do anyway?"

As time moved on, I struggled to hold on to my faith. After all, I had waited and prayed faithfully, not for one year or two years or five, but for almost a decade. During those long years I wouldn't even consider anyone else. Now my world had turned completely upside down, and I was broken—broken spiritually, emotionally, mentally, and even physically.

For the next year I fell into such deep depression that at times I didn't even want to go on living. But God did not give up on me during those dark months, even though I temporarily gave up on Him. He took the dreams I thought were shattered and began to build a better love story for His purpose and His glory.

I still remember one of the darkest days, before I came out of the depression, and how God tenderly showed me His great love.

I had gone for a long walk outside in the rain without an umbrella. I didn't even want to live. Tears were streaming down my face, and I was soaked, but I didn't care. I felt completely hopeless. I knew I didn't deserve God's grace and mercy. I just wanted to give up, to end it all.

"God, do You still have a plan for me? Can You still do something beautiful in my life?" I silently cried.

As I prayed that brief prayer, the first real prayer I'd prayed in some time, the dark clouds above me parted. Sunshine streamed down all around me in a large warm circle of love. I stopped and looked up in awe at the beautiful sunshine. As I did, I felt fresh hope shining into my broken, bleeding heart.

"Does that mean yes?" I asked God, as a faint glimmer of faith began to grow.

Just then the promise of Hebrews 10:35 came to my mind. I had memorized the verse years before: "Cast not away your confidence which has great recompense of reward."

"Melody," I heard God's gentle voice whispering. "If you give up now, you'll never know what beautiful plans I have in store for your life. Don't you want to see what I have prepared for you in the years ahead?"

God's question startled me. I knew it was Him speaking. I wept fresh tears as I realized He had not forsaken me. He still had something good planned for my life. Despite my seeming failures, my story wasn't over.

My friend, your story isn't over either, no matter what you are going through. If you think you've completely blown God's plan for your life, know this. You are not that powerful! God can create beauty out of any messed-up story. He tells us in His Word, "To appoint unto them that mourn in Zion, to give unto them beauty for ashes, the oil of joy for mourning, the garment of praise for the spirit of heaviness; that they might be called trees of righteousness, the planting of the LORD, that He might be glorified" (Isa 61:3).

You may feel so broken that you believe nothing good can come out of your life, but God isn't done writing your story, and He has a beautiful way of healing broken hearts.

As I began to turn my heart back to God, He began giving me beauty for ashes. He started to fulfill His promise of giving me the oil of joy for mourning, and the garment of praise for the spirit of heaviness. While the process was slow and gradual, my dry desolate wilderness began to blossom as the rose as God brought me back to spiritual life and set my feet again on solid ground.[1]

Unanswered Prayers and More Disappointments

As I continued driving south through the Wyoming prairie, my tears began to dry. I smiled to myself with fresh awe and wonder. I thought back over the years of how God had delivered me from tha pit of depression and despair, and how He had blessed in the years since I turned my heart back to Him.

"God, thank You for how You revived my heart and renewed my relationship with You all those years ago," I prayed. "Thank You that You didn't answer my prayers the way I hoped back then!"

But then, I thought about the next man and the next big heartbreak.

The next man and I had worked together in ministry even more extensively than the first. Along with other ministry teammates, we had traveled thousands of miles together in overseas missions. We had preached dozens of sermons together and had been on many amazing, exciting adventures. He was a wonderful friend and confidant, and once again everything seemed to be matching up in the romantic department. So, I eagerly prayed, waited, and prayed some more. Then, at long last, he too walked away and married another. Again, I was devastated. I had faithfully waited and prayed another eight long years.

However, this time I did not lose my faith or my grip on God. God was my foundation, and I was firmly rooted in His Word. So, instead of giving up in despair, I praised Him for *finally* making His will clear. But with fresh tears and questions, I cried out to Him once more, "Do You still have a beautiful love story for me?"

I knew that God could write the best love story if I let Him. I had watched Him do it for many others. When friends married, I rejoiced with them, and I stood up in their weddings, more weddings than I can count. But I was still just a bridesmaid, never a bride.

"Have You forgotten about me, Lord?" I sometimes prayed, as silent tears would slide down my cheeks.

"Just trust Me and be patient!" was all He would say.

And so I went on praying, went on claiming the promises, and went on hoping that maybe, just maybe, someday, there would be a love story for me too.

Twenty years went by, then twenty two. I kept praying and surrendering, praying and surrendering, as I sought to serve the Lord, throwing my heart into full-time ministry. Twenty five years passed, bringing more heartaches and even some ill-fated marriage proposals. But God knew best, and He strengthened me to move on.

I kept waiting and praying, asking God to take all my prayers of the years and make them effective for the right man, *His man,* wherever he was. I believed deep in my heart that God still had someone special out there for me. And I was determined that no matter how long it took for God to bring us together, I would faithfully wait and keep praying. But after many disappointed hopes and a trail of broken dreams and rejected love, my faith in God's matchmaking skills was starting to wear a little thin.

"What a blessed life you live," people would sometimes say. "You are free to go wherever God calls and do whatever you want without worrying about the responsibilities of a husband or family." Their attempts at encouragement didn't help.

Yes, I loved serving Jesus, and my relationship with Him was sweeter because of all the heartache of the years. My single journey had pressed me deeper into His arms. And I loved the freedom I had to serve Him. But I still longed to get married. Did the two have to be mutually exclusive?

Trusting God in the Middle of the Story

So, what are we to do when God doesn't seem to hear our deepest heart cries? What are we to do with unanswered prayers and closed doors? I know I'm not the only one who has wrestled with these hard life questions. I hear from people all the time dealing with heartache and difficult life challenges, some more painful than I can comprehend.

I also get a lot of messages from singles around the world, struggling with waiting on God in the midst of their difficult and solitary seasons. Knowing that I share on the topic of prayer, they write me earnestly, "Miss Melody, I really want to get married. Can you please pray for me?" I can't tell you how many such messages I have received.

Recently, I received a message from a young woman from Chile. She wrote:

> I am going through a difficult situation that has broken my heart. When I started the relationship, everything indicated to me that it was the will of God, until we broke up. A few months ago, God told me to wait for him as we will get back together. But now I despair, as God is not answering my prayer. I have read in your book

that He answers your prayers quickly. Please pray for me and pray for my heart. Thank you.

Although I understand her struggle and pain all too well, I had to chuckle when she said that God answers my prayers quickly. Yes, sometimes He does . . . but other times . . . well, that's why I'm writing this book! However, knowing the struggle such heartache brings, let me share how I responded to this precious young woman.

I wrote:

My friend, sometimes God answers quickly . . . but sometimes He says wait! I've been waiting 30 years now for Him to answer "yes" to my prayers for a husband. But these years have been good years. And God has used these years to grow my walk with Him to a place it would have never been otherwise.

Sometimes life is lonely working as a single in ministry, but I'm so thankful He didn't let me marry the different men I prayed for over the years. They were all good men. All of them are still friends. But they weren't God's choice for me. And so, I continue to pray, and I continue to wait.

Waiting is a special part of the journey. Embrace it and surrender it to Him. And don't worry! I doubt He will ask you to wait 30 years, like He has me. But if He does, He will give you strength . . . one day at a time!

Dear reader, do you, like me, have many why questions about your life? Maybe you don't understand why you've had to walk through heartbreak and hardship, or why you've had such difficult trials with ministry or work. Maybe you struggle in your family relationships, with your children, your marriage, making financial ends meet, or with your health.

Maybe you're hurting over losing a loved one unexpectedly, or wondering why God isn't answering your prayers to give you a child. I can't answer all these difficult questions. Some heartaches in life won't ever make sense.

However, we are told, "All that has perplexed us in the providences of God will in the world to come be made plain. The things hard to be understood will then find explanation. The mysteries of grace will unfold before us. Where our finite minds discovered only confusion and broken promises, we shall see the most perfect and beautiful harmony. We shall know that infinite love ordered the experiences that seemed most trying. As we realize the tender care of Him who makes all things work together for our good, we shall rejoice with joy unspeakable and full of glory."[2]

Corrie Ten Boom, who was arrested and held in a Nazi prison camp during World War II, for hiding Jews, once shared a beautiful illustration how we can always trust that God knows what He's doing, even in the midst of great suffering.

As Corrie talked with a group of young people one day, she slowly unfolded a large purple cloth, covered with hundreds of different colored threads, all tied in knots and pulled through the cloth. All the different tangled threads looked so random and out of place. The threads didn't seem to have any order or make sense at all. But then she turned the tangled mess of threads over to reveal a beautiful tapestry: a crown of pure gold with multicolored jewels.

As Corrie shared the illustration, she also quoted a poem called "The Weaving." The poem goes like this:

My life is but a weaving
Between my God and me.
I cannot choose the colors
He weaveth steadily.

Oft' times He weaveth sorrow;
And I in foolish pride
Forget He sees the upper
And I the underside.

Not 'til the loom is silent
And the shuttles cease to fly

Will God unroll the canvas
And reveal the reason why.

The dark threads are as needful
In the weaver's skillful hand
As the threads of gold and silver
In the pattern He has planned.

He knows, He loves, He cares;
Nothing this truth can dim.
He gives the very best
To those who leave the choice to Him.[3]

Life may not feel very good right this moment, because you and I can't see what all those dark threads are all about. But the end of our story will be beautiful, because God is the Master Weaver. He is writing a beautiful ending to our story. In fact, I believe that He is weaving our lives into such an amazing tapestry, for His glory, that one day we will be lost in complete wonder and awe when we finally see the other side.

Truly, His ways are higher than ours. All He asks is that we keep trusting Him today, in the middle of our story, *one day at a time.*

Steps to Deeper Joy!

(Bible passages, heart questions, and activities for going deeper)

Closed doors are painful and often confusing, but someday we will understand why a certain door didn't open or why the answer from God over a specific situation was "No." We will praise the Lord that He didn't give us a "Yes" that would have led us away from His best plan.

1. Take some time to reflect on the ways God has intervened or saved you from making an unwise choice that you would have later regretted. Then reflect on the ways He's been with you through difficult circumstances or seasons, even when you made choices that cost you dearly.

2. Look up the following Bible passages and ask how God's Word is speaking to your own difficult or solitary season: Psalm 56:8; Matthew 10:29-31; Jeremiah 29:11; Isaiah 55:8-9; John 20:29.

3. Are you willing to receive God's plan for your life, even if it doesn't fit your agenda or expectations? Could His plan actually be a great gift in disguise? Pray about your answer to the Lord as you read Luke 1:38, 45.

4. Is any situation too hard or impossible for God? Read Romans 4:17-22 and 2 Kings 6:15-17.

We must put away all doubts and trust Jesus, in the darkness as well as in the light. We may not always feel His love, but we must trust that He loves us still. We may not always see His working, but we must believe that He is working still.

I love the following quote from *Thoughts from the Mount of Blessing:*

> When we really believe that God loves us and means to do us good, we shall cease to worry about the future. We shall trust God as a child trusts a loving parent. Then our troubles and torments will disappear, for our will is swallowed up in the will of God. Christ has given us no promise of help in bearing today the burdens of tomorrow. He has said, "My grace is sufficient for thee" (2 Cor 12:9); but, like the manna given in the wilderness, His grace is bestowed daily, for the day's need.[4]

God's grace is enough for today's need. Lean on Him, even in the middle of the story, even when you don't understand what He is doing. Just because you don't clearly understand God's plan doesn't mean He is confused too. The Bible tells us, "A man's heart plans his way, but the Lord directs his steps" (Prov 16:9). God knows what He's doing!

CHAPTER 2

Jungle Reflections

"For I consider that the sufferings of this present time are not worthy to be compared with the glory which shall be revealed in us." Romans 8:18

When one is traveling alone across vast stretches of empty prairie, it's a great time to reflect on your life as you talk with God. My deep heart-to-heart conversation with God was far from over. I still had many hours remaining on my journey home, and more serious surrendering I needed to do.

As the miles continued to fly by, a sign announced that I was nearing the Colorado border. I pressed the gas pedal closer to the floor, as if going faster might speed up God's plans for my life. Once again, my questions to God began to overflow.

"Lord, is it wrong to want a human hand to hold, a human ear to listen, and a human heart to share with?" I prayed, as fresh tears started to fall once again. "I love You Lord, but You made me with physical longings and desires for a reason. You created me to love and be loved, to hug and be held, to be someone's best friend and teammate. It's not for an elusive dream I pray, but for a real man in flesh and blood."

I reached for a fresh tissue.

"Lord, if You say it's not good for man to be alone, it's *certainly* not good for woman to be alone. You even sent Your disciples out two-by-two. What happened to two-by-two for me? Why must I keep walking this journey alone?"

I blew my nose again, thankful that only God could see my red puffy eyes and my messy tears. Of course, deep down in my heart, no matter how hard I prayed or how hard I cried, I only wanted God's best. So, if marriage was not His best for my life, I sincerely didn't want it, but oh how I wished He would at least take the desires away.

As I crossed the Colorado border, leaving Wyoming behind, my mind drifted back to a remote village deep in the jungles of South America, where I had once lived as a student missionary.

Over the summer of 2001, I served in Guyana, in a little village called Kaikan. I was filling in as a teacher in a small jungle school until the next student missionary teacher would arrive in the fall. It was just me, and one other missionary girl named Martha, living in a village with a hundred or so native Amerindians, as they were called.

While Martha had come from Brazil and I from the United States, the struggles of jungle life drew us close quickly. We shared priceless adventures during our brief summer in that remote village.

Both in our twenties, we had been dropped off on the jungle airstrip and left to fend for ourselves *alone.* We cooked our daily meals over an outdoor fire, surrounded by the inquisitive eyes of many curious children. We washed our clothes in the river by hand, taught classes in the village school with meager supplies, tended to the sick, and trudged through many jungle trails filled with howler monkeys, anacondas, and evil spirits who desperately wanted us to leave. Was God with us? Yes! We saw Him answering our prayers on every side. Did we enjoy the experience? Yes! It was the adventure of a lifetime. But was it easy? No! We were getting a crash course in hard-core survival, deep in the jungles of South America, with no easy way to escape.

While the distinct memories of that adventurous summer have blurred with the passing of time, I will never forget a long conversation I had with God, one dark, lonely night.

"God, I need a husband!" I cried boldly. "I need a man to stand with in ministry. I can't be a missionary like this *alone.*"

I was exhausted from trying to teach the children who would much rather be out climbing mango trees than sitting at a desk learning to spell. I was weary from early morning treks through the dark jungle to pray away evil spirits, and exhausted from battling to save lives from malaria. I was tired of hearing the screams of drunken brawls or fearing that an intoxicated soldier might break into our tiny house and rape us. (A drunk soldier had tried to break in before.) I was tired of fighting stomach issues and chasing away dozens of huge roaches and spiders—and sometimes even snakes—*every time* I wanted to use the outdoor outhouse. Mission life was not romantic!

"God, don't You see that I need a strong man here to protect me and work with me? Doing this as two young women alone is not safe or easy!"

I cried and prayed for several hours deep into that night. As the tears finally lessened, and I surrendered my heart to God, the Holy Spirit impressed me to open my Bible. My Bible fell open to a passage in Hebrews. The passage was so pointed, so specific and timely to what I had just been praying, that I felt in my heart that it was God's answer for me.

God has heard my prayer, and He does have someone for me, I thought joyfully as I dried my tears. *If I stay in the center of His will, He will bring that man into my life.*

With peace and joy flooding my heart, I finally went to sleep. From that day on, I grasped the special promise God had given me as a leaf from the tree of life. I felt in my heart that it was His promise of a coming husband.

But the years continued to go by, and there was no husband. As time dragged on, I began to feel more and more like Joseph trapped in that dark dungeon in Egypt. While I felt God had shown me that He had someone for me, the answer seemed illusive and far away. I felt invisible to the world of men, like a prisoner of love locked away and out of sight. As the years went by, the dream seemed more and more impossible. Would God's promise to me ever come true?

A semi truck swished past, the wind from the truck's long trailer whipping my van dangerously towards the edge of the road. I steadied the steering wheel as my thoughts jolted back to the present.

I was driving home from a vacation with my family in the Pacific Northwest. I was also on my way home from yet another romantic disappointment.

Just a few weeks earlier, a sweet friend had tried to match me with another single man about my age. After hearing about his amazing qualities for some time, he and I had finally been introduced. I had prayed all night before our meeting, asking God to make it clear if this was finally *the one*. He was handsome and talented and loved the Lord. We seemed to hit it off. But afterwards he told me that he didn't have peace to press forward with our friendship, so we parted ways. It was over as fast as it had started, and once again, my hopes were deflated. As I thought of this fresh disappointment, tears welled up again in my eyes.

Then the Holy Spirit's question came back to my heart with fresh force. "Are you willing to let Me choose the man in My own time and way, if I decide it's best?"

"Oh Lord, forgive me," I sighed. "Forgive me for holding back! Yes, You must choose. You must be my matchmaker. I haven't waited all these years just to go and make a terrible mistake now. I only want Your best. If You still have a man for me, then please bring Him into my life in such a way that I will know very clearly that He is sent by You."

It wasn't the first time I had prayed this prayer of surrender, and it wouldn't be the last. God's mercy is fresh every moment as we re-surrender our wants and desires back to Him. But the Holy Spirit had one more question for my weary heart. "Are you willing to accept God's plan for your life, Melody, even if there's never a husband?"

"Yes, Lord," I replied softly. "Not my will, but Your will be done. I only want Your way, even if it means no husband. I've told You many times over the years, if my life can be more for Your glory and honor working and serving alone, then please keep me single."

Fresh peace flooded my soul as I reminded myself of a promise that God had given me just a few days earlier.

"All the paths of the LORD are mercy" (Ps 25:10), He had told me. *And all means all!* That meant, if He led me to meet and marry a godly man someday, it would be in mercy. It also meant that if He asked me to keep walking life's journey alone, it was because that was His path of mercy, for had He not promised, "No good thing will He withhold from those that walk uprightly" (Ps 84:11)?

Yes, I was at peace at last. I only wanted His best gift. If He chose to withhold a husband, it meant a husband was not His best plan for me, and in that case, I didn't want one anyway.

Blooming Where You Are planted!

Author Elisabeth Elliot once gave a poignant definition of suffering. She said, "Suffering is having what you don't want or wanting what you don't have."[1]

Is there something in your life that you desperately want that you don't have? Or is there something in your life that you have that you really don't want? Are you confused or hurt by God's slowness to work on your behalf?

It's okay to be real with God about your frustrations when you don't understand what He's doing. It's okay to have unfulfilled longings. We all have them. It's okay to cry and let the tears roll. The Bible says, "Blessed are those who mourn, for they shall be comforted" (Matt 5:4). Tears can be healing. As one author writes, "Tears are not the enemy. Tears do not reflect a lack of faith. Tears are a gift from God that help to wash away the deep pain of loss."[2]

I'm thankful for the gift of tears. But ultimately, after we have had our good cry, we must wrap all those tears, heartaches, disappointments, unfulfilled longings, and broken dreams up in one big bundle, and lift that bundle up in surrender to God. Such gifts are precious material for sacrifice to our King. They also give us a fresh opportunity to say, "Lord, I may not understand, I may not feel very good right now about my current situation, but I choose to trust You anyway. I choose to joyfully worship You and be thankful for what I have."

Having joy in your heart doesn't mean that there is no suffering in your life. Having joy just means that you know God is with you, even in the middle of that suffering. His Word fills you and sustains you and gives you peace. Having joy also means that you have the quiet assurance that, *someday*, God will bring far more glory than you ever experienced in all your suffering.

The Bible says, "For I consider that the sufferings of this present time are not worthy to be compared with the glory which shall be revealed in us" (Rom 8:18).

Lilias Trotter, a single woman who left her comfortable Victorian home in England, as well as her prospects of marriage, to go as a missionary to Algeria in the late 1800s, once wrote, "Take the very hardest thing in your life, the place of difficulty, outward or inward, and expect God to triumph gloriously in that very spot. Just there He can bring your soul into blossom."

No matter our age, relationship status, or circumstances, God wants to teach us how to bloom and blossom exactly where He's planted us in life's journey. As I've discovered, the most difficult and painful experiences of our lives are often the fertilizer that give growth to God's most precious heavenly fruit. We may feel forgotten, but God's love for us during our toughest trials is not diminished. It is just as strong and tender as in the days of our sunniest prosperity, and He wants to grow something beautiful and glorious even in our times of brokenness.

You know, the wonderful thing about God is that even a "No" from Him has goodness written all over it. Looking back, I realize that if I had received the love story I prayed for all those years ago, my life and ministry would be very different today. In fact, if it weren't for all the solitary seasons that I've walked alone with God over the years, I probably would not have such a special testimony of His faithfulness to share. The bittersweet reality is that the very pain that broke my heart is the same pain that pushed me deeper into the arms of Jesus. The places that sorrow carved deep in my soul have become places for more abundant joy to fill. If it weren't for my disappointments and heartaches, I might have taken God's blessings for granted, and been content with a superficial, lukewarm spiritual experience. I wouldn't have understood the beauty of persevering prayer and faith, and my first book, *Daring to Ask for More,* might never have been written.

I'm thankful for the way God has led me over these past four decades. Of course, I'd still like to be married. *But I actually want God's will most.* And whatever will bring God the highest glory and honor is my greatest desire.

Steps to Deeper Joy!

(Bible passages, heart questions, and activities for going deeper)

I've heard it said, "To pray 'Thy will be done,' I must be willing, if the answer requires it, that my will be undone." Are you willing for your will to be undone? Are you willing to pray, "Lord, take my will and make it Your will! Not my will, but Your will be done."

1. Ask God what He wants to tell you as you meditate on the following passages: Luke 22:42; Proverbs 3:5-7; 14:12; Psalms 18:30-32.
2. Why is it best to trust in the Lord and follow His Way? How could "not withholding any good thing" apply to your current situation? See Psalm 84:11.
3. Take time, when you are not rushed, to do the following:

- Take an empty sheet of paper and write out those things about your life that you wish you had or that you wish you didn't have. In just a few words or phrases, write out your heartaches, disappointments, confusion, unfulfilled longings, or unanswered prayers.

- When you are done writing these difficult things out, take that piece of paper and roll it up, and scrunch it together, into a tight ball.
- Get down on your knees, if possible, and lift that ball of paper up to God with upturned palms. Lift it as high as you can over your head as a symbol of fresh surrender to Jesus.
- Then pray, "Lord, I don't understand the circumstances of my life, but I give You this offering. I surrender my questions and my hurt and my loneliness to You. Take it! I cannot carry all these things any longer. Please give me Your heart, a heart of gratitude for the gifts You have given me. Fill my heart with Your abundant peace and joy."
- Next time all the hurt and questions of life threaten to overwhelm you, do the same thing again, surrendering all your heartache as a precious offering back to Jesus.

4. Now take a few moments to meditate on Psalm 61:2; 23:4; and 27:14. Which passage is the most meaningful to you, and why? Have other scriptures been especially meaningful to you during the dark valleys? What are those?
5. If you are someone who skips over introductions in books, please go back and read my introduction titled, "Summer Storms" on page 15. It's very important as we continue this journey together.

If we really trust that God is on the throne, surrender will become a joy, and the sacrifice of our desires will become a pleasure. I love the following quote, as it helps keep everything in perspective:

> We are never called upon to make a real sacrifice for God. Many things He asks us to yield to Him, but in doing this we are but giving up that which hinders us in the heavenward way. Even when called upon to surrender those things which in themselves are good, we may be sure that God is thus working out for us some higher good. In the future life the mysteries that here have annoyed and

> disappointed us will be made plain. We shall see that our seemingly unanswered prayers and disappointed hopes have been among our greatest blessings.[3]

I don't know about you, but if a "No" from heaven right now means an even greater joy and blessing in the future, I'm all in. Let's keep surrendering and let God write our life story.

CHAPTER 3

And If Not, God is Still Good

"We are hard-pressed on every side, yet not crushed; we are perplexed, but not in despair; persecuted, but not forsaken; struck down, but not destroyed." 2 Corinthians 4:8-9

As I've had the privilege of traveling the world and ministering to many people over the last twenty-plus years, different ones have shared precious stories with me, stories of their personal life seasons. Some of these stories have overflowed with praises to God for all His abundant blessings, while other stories have been mixed with unanswered questions, tears, and great heartache.

I remember one young woman who, after a childhood of pain and disappointment, had finally found the man of her dreams. He was a good man, loyal and hardworking, and he loved the Lord with all his heart. She was a godly woman who had waited many years for such a man. They were a heaven-made match, and their love story was beautiful. My parents and I helped them celebrate their wedding. We all cried tears of joy on their big day. They were so happy, and the future ahead of them looked bright.

Two years into their marriage, their first child was born: a beautiful baby girl. They were such joyful, proud parents. Then, while they were still adjusting to this beautiful new life season, that new daddy and loving husband died in a tragic car accident. His baby daughter was only one month old. I will never forget the utter horror, the raw pain and anguish, that ripped through that home as the still-young bride tried to comprehend the dreadful news.

The months and years since that tragedy have been difficult. They still are, as my friend Katie now lives life as a single mom, doing her best to make ends meet and be both a mother and father to her young girl.

As I think about such tragedies, there are many unanswered questions. No one, unless you've walked through the deep valley, can pretend to understand the pain and suffering such experiences bring—no one, that is, *except God.* However, even through our deepest and darkest life seasons, God is still with us, His tears mixing with our own.

I take comfort in the fact that even the Bible writers didn't whitewash the raw emotions they experienced through life's difficult and hard seasons. Again and again, they are shockingly honest as they share their fears, their struggles, and their cries of anguish.

Because they are so honest and real in their journey, we can be honest and real in journey too. Even in life's darkest seasons, these great men and women from Bible history still remained true to God.

The Joy of the Lord is My Strength

I think of another friend named Shelly, a mother of four, not much older than me, who has always been happy, active, and healthy. A few years ago she suddenly found herself dealing with unexplained slurring of speech. It wasn't long after that she found out she had Amyotrophic Lateral Sclerosis (ALS), also known as Lou Gehrig's disease. This rare progressive neurodegenerative disease affects nerve cells in the brain and spinal cord. Victims gradually lose muscle strength until they become completely paralyzed from head to foot. Shelly prayed earnestly that God would heal her or remove this bitter cup from her lips. But after much wrestling prayer, in sweet faith and childlike trust, she submitted her life and future into God's hands.

Recognizing that in the days ahead, it might be difficult for her to communicate, Shelly began recording little messages of encouragement on video so her loved ones would always be able to hear and remember her voice. A few weeks after her initial ALS diagnosis, Shelly shared the following words of joy that God had given her one morning during her time with Him.

> It doesn't matter what our circumstances are, we can always find joy in God's presence. This is one of those days when I feel God's presence especially close. His joy is all along my pathway, sparkling like beautiful dewdrops in the morning's sunshine. I still feel great. Except for a little slurring of my speech and slowness in talking, you would never even know that I had ALS.
>
> Today I choose joy, I choose healing, and I chose not to let my diagnosis rule my life. Who knows what the next few years will hold, but I can trust the One who led me in the past, the One who brought so many good things into my life.

Well, God didn't remove the disease, and He didn't heal her. Today, four years later, Shelly is completely paralyzed, lives with the aid of a ventilator and feeding tube, and is dependent on her family and loved ones for complete 24-hour a day care. She can no longer speak or move, and her only method of communication is through an "Eyegaze" device that tracks her eye moments. Through this device, she is able to write out what she wants to say *one letter at a time*. And yet despite these overwhelmingly difficult circumstances, Shelly continues to share words of hope and encouragement with anyone who will listen.

On her blog "Mounting up with Wings," she recently shared the following words:

> My life as it is, might not be classified by most as "life more abundant." It's crazy, plain hard, and not picture perfect, but who said you have to walk and talk to have a fulfilled life?
>
> There are many potential life threatening complications that could occur since I now live, imprisoned within my own body, depen-

dent on the support of a ventilator. So, basically (as with any of us), only God knows the length of my days. However, as long as He has a work for me to do, He will preserve me. Nothing can take me out without His permission.

Thank you, dear Lord, for your many blessings to me, especially my loving family! Grow us all together through this journey to have the strength we need to be a greater witness and blessing to others. And help me have wisdom to know how to encourage others who are struggling, discouraged, or tempted to give up.

Shelly then closed her blog with the following Bible promise:

"May the God of hope fill you with all joy and peace as you trust in Him, so that you may overflow with hope by the power of the Holy Spirit." (Rom 15:13 NIV)[1]

Early in Shelly's diagnosis, her husband Kevin coined a new meaning for ALS—A Loving Savior. "There's always someone who has things worse than we do," Kevin said during a recent video testimony he and Shelly shared together. "We have so many reasons to praise God and rejoice. He truly is a loving Savior."

Kevin and Shelly Powell have been married almost 35 years, and what a vibrant testimony of faith, love, and commitment, both to each other and Jesus, they share, even in the midst of such hardship. As I think about their story, and all that their family is going through together, I realize that my own challenges, tears, and life heartaches are hardly worth mentioning. And yet, I know that God sees and cares about every tear that falls from our eyes. To Him, no sorrow or difficult season is ever overlooked.

As I type the words for this chapter, I'm lying flat on my back in bed. I'm writing in this position because of severe lower back pain that makes it difficult for me to sit up for long periods of time. Back pain is no fun, and it's especially difficult when I need to work for hours at a time on my computer. To add to this small trial, just yesterday I smashed my fingers in my car door. Nothing is broken, but my entire left hand is now throbbing, which means I'm typing today with only my right hand. So much for speed and efficiency in writing. But what an interesting backdrop for writing a book on the topic of joy in the midst of suffering. *Surely this can't be for God's glory,* I'm tempted to think to myself. *Should I rejoice and give thanks even in this?*

Yes, I am learning to rejoice even in the middle of these minor, but painful, life hardships. You see, I also serve a loving Saviour. And, as I read God's Word, I discover that God has much to say about joy. However, the joy He speaks of has nothing to do with the seasons or circumstances of our life. It has nothing to do with our feelings, whether we are dancing up and down with happiness, lying flat on our back in pain, or completely paralyzed and not able to move at all. The joy He's talking about is all about the position of our heart. It's about having an ongoing love relationship with Him.

In John 15:9-11 we read:

> As the Father loved Me, I also have loved you; abide in My love. If you keep My commandments, you will abide in My love, just as I have kept My Father's commandments and abide in His love. These things I have spoken to you, that My joy may remain in you, and that your joy may be full.

As I look back over the many years, I realize that it was "in faithfulness" that God has allowed trials and suffering to cross my path (Ps 119:75). For it has been in the tough times of life that I have most grown in my walk with God. Perhaps that's why, in the face of great difficulties, and even heartache, we are told, "Count it all joy when you fall into various trials, knowing that the testing of your faith produces patience. But let patience have its perfect work, that you may be perfect and complete, lacking nothing" (James 1:2-4).

Obviously, much that happens in our lives is *not good.* Some of it is downright ugly, heart-rending, and tragic. Katie and Shelly's stories are examples of that. And yet God's Word tells us, "And we know that all things [not some things, not just the good things, but *all things*] work together for good to those who love God, to those who are called according to His purposes" (Rom 8:28). Right now we may not see the suffering and hardships of life working together *for good*, however it is His promise that *someday all will be good* as He wipes the last tear from our eyes (Rev 21:4).

Adina's Healed Garden

This past summer I had the privilege of traveling to Scotland to hold a prayer ministries retreat. What a blessing to share and fellowship with the precious believers who gathered there.

While in Scotland, I shared my story about the summer storms and our battered garden. *(If you missed this story, read the introduction to this book.)* Little did I know how this simple miracle story would affect one precious woman's life.

From the moment I first met Adina, her joy and love for Jesus overflowed. She was serving as one of the prayer coordinators for the Scottish Mission, and her hunger for deeper revival for the people of Scotland was beautiful to witness.

Adina picked me up at the Edinburgh airport on a bright, sunshiny Friday morning. From the airport we took a one-hour bus ride, and then a thirty-minute train ride, to reach our destination. As we started our journey together through the beautiful Scottish countryside, Adina began to share some of her testimony about the adventures she had experienced with *her* loving Saviour. As she shared, I sensed in my heart that we would probably become life-long friends.

Adina was born and raised in a communist country, by a family who did not worship God. Her childhood left her with many wounds and scars. However, as a young girl, her grandmother took her to a Catholic church. There she began longing to become a bride of Christ. She also experienced her first communion service. While she only wore a simple white robe, unlike the fancy, sparkling white dresses of other girls, she was so happy to take part.

While Adina didn't always attend Mass, for most of her youth she stayed connected to church. Whenever she saw a Catholic church, she would reverently step inside, light a candle, and pray. She longed to be close to God.

As Adina entered her young adulthood, she experienced difficult and painful things that caused her much hurt, anger, and bitterness. She began to withdraw and lose her connection with God. For four long years, her spiritual life spiraled downhill. Then a small ray of light came back into her life when a friend invited her to an Adventist church. There, for the first time, Adina learned about how Jesus loves us, washes us clean from all our sins, and helps us to forgive. With God's help, Adina was able to forgive those who had deeply wounded her. Still, the wounds and effects of those scars on her emotional health remained.

More time passed, and Adina moved to the United Kingdom, and then to Scotland. Although by this time she had been baptized, there were no Adventist churches nearby, and she had no close friends or spiritual support. Once again she began to drift spiritually.

Adina longed to love and be loved, but she had never experienced genuine love by a godly man. The world's standards of "cheap, superficial love" were all she knew. The ways of the world became her way of life.

Nearly ten years passed, and she realized that she had become a dry, desolate woman, a shattered garden. Life had no meaning, and her joy and purpose for living were gone.

In 2020, as the Covid pandemic spread around the world, Adina watched as fear consumed people. It proved a spiritual wake-up call, but instead of her heart filling with fear, she had great peace. She had studied the Bible in her younger years, and she knew how the final story ends. She knew Jesus was coming soon, and that He had prophesied many bad things would happen before His coming. All around her, she saw evidences of these prophecies being fulfilled.

As if God's still small voice was speaking to her heart, Adina heard the Holy Spirit telling her: "God has chosen you, Adina. Walk away from the empty life you're living and return to Me."

Adina obeyed. She broke off her ungodly relationships and walked away from her worldly lifestyle. Not long after that, she signed up for an initiative called "100 Days of Prayer," that I was coordinating for the General Conference. Our focus was on praying for revival, reformation, and peace in the midst of the worldwide pandemic.

As Adina participated, she began to grow in her walk with Jesus as never before. She also realized for the first time that Jesus didn't just die for our sins; He didn't just want to forgive us; but He also wants to sanctify us, cleanse us, and make us new creatures in Him. She realized He wants to teach us how to love righteousness and hate sin, and most of all, be in an intimate relationship with Him.

As Adina's heart slowly revived, she prayed, "Lord, how can I serve you? I have no idea where to begin."

About that time, she watched a program called "Prayer Evangelism" on the Three Angels Broadcasting Network. The guests on 3ABN that day were my friends Jerry and Janet Page, along with Jonathan Walter. The whole program was about the power of intercessory prayer. One of the team shared the story of an elderly woman who could do nothing for Jesus but sit home and pray daily over the names of 100 people in the local phone book. It seemed so small; the older woman wasn't sure what difference her prayers could make. However, as it turned out, 99 of those prayed-for names ended up giving their life to Jesus.

Adina was mesmerized. *Perhaps prayer ministry is where God is asking me to start,* she thought to herself. *But I'm so unworthy. I've failed in so many ways. How could God use me? What can I really do for Him anyway?*

Just then, J.D. Quinn, one of the 3ABN hosts, prayed a very specific prayer.

> "Father, right now, there are people around the world who are looking for something to do. Help them to know that they can become prayer warriors. Don't let them be afraid. Let them step out in bold faith and give You a chance to work. Father, You created each one of us to be a disciple for You, and sometimes we don't think we are worthy for that. Help us to trust You and be who You created us to be."

At that moment, while Adina didn't know much of anything about ministry, and her own prayer life was still rather superficial, she knew that prayer ministry was her calling.

Not long after, she was invited to participate in the 24/7 United Prayer ministry Zoom calls. From there, through the kind support and mentorship of the leaders, she became a prayer facilitator and coordinator for prayer calls across Europe. A year later, she was asked to assist with prayer leadership for the Scottish Mission. Truly, God was calling Adina, and beginning to use her in a very special way.

Yet, even as God continued to work miracle after miracle in Adina's life, Adina still felt the deep pain of her scars and the brokenness from her past. Sometimes even a simple conversation would trigger Adina emotionally. She sank deep into her negative thoughts and emotions for days on end. She did not know how to handle herself during these times and kept crying out to God for deliverance.

Unbeknownst to me, when Adina heard the story about our battered garden, destroyed by the hail, she wept as she began to pray that her heart would also be healed and restored.

"God," she prayed, "If you can restore a destroyed garden, You can also restore my destroyed heart. All the damage from those icy hail stones over the years, all the wounds that have laid my life a waste, You can restore. You can make me a flourishing and vibrant garden once again!"

A few months after our initial meeting, Adina came to the United States for a ministry training event. For the second time we had the joy of meeting together, this time as friends and co-laborers. At the event, Adina asked for special prayer for emotional healing. A small group of us surrounded Adina and prayed. When it was my turn, I claimed Psalm 107:20 for Adina.

"Lord, You said that You sent your Word and healed them and delivered them from their destructions. Please, God, heal Adina's heart through the power of Your Word. Make her a new creature in You."

I had no idea that Adina had been claiming that very promise for the past few months, since my visit to Scotland. However, at that moment, Adina knew that God had answered our prayers and healed her heart and mind.

Today, Adina Lupu is no longer a broken and shattered garden. She has been healed by the power of God's Word, and she is flourishing in the joy of the Lord. She has discovered personally the beauty of her loving Saviour.

In Proverbs 31:24 we read, "Who can find a virtuous woman? For her price is far above rubies. Strength and honor are her clothing; and she shall rejoice in time to come."

Adina, just like me, is still living in the middle of her story as a single woman, not knowing what lies ahead. However, because of her loving Saviour, she can look toward the future with joy, because God is in charge of every tomorrow. He knows how to bring beauty out of the bleakest wilderness.

Ellen White wrote, "In the human heart [God] sees more than sin, more than misery. In His infinite wisdom and love He sees man's possibilities, the height to which he may attain."[2]

My friend, no matter what you've been through, your difficult life is not too much for God. You may be "hard-pressed on every side, yet not crushed." You may be "perplexed, but not in despair; persecuted, but not forsaken; struck down, but not destroyed" (2 Cor 4:8-9).

Out of the fiercest storms and the driest wilderness, He can grow rich, flourishing plants that bear fruit for His glory.

The Fiery Furnace Test

One of my favorite Bible stories comes from Daniel 3, the story of the three Hebrews facing the fiery furnace. You probably know how the story goes. While King Nebuchadnezzar is threatening the "three worthies" with death by fire if they don't bow down to his golden image, they are not the least bit moved or intimidated.

"Our God whom we serve is able to deliver us from the burning fiery furnace," they respond bravely, "and He will deliver us from your hand, O king. *But if not*, let it be known to you, O king, that we do not serve your gods, nor will we worship the gold image which you have set up" (Dan 3:17-18, emphasis added).

No matter what happened, they knew their God was in control and very much on heaven's throne. Nothing could sway their allegiance, their trust, or their worship, not even the threat of death.

Are you struggling with a fiery furnace experience? Are you walking through a life season that is testing your faith? Do you have unanswered questions? Welcome to the club! You are not alone! We are all going through the furnace to one degree or another, and we all have unanswered questions.

1 Peter 4:12-13 tells us, "Beloved, do not think it strange concerning the fiery trial, which is to try you, as though some strange thing happened to you; but rejoice to the extent that you partake of Christ's sufferings, that when His glory is revealed, you may also be glad with exceeding joy."

On my bedroom wall hang two meaningful plaques. One has big, bold letters that spell out the word, "PRAY." Underneath, another plaque reads, "And if not, God is still good!" That has become the theme of my life.

Of course, we should always keep praying. God loves it when we give Him our burdens, our heartaches, and our deepest heart desires. We are told, "The prayers [we] offer in loneliness, in weariness, in trial—God answers, not always according to [our] expectations, but always for [our] good."[3] You see, it's when we still choose to trust His goodness, even if He doesn't answer every prayer according to our desires, that true faith is really grown.

Suffering is not for nothing. We are on the borders of our heavenly Promised Land. God is giving us one final period of probation to grow our faith as we prepare for Jesus' soon return. Will you trust Him even when you cannot see the way? Will you trust Him even when you can't understand why? Will you run your race with joy?

Steps to Deeper Joy!

(Bible passages, heart questions, and activities for going deeper)

Consider this: Every miracle in the Bible started out as a gigantic problem. So, if you've got a big problem, you've got the perfect recipe for the makings of a big miracle. Remember that true faith has nothing to do with circumstances and everything to do with the Word of God. Let's live by His Word! Let's live with a heavenly perspective, even when called to endure life's storms.

1. Prayerfully read Isaiah 42:3. What does this passage convey about God's tender love for the struggling and broken hearted?
2. Prayerfully read Isaiah 35—the entire chapter. What does this tell you about how God loves to work with desolate wildernesses? How does this speak to you about what He longs to do in your own life? Journal your thoughts.
3. Where do you need healing in your heart or life? Claim the following promises for any broken or destroyed gardens! These promises are for you. Look up Jeremiah 30:17; Jeremiah 17:14; Malachi 4:2; Psalm 107:20.

   Ellen White wrote:

   > God's word for the sorrowing is, "I have seen his ways, and will heal him: I will lead him also and restore comforts unto him and to his mourners." "I will turn their mourning into joy, and will comfort them, and make them rejoice from their sorrow." Isaiah 57:18; Jeremiah 31:13.[4]
   >
   > Instead of the thorn shall come up the fir-tree, and instead of the brier shall come up the myrtle-tree." We behold life's desert "rejoice, and blossom as the rose." [Isaiah 35:1.] Christ delights to take apparently hopeless material, those whom Satan has debased and through whom he has worked, and make them the subjects of His grace.[5]

My friend April MacLafferty, who has experienced a difficult battle with cancer, continues to shine with the joy of Jesus. Even when she has long sleepless nights, and her energy is running low, she still radiates peace. She is an inspiration to so many of us. Recently she shared the following quote with me: "Life isn't about waiting for the storms to pass, but about learning to dance in the rain." What profound wisdom! It reminds me of a beautiful song by the Collingsworth family titled, "Redeemer of the Rain." You can watch it on YouTube. As you watch it, ask God how He wants to redeem your current storm.

CHAPTER 4

Songs in the Night

"The LORD will command His lovingkindness in the daytime, and in the night His song shall be with me—A prayer to the God of my life."
Psalm 42:8

Looking back over the years, I am reminded again and again how blessed I have been. When I compare my heartache and struggles with the suffering and trauma many others have experienced, I sometimes ask myself, "Why am I even telling my story?"

However, I've realized over the years that *pain is pain*, and when it comes to suffering, we all speak the same universal language. No matter the pain or night season we walk through, we all cry the same salty tears. Although each story or circumstance is unique, only God's grace enables any of us to get through. The truth is, we shouldn't compare our night seasons or heartaches, but rather celebrate the grace of God that helps us maintain joy even through these difficult seasons. This is why I continue to share my story.

I was raised in a wonderful, supportive, and God-fearing Christian home. My parents loved each other and led our home in love. They also modeled what it means to live practical Christianity in everyday life. I remember as an adolescent waking up to my father's voice praying at 4 a.m. everyday. At first, I was not happy to be awakened so early in the morning, but as I began listening to my father's prayers day after day, I longed to know God more and have my own meaningful time in prayer. Even now, years later, my parents continue to inspire me. They are still committed to getting up early each morning and praying together before they start their day.

I've heard it said that couples who daily pray together have a less than one-tenth of one percent chance of divorce.[1] My parents just celebrated their 52nd wedding anniversary, and my daddy (now 74 years old) still picks my mom up in his arms and waltzes with her playfully around our living room. They make me smile, and seeing their love for each other and for God brings me great joy. While no family is perfect, I consider myself to have been unusually blessed by the example of their love for God and for one another.

I made the most monumental decision of my life when I was only twelve years old—to give my life to Jesus. I still remember that special, life-changing evening. My mom was playing the song, "I Have Decided to Follow Jesus," on the piano. I had been struggling because of some difficult things going on in my life, and my heart was bleeding. But when I heard my mom playing that song, I knew God was calling me to make a choice.

"I have decided to follow Jesus," I told my mom simply, as I sat down beside her on the piano bench. She was overjoyed to tears and hugged me as we prayed together. Then we sang, "I Have Decided to Follow Jesus." Although I didn't really understand what following Jesus would look like, and I had many difficult challenges to work through, from then on, I made the intentional choice to serve Jesus and to live for Him.

In addition to my precious parents, God brought other godly mentors into my life, who also believed in me, and showed me what it means to really love and live for Jesus. As a result of these positive spiritual role models,[2] through my teen years and into my young adulthood, I became more and more earnest in seeking the Lord. I also became active in ministry, as my desire was to someday be a missionary.

When I experienced unexpected heartbreak in my twenties, my focus and vision grew clouded as I tried to work through what had happened. Yet, even during the long dark nights that followed, when I couldn't sleep, when I couldn't pray, and I wasn't living for Jesus as I should, God didn't give up on me. He was still speaking and trying to show me that He was with me. And He gave me special songs in the night.

One especially meaningful song to my life came during that dark night season.

On October 5, 2002, some college friends and I gathered on a friend's porch for vespers. After we sang a few different songs, someone picked the hymn, *Be Still, My Soul.* I had never heard the song before, but as I listened to the words, tears slowly slid down my cheeks. I knew God was speaking directly to me in the midst of my heartache. He was reminding me to be still and know that He is God, and that He is still in control (Isa 46:10).

I've written the lyrics in the back of my Bible and still treasure them to this day:

Be still, my soul: the Lord is on thy side.
Bear patiently the cross of grief or pain.
Leave to thy God to order and provide.
In every change He faithful will remain.
Be still, my soul: thy best, thy heavenly friend.
Through thorny ways leads to a joyful end.

Be still, my soul: thy God doth undertake.
To guide the future as He has the past.
Thy hope, thy confidence let nothing shake.
All now mysterious shall be bright at last.
Be still, my soul: the waves and winds still know.
His voice who ruled them while He dwelt below.

Be still, my soul: the hour is hastening on
When we shall be forever with the Lord,
When disappointment, grief, and fear are gone,
Sorrow forgot, love's purest joys restored.
Be still, my soul: when change and tears are past,
All safe and blessed we shall meet at last.[3]

Ever since that day, *Be Still, My Soul* has been etched upon my heart. Whenever I'm feeling discouraged, I look back to the lyrics of this song, reminding myself that God is still on my side, and He promises that thorny ways lead to a joyful end.[4]

From Single-Focused to Service-Focused

If we aren't careful, it's easy to get stuck in the solitary seasons. It's also easy to become rather self-focused and self-absorbed as a single. After all, we live alone, we work alone, we shop alone, we travel alone, we sit alone, we do ministry alone, we feel alone.

Going to church or to conferences and meetings has sometimes been a struggle for me, especially as I look around and see couples with arms draped around each other. *Here I am again, all by myself,* I am tempted to think to myself. *There's no arm around me, no hand to hold, no one by my side.* At times, I've found myself sitting in church crying, just longing to feel a strong, protective arm wrapped around my shoulders. At times like this, when I feel like the "outsider" in a world filled with love, it's so easy to indulge in self-pity.

We must refuse to wallow in self-pity or be controlled by our emotions. We must refuse to become bitter or angry about life's circumstances, whatever they are. Instead of focusing on what we don't have, we need to praise God for what we do have. We also need to consider what we have to give others who are struggling much more than ourselves. When I start looking for others to serve and pour my love into, my whole perspective changes.

By the way, you know, it's not just singles who feel like "outsiders." Most people today feel alone and like an "outsider" in one way or another. The newly married couple feel like outsiders. A new nursing mother feels like an outsider. The widow or widower whose partner has passed away feels like an outsider. The new family that's moved to town with six kids feels like outsiders. The pastor's wife might even feel like an outsider at her own church.

If we start approaching life from a "What can I do for others?" mentality, rather than a self-centered "Poor me, I'm just an outsider" mentality, what a difference it makes.

Nowadays, people tend to isolate themselves. They get stuck on their phones, browsing social media, or reading the news. They get stuck in their own little world. Instead of growing practical life skills or looking for ways to serve, they turn inward. My friend, don't waste the gift of life or singlehood playing games on your phone or isolating yourself when there is so much you could do. There are gardens that could be grown, practical life skills that could be developed, lonely people who could use a friend, young people who could use a mentor, cards that could be written and mailed, songs that could be sung, hobbies that could be developed, a piano that could be played, creative gifts that could be given, leaves that could be raked, a mission field that could be reached, and much more. On all sides, there are people just waiting for our love and care. Give your life in service to others. Lay up treasures in the Kingdom while you still can.

Author Ty Gibson writes, "Get to know people. It's all about people. Notice people. Tune in to people. Be good to people. Jesus died for people. Take people out of the equation and life has no meaning. If you're too busy for people, you're missing the whole point of your existence."

The more healthy you are as a single, the more diverse your friendship base will be. Don't let yourself get stuck in the "singles only club." Mingle with the elderly, with couples, with families, with those who have no friends. Find those in need whom you can pour your life into. Give lavishly, instead of trying to live lavishly. Not only will you find greater joy, but you will bring joy to others.

Journals of His Faithfulness

As I healed from the deep wounds of heartbreak and depression, my walk with God came alive in a whole new way. I saw God's great love for me afresh through Jesus' death on the cross, and my purpose in living began to come back into focus. Heavenly joy overwhelmed me.

I couldn't get enough of Jesus. I poured over my Bible for hours each day, often with tears running down my cheeks, as I begged Him to do a deeper work in my heart. I began asking Him to wake me up early each morning, no matter what time, whenever He was ready to meet with me. I was so hungry to know Him, and I determined not to settle for a superficial, lukewarm Christian experience like so many around me had done. I wanted *more, much more*!

I also began praying earnestly for a baptism of the Holy Spirit. I was so eager for this gift that sometimes I went to sleep with my Bible on my chest, hugging it close.

While I never stopped praying for a life partner, and the romantic hopes continued to come and go, I focused more and more on growing a deeper relationship with Jesus, and looking for ways to be used for the Kingdom. God opened many doors in ministry as a result. I found my purpose again in serving others, and my heart filled with deep peace and joy.

In August 2003, I wrote the following journal entry:

> My questions from all the heartaches still aren't completely answered, and maybe they never will be this side of heaven, but this much I know, I will hold on till my dying breath because God knows best. He knows what He must lead me through to make me who He wants me to be. And He is in control. While my heart aches for human companionship, Jesus truly has been all that I need. No one can truly satisfy like He does, and I will continue to look to Him for my fulfillment.

While I prayed for God's leading, I got more involved in overseas missions, working with orphaned children, doing evangelistic meetings, and assisting with jungle health clinics. When I wasn't traveling,

I served as an assistant girl's dean and mentor to young women on my old high school academy campus. I also worked in the hospital as a nurse, trying to be the best witness I could be. When I began to see my patients' making decisions for Jesus, I was overjoyed. Truly God was at work, and I was thrilled to see the many divine appointments He gave in answer to prayer.

As time passed, my love story with Jesus continued to grow and blossom, as I found more and more of my strength in Him.

In May 2007, I journaled the following words:

> I'm growing, and my life is so full of joy and meaning now. I've been coming to trust God at a deeper level than I ever did before. I believe that I'm finally beginning to see the beautiful plan that God has been preparing for my life . . . so far beyond my wildest dreams. It's been fourteen years since I started praying for my future husband. Although I still long for companionship and love, if God wills, I'm also content to be single for the rest of my life. No matter the cost, no matter the pain, even if my earthly dreams don't all come true, I will be faithful to my true Heavenly love.

About this time, I moved to Loma Linda, California. I began leading prayer ministry for the Advent Hope young adult group. God gave me many wonderful ministry opportunities, and much precious fellowship during my four years in Loma Linda. I began to realize that being single was not a curse, but actually a great blessing, as I could spend undistracted time with Jesus and dedicate all my time to mission opportunities and service. While I had no idea what the future would hold, I knew one thing—I wanted to stay in the center of God's will.

So often it's easy to get stuck in the "If only" world, and put our life on hold while we wait for certain circumstances in our life to change. This mentality robs us of present joy, and paralyzes our ability to accomplish the specific mission God has for us in the here and now. We are always thinking, "When this happens, then I can . . ." or "When he/she comes into my life, I will . . ." or "When I get this, I can . . ." about whatever it is you are waiting to happen.

I love what Nancy DeMoss Wolgemuth wrote about the "If only" mentality:

> The enemy has robbed many of us of joy by getting us to live in that foolish realm of "if only . . ." We feel that we would be happy, "if only . . ." "If only I had a husband . . ." "If only I didn't have a husband . . ." "If only I had a different husband . . . " "If only we had children . . ." "If only we didn't have so many children . . ." "If only I had a different job . . ." "If only I lived in a different place . . ." "If only I could own my own home . . ." "If only I made more money . . ." The fact is, if we're not content with what we have, we will never be content with what we think we want.

She goes on to write:

> Generally, there is an expectation that marriage will make [a person] happy. But marriage can't make anyone happy! In fact, sooner or later, every man or woman who marries so he or she can be happy is bound to be miserable. Marriage is not about finding someone to make us happy; it is about learning to make someone else happy. It's not about getting; it is about giving. It's not about finding fulfillment; it is about self-denial and sacrifice. The man or woman who does not learn contentment as a single is highly unlikely to be content once married . . . The key to joyous living is to embrace the will of God and to receive with gratitude whatever gift He has given us.[5]

Recognizing that, as a single, I could dedicate myself more fully to God without distractions, I determined to use all my energy for His glory. Already some of my friends were having marital problems, and sadly some had divorced. In contrast, I was still happy and free to serve the Lord however He called me. I realized this was a precious gift!

New ministry opportunities continued to open. In February 2011, I wrote:

> These last few years, while not always free of trials or hardship, have been truly the happiest of my life, and they only keep getting better. I'm so full of satisfaction and joy in what God has called me

to do . . . It's kind of strange, but I feel like God has put my desires for a future husband to sleep to a large extent . . . I am happy and fulfilled. I've decided, if I'm going to be single, I just want to be a blessing to others, because I know for myself that God can more than meet all our needs.

By 2011, I had spent two years on the leadership team of a revival ministry focused on helping people go deeper in Bible study. It was fulfilling to see the Holy Spirit change hearts of both young and old. I felt like I was finally finding my true purpose in ministry.

Around this time, I quit my job working as a nurse and started traveling by faith, as God opened the doors and provided, testifying about a prayer-hearing, prayer-answering God. Highlighting Ephesians 3:20-21, a text that had radically changed my own prayer life, I encouraged people everywhere to "dare to ask for more" in their walk with Him.

"Why settle in the wilderness spiritually," I challenged, "when God wants to take us to the Promised Land in our walk with Him. Ask Him for more, ask Him for big things! He has more He's longing to do in our lives, especially spiritually!" (As many know this whole testimony is another book all in itself![6])

God worked above and beyond my expectations, and my heart soared with gratitude. During this time, another song also spoke powerfully to my soul, called "With All My Heart." I loved it because it reflected my own heart cry and relationship with Jesus. It is still a reflection of my desires today.

The lyrics go like this:

In this quiet place with You
I bow before Your throne
I bare the deepest part of me
To You and You alone
I keep no secrets for there is
No thought You have not known
I bring the best and all the rest
To You and lay them down

With all my heart
I want to love You Lord
And live my life
Each day to know You more
All that is win me
Is Yours completely
I'll serve You only with all my heart
You faithfully supply my needs
According to Your plan
So help me Lord to seek Your face
Before I seek Your Hand
Then follow in obedience
In every circumstance

With all my heart
I want to love You Lord
And live my life
Each day to know You more
All that is win me
Is Yours completely
I'll serve You only with all my heart[7]

Of course, there were still moments when loneliness and longing overwhelmed me. After brushing the tears away, I would again surrender my dreams to Jesus as a fresh offering of sacrifice. As I spent time in God's Word and reminded myself daily of His love, He kept giving me new songs in the night.

In August 2013, I wrote the following journal entry as I celebrated twenty years of praying and waiting on God:

> It's hard to believe, but it's been twenty years this month since I started praying for my future husband. This month marks many years of prayers, tears, and much waiting. But God has been faithful. God has given me complete peace. I wonder at times if it's even His will for me to ever marry.

> The last years have been busy and fulfilling . . . Sometimes in the quiet moments, I still find myself longing for that godly man who will just hold me in his arms and be there, but most of the time I haven't noticed the passing of time. I don't know what God is doing, but I trust Him.
>
> I just read this evening, "Often God delays purposely, and the delay is just as much an answer to your prayer as is the fulfillment when it comes."
>
> I'm not a little girl anymore, and I'm realizing that life is fleeting. Before I know it, it will be gone. But I'm seeking to put the remaining energy of my youth into serving Him. I'm praying that God will give me many trophies, souls for the Kingdom.

In September 2023, I wrote another journal entry as I celebrated the thirty-year mark:

> Can't believe it's been over thirty years now. But I'm willing to wait another 30 years if that's what it takes, because I know God's best plan is always worth the wait! This year, for my 30th anniversary of waiting and praying, God surprised me. He took me to Switzerland. It has always been my dream to go hiking in the Swiss Alps, and that dream has finally come true. "Delight yourself also in the Lord and He shall give you the desires of your heart" (Ps 37:4).[8]
>
> I'm in total AWE of God and His amazing ways. Truly Jesus is ENOUGH! And He keeps giving me Himself in greater and greater abundance. How could I ask for more? He is my joy and my song, and He makes my way perfect.

And so, the years continue to pass. I don't know what tomorrow holds, or where I will be in yet another ten years, let alone another thirty years. But one thing I do know, God will be with me. And He will keep giving me fresh songs in the night, fresh songs from my time with Him, and fresh songs from His Word. Month by month, journal after journal is being added to my bookshelf, all testifying to the fact that while heartbreaks may come and go, Jesus' love remains, and truly *He is enough.* He is faithful, and He walks with us through every season.

Hearing God's Voice in the Night

Do you sometimes feel like you are in the middle of a long dark night season? If you ask yourself, "Who are the people who have most profoundly influenced my life?" you will probably find that every one of them has endured a dark night season of their own. In fact, all the great men and women of God from Bible times walked through night seasons in their faith journey. And that's what made them *great!*

Facing loss after loss, Job cried out to God, "When will the night end?" (Job 7:4). I have often cried the same prayer over the years. Maybe you have too.

I have discovered that the night seasons are often sacred opportunities to meet with Jesus and hear His voice in ways I might not have heard otherwise. The Scriptures show that God often gave His most precious messages of love in times of apparent darkness.

God gave His most beautiful promises and revelations to Abraham at night while he was hurting, longing for a son (Gen 15:1; Gen 26:24). Jacob received his vision of the ladder to heaven while running for his life (Gen 28:11). He had a heavenly wrestling match with Jesus Himself during a dark night of fear (Gen 32:24). Joseph received amazing dreams about his future at night (Gen 37:5-9). He went through a dark night season in slavery and in prison in Egypt, but God spoke to him even in his captivity (Gen 39-40). The shepherds on the hills surrounding Bethlehem received the news of Jesus' birth during the middle of the night while they watched their sheep (Luke 2:8). In hindsight, I am sure they were so glad that they hadn't been sleeping! Jesus received wisdom on how to choose His twelve disciples after a dark night alone in prayer (Luke 6:12). He was also strengthened for His great battle on the cross during His lonely night in the Garden of Gethsemane (Luke 22:41-43). Some of the timeliest messages the prophet Daniel received came in the night (Dan 2:19, 7:7). God spoke to the Apostle Paul during the night (see Acts 16:9; Acts 18:9; Acts 23:11; Acts 27:23) and gave Paul and Silas a special song of praise to sing even at midnight (Acts 16:25).

There are numerous stories of God's faithfulness in the night seasons through the lives of Gideon, David, Samuel, Solomon, Elijah, Nehemiah, Naomi, Ruth, Esther, Job, Nicodemus, and many others. The stories of God's voice in the night and His faithfulness to His children—whether to the Israelites wandering for 40 years in the wilderness, or to His people today preparing for Jesus' Second Coming—go on and on.

Aren't you glad God allowed David to struggle through many night seasons, which inspired so many beautiful psalms? David wrote, "The LORD will command His lovingkindness in the daytime, and in the night His song shall be with me" (Ps 42:8).

Perhaps David's many tears and conversations with God gave him the confidence to say, "Don't be afraid of the terror by night. Don't be afraid of the pestilence that walks in darkness" (Ps 91:5, 6). It's as if he was saying, "Don't be afraid of the night season. God is with you. Keep singing songs of praise, because you will be okay!"

My friend, you too will be okay. God is going to bring you through your night season. As I've heard it said, "Divine daybreaks often follow the darkest nights."[9] In the meantime, instead of cursing God in the darkness, or doubting His love, what if we praised God more? What if, instead of speaking words of despair, we sang songs of God's faithfulness? There is so much power in singing songs of praise!

As my favorite author wrote, "When the enemy comes with his darkness, sing faith and talk faith, and you will find that you have sung and talked yourself into the light.[10] She also wrote, "[God] has a song to teach us, and when we have learned it amid the shadows of affliction, we can sing it ever afterward."[11]

Let's pray that God would teach us His love songs in the night—songs that will last throughout all eternity.

Steps to Deeper Joy!

(Bible passages, heart questions, and activities for going deeper)

Each life season is a sacred gift from God. Pray that God will help you be joyful and satisfied in your current season. Remember, true joy is not found in having everything we think we want, but in choosing to be satisfied with what God has already provided. It is the wholehearted surrender of all life's "What ifs?" as we seek God's Kingdom.

1. Prayerfully read Psalm 92:1-2. Then, take some time to look back and reflect on God's faithfulness through your own night seasons. How has He spoken to you during these times of darkness, whether stretching over weeks, months, or years? What songs (or promises from God's Word) has He given you in those nights?
2. Pray over the following passages and ask God how they apply in your own life circumstances: Psalm 17:3; 77:6-9; 119:148; Isaiah 26:9; Lamentations 3:21-23; Luke 18:7-8.
3. What practical encouragement do you find from the following passages? Psalm 51:8; Nehemiah 8:10; Revelation 22:1-5. What promises do you find for your future?
4. The next time God wakes you in the night, get up and listen like Samuel or pray like Solomon, "Lord, help me! I'm a little child who doesn't know how to go out or come in!" See 1 Samuel 3:8-9; 2 Chronicles 7:12-14.
5. For a list of musical melodies that have been extra meaningful in my journey through my night seasons, see Appendix 5. Perhaps you will find a new song that will speak to your heart as well!

As you reflect on the following quote, what are we told is behind the darkest clouds?

> You may be disappointed, and your will and your way may be denied; but be assured that the Lord loves you. The furnace fire may kindle upon you, not for the purpose of destroying you, but to consume the dross, that you may come forth as gold seven times purified. Bear in mind that God will give you songs in the night. Darkness may seem to enclose you; but you are not to look at the clouds. Beyond the darkest cloud there is an everlasting light. The Lord has light for every soul. Open the door of the heart to hope, peace, and joy. Jesus says, "These things have I spoken unto you, that my joy might remain in you, and that your joy might be full." [John 15:11.][12]

As I've heard it said, "God hides His most precious treasures in our most difficult and painful experiences."[13] He can bring the deepest joy out of the darkest nights, because He is the source of our joy. His joy can never be taken away.

CHAPTER 5

The Best Place to Fall

"Therefore, if anyone is in Christ, he is a new creation; old things have passed away; behold, all things have become new." 2 Corinthians 5:17

Many have come to me over the last few years, after reading my first book *Daring to Ask for More,* and told me with shining eyes, "It must be so amazing to be a published author! I hope to write a book someday too!"

I can understand their aspirations. From my earliest years I dreamed of becoming an author. However, writing books, as I've discovered, is not glamorous or easy. Far from it. It's hard work, very hard work—perhaps somewhat like giving birth to a baby. Only, a book isn't born in a matter of hours. It's usually weeks, months, and sometimes years' worth of hard labor. Then with the passing of time, you realize that what you wrote needs major editing, and you painfully crop and cut out half of what you spent so much time trying to birth. *Now what was that all about?* you wonder to yourself. *Was all my hard work for nothing?*

Well, I firmly believe that nothing is ever wasted in this life, no matter how painful or discouraging, especially if it adds to the person that we are, or can be used to point others to Jesus. While writing books is hard work and often tiring, it's part of my personal journey learning to give glory to my King.

However, this is a chapter that I wish I didn't have to write. Perhaps as you've been reading, you've thought, "Well, Melody may have had a few heartbreaks in her lifetime, but what does she really know about scars and suffering? After all, she's had a sheltered life, she comes from a great family, and she's been praying and saving herself for her future husband for many years now. How could she understand *my pain*?"

My friend, we need to be careful about judging a book by its cover, for most everyone we meet has private struggles and hidden scars that no one else knows about. These struggles and painful scars come in various shapes and sizes, and in varying degrees of intensity. But often times they are so deep, so painful, so personal, that we can't begin to talk about them even with those closest to us, let alone with the world.

"What would others think if they only knew the struggles I have?" we ask ourselves, hanging our heads in shame. "What would they think if they knew what happened to me, or what I've done? Where do I go from here? Can God still forgive me and love me?"

If you are asking yourself these tough questions, you are not alone.

"So, where do I go from here?" The answer is simple. *Fall at the feet of Jesus!*

If you want to start anew in your walk with God, if you want to find the pathway to abundant joy, fall broken and bleeding at the feet of the One who loves you most. *There is simply nowhere else to go!* Jesus' arms are open wide. There's nothing about your life that He can't handle. He takes you as you are, and He loves you fiercely. While you cannot begin to turn your messed-up broken life around, Jesus can.

Truth be told, we are all broken vacuums for love. Unless Jesus becomes our first love, we will probably look for love and comfort in all the wrong places and with all the wrong people. Or we will fill our life with superficial pleasures to numb our pain and disappointments. But nothing and no one can fill the vacuum in our hearts that only

Jesus can fill. That's why we must continually come with all our brokenness, with all our need and failures, and fall at Jesus' feet.

Go and Sin No More!

As we read about the life of Jesus in the gospels, there is one woman's name who you will see again and again wherever Jesus goes. The woman I'm thinking of was single, and had spent much of her life looking for love and attention in all the wrong places. Of course, I'm referring to Mary Magdalene.[1]

Mary was the sister of Martha and Lazarus, and the three siblings together became close friends to Jesus. However, while they were religious and had means, they weren't exactly the kind of people you would expect Jesus to buddy up with. Martha had major workaholic tendencies, and Mary had messed up her life royally. The Bible tells us that Jesus not only cast seven demons out of Mary Magdalene, but many believe that she was *the woman* caught in the act of adultery whom the scribes and Pharisees threw at Jesus' feet.

Imagine how it would have felt that day to be the one whom everyone was staring at with contempt and disgust.

Not only was Mary caught in bed with a married man, but the ones who found her were, of all people, the elders of her synagogue, and even the high-up religious leaders of that region. While her customer slipped away unscathed, these religious leaders, whom she had respected and looked up to, proceeded to drag her half-naked through the streets. It was obviously a set-up, and their destination for interrogation was, of all places, the holy temple. If only they could have taken her anywhere, *but there.* But they seemed to be enjoying making a spectacle of her, and that is exactly what Satan loves to do in response to our sins, the very sins *he* prompted us to commit.

Arriving at the temple, the priest and leaders threw Mary, down at the feet of the One who is sinless, and the One who reads the motives behind every thought and deed.

"Teacher," they began, as they piously addressed Jesus, "This woman was caught in adultery, *in the very act.* Now Moses, in the law, commanded us that such should be stoned. But what do *You* say?"

It was obviously a trap for Jesus as well. But what Mary would soon discover is that, when you are in trouble or you have messed up your life royally, the best place to fall is at the feet of Jesus.[2] *This is the best place for you and me to fall as well!*

As the scribes and Pharisees gloated that they were about to pull a fast one on Jesus, they had no idea that they were even more naked than the woman trembling on the ground before them, for all things are open to the eyes of God. Jesus knew Mary's heart. He also knew their thoughts and corrupt motives. Stooping down, Jesus wrote in the sand. What He wrote, we aren't exactly told, but when He stood up and responded to their question, their consciences were immediately smitten.

"He who is without sin among you, let *him* throw a stone at her first," Jesus said simply.

Mary was still trembling with fear, waiting for that first stone to hit her body. But it never came. One by one her accusers slipped away, their heads down in shame. Then she was left alone with Jesus.

"Woman, where are those accusers of yours? Has no one condemned you?" Jesus gently asked.

She responded, "No one, Lord."

"Neither do I condemn you," Jesus told her. "Go and sin no more."[3]

Think of the sense of exhilaration and holy joy that must have burst through Mary's heart and soul. Just moments before she had been filled with fear, preparing herself to die. Now her death sentence was lifted. Just moments before she was bowed low in shame under the men's loathing eyes. Now that shame had been wiped away.

Mary knew well the feelings of fear and shame. Every man looked at her either in lust or disgust. But now, standing before her, was a man who didn't lust. He loved. He was not blind to reality. He saw her sin and shame, yet set her free with a simple message of grace.

As she looked into His eyes of love for the first time, she read a message that went far deeper than actual words. He was speaking to her heart and soul the same message He speaks to us today: "I don't condemn you. I forgive you. I believe in you. I intend to take your shame and punishment, so you can have a fresh beginning with Me—not just today, but for all eternity. So, go, and don't live this sinful life anymore—because I love you."

It is no wonder that Mary became one of Jesus' closest followers in the days to come. Jesus' message of love and grace seemed too good to be true! But it was true.

Some of us can resonate personally with Mary's experience. However, even if we haven't committed physical adultery, how often have we been guilty of *spiritual adultery*, or of lusting after someone, or even coveting someone else's property, romance, or marriage? In today's world, no one blinks an eye at such "thought sins," but according to God's Word, these thoughts can be just as dangerous as *real physical adultery*.[4] When we are consumed with lust or coveting that which God has not given, it's called idolatry. We may not bow down to images of gold or silver, but we have chosen a counterfeit god and lover before the Lover of our soul.

Consider the following:

Anything I put before God is an idol.
Anything I want with all my heart is an idol.
Anything I can't stop thinking of is an idol.
And anything I give all my love to is an idol.[5]

Have you at times been guilty of idolatry? Are you even now putting your desires for something that you desperately want above your pursuit of God? Do you find yourself trapped in some type of bondage or sin? If so, maybe you hear the enemy taunting you right now, "Sinner!" as he looks for an opportunity to *stone* you. My friend, when your heart is overwhelmed by stones of condemnation, look up to *the Rock* that is higher than you (Ps 61:2).

Thankfully, the appeal that Jesus gave Mary is also for you and me today. "Go and sin no more," He softly whispers. He's also given us a special promise: "Then I will sprinkle clean water on you, and you shall be clean; I will cleanse you from all your filthiness and from all your idols" (Ezek 36:25).

This promise is for all of us, and we can claim it with joy!

Purity from the Inside Out

Now let's talk about purity for a few more moments. Purity by definition means the condition or quality of being pure. It means freedom from anything that debases, defiles, contaminates, pollutes, etc.

I've met some singles who pride themselves on their virginity, on the fact that they have kept themselves pure by not crossing certain physical boundaries. But if you listen to them talk, well, you can tell their heart is anything but pure. As I've come to realize over the years, being pure is more than just being a virgin. While virginity is a physical condition, purity is a heart condition. We are called to be virgins until we enter a covenant relationship called marriage. However, staying pure in heart is a life-long calling, whether single or married. It doesn't start when we get married, it starts now.

Staying pure isn't easy in today's world. If we aren't intentionally making a choice to keep our heart and body pure, as unto the Lord, our heart and bodies can easily wander. That's why the Bible tells us, "Keep your heart with all diligence, for out of it spring the issues of life" (Prov 4:23). Once again, we discover that holiness of heart is what God is really after.

In Matthew 5:8 Jesus tells us, "Blessed are the pure in heart, for they shall see God." I love how one pastor describes what true purity means:

> Purity is not a point you cross. You might say, "Oh, I no longer watch porn. I no longer mentally undress women. I no lunger lust. Now I'm pure." No! True purity is a pursuit after God! If you aren't pursuing God, you are not pure. Even if you aren't acting out sexually, watching porn, or other

things. If you aren't pursuing God, you aren't pure. Purity is a heart issue. It's the foundation of all relationships.[6]

Perhaps staying pure in heart and body is a constant struggle for you. Perhaps, because of your sins, or because of scars from your past, you wonder if God can make you pure and clean once again. He can! Let me share a personal testimony. It's a testimony that few know.

Long before I knew anything about the birds and bees, I had already experienced what no child should ever experience. You see, I lost my purity and innocence when I was only seven or eight years old. This started a whole chain of tragic events, events that I wish I could erase from the pages of my childhood history.

"How could a sweet little girl, who obviously was raised in a good home with godly, loving, protective parents lose her innocence at such a young age?" you ask. It's simple! The answer is "Sin!" Unfortunately, bad things can happen quickly and in ways least expected. The reality is that we've all been wounded in the battle in some way, by living in this war zone called Earth. I am no exception.

Thankfully, as I entered my teen years and gave my life to Jesus, God began to heal my heart and repair the damage that the enemy had done. However, as I got older, I was shocked to discover that I was not alone in carrying battle scars, as many of my friends had also suffered similar losses. Some of them continued to struggle with deep wounds and ongoing private addictions. Some of them also battled depression.

Did you know that any sexual activity that happens outside of the sanctity of marriage (whether private or with another partner) damages the frontal cortex of our brain? The frontal cortex is the part of the brain that regulates our thoughts, actions, emotions, and self-control. Private sin and sexually promiscuous behaviors not only increase our risk of depression, and give an open door for the enemy to come into our life, they also interfere with our ability to hear the Holy Spirit's voice.

God pleads with us in His Word, "Beloved, I beg you as sojourners and pilgrims, abstain from fleshly lusts which war against the soul"

(1 Pet 2:11). In Ephesians 5 we are admonished, "But among you there must not be *even a hint* of sexual immorality, or of any kind of impurity, or of greed, because these are improper for God's holy people" (Eph 5:3, NIV, emphasis added).

As I've already shared, my own journey into depression was not pretty—depression never is. During my months of great discouragement, instead of finding my comfort in Jesus, I started turning to unhealthy distractions and worldly substitutes for the love I longed for—things like romance movies and stories, online dating, and of course junk food. Of course, none of these things brought the love or comfort that I needed.

Thankfully, Jesus didn't give up on me. In Hebrews 7:25 we are told, "Therefore He is also able to save to the uttermost those who come to God through Him, since He always lives to make intercession for them." No matter how deep we sink, Jesus is deeper still. And He loves to come to our rescue.

As I opened my heart again to Jesus, and repented of my sins of spiritual compromise, He began to breathe fresh life back into my soul. As I spent more and more time in His presence, I found that I no longer desired the superficial substitutes for love the world offers. Slowly, through His grace, He healed the brokenness in my life, and He made me pure and whole once again.

I do not wish to emphasize or talk about the painful things in my past. Those experiences do not define my life. I'm no longer a victim of sin, but a victor in Jesus. He has made all things new. He continues to make all things new *even today*. He will do the same for you.

I love the promise of 2 Corinthians 5:17: "Therefore, if anyone is in Christ, he is a new creation; old things have passed away; behold, all things have become new."

Does this mean I never weep over the wounds from my past? No! I'm human, and God created our tear ducts for a reason. Sometimes I've struggled, wondering if a godly man will be able to accept me when he learns the truth about my scars. But I must leave the future (and my future-husband if there is one) in God's hands. Until Jesus comes, we will always carry the scars of sin and suffering, and with those scars the tears of pain and regret. One thing I know though, when we get to heaven, our scars won't have the final say over our lives anymore—His scars will!

Thankfully Jesus can bring beauty in place of ashes. While I have yet to experience the joy of loving physical intimacy, I still look forward to enjoying this precious gift in marriage *someday*, if God so wills. I also have yet to be kissed! And trust me, I didn't wait this long just to go and kiss *any* good looking, sweet-talking man. I'm saving that kiss for the right man—*for God's man!* I hope to share my "first kiss" with my husband at the altar.

But what about getting through *today?* Well, today, God hasn't given me a husband. And the reality is that He might never give me a husband, so that means I do not indulge my desires, and I surrender all my physical longings to Him. Until God opens the appropriate doors, these longings and desires are more offerings for fresh sacrifice to Jesus, my King.

Guarding Hidden Treasures

I'd like to pause a moment and talk straight to all my sisters and brothers. Women, consider this: Where do you find the most costly diamonds? They are found deep down in the ground. Where are the biggest pearls discovered? Deep down in the bottom of the ocean. Where do you find gold? Deep inside a mine.

Your body is sacred. You are far more valuable than diamonds, pearls, or gold. If you keep your treasures covered, someday, a godly man (who is worth his weight in gold), will be willing to dedicate great time, commitment, and investment to "mining" the treasures of your heart. His love will be far better than all the love you could have experienced along the way with superficial lovers. Don't live like an imitation jewel. You are of infinite value to God, and you will be of infinite value to the right man. Guard your heart. Guard your physical treasures. Don't cast your pearls before swine.

Men, I encourage you to also guard your eyes and your heart. Psalm 101:3 says, "I will set nothing wicked before my eyes; I hate the work of those who fall away; It shall not cling to me." Guard each woman you meet as if she is someone else's wife and property—because she is, until you make the choice to marry her! Don't let your physical desires and longings lead you into bed before you've been to the altar. Many strong men have been destroyed by unruly passions (Prov 7:26). "Can a man take fire into his bosom and not be burned?" (Prov 6:27). Don't give any footholds to the enemy. Unrestrained passion can be an avenue the devil will use to destroy you, and to destroy others.

Keep in mind that women are often led into temptation through their emotions. As a man, ask yourself, "Are there ways that I talk, that might cause a women to stumble in moral purity?" Do you say things to draw out a women's affections, before you are ready to commit? This is stealing! Guard the hearts of your sisters in the Lord and treat them with respect and dignity.

Women, take note if the man of your choice has a wandering eye, even after you start a relationship. Is he constantly checking out other girls? Who does he follow on social media? Does he follow swimsuit models, celebrities, and half-naked women? If so, he may be dealing with an ongoing issue with lust or pornography. You shouldn't try to control him or mother him, and he shouldn't try to control you, but you should observe what you each look at and enjoy. These things provide windows into the heart and soul.

My sisters, we should do our part to help our brothers by guarding our bodies and treating them as God intended—as a sacred gift intended for one man. Flirtatious or provocative behaviors and tight, revealing, and immodest clothing do not attract men of noble character. A real man of God, wants a woman of dignity, not a playgirl.

Are you dressing to draw attention to your body, or to flaunt certain features of your body? Are you trying to show the men out there, "Hey, I may be getting older, but I'm still sexy! I still got the goods. I still have something to give." Or are you seeking to bring glory to God?

Think about this: Outfits are either a frame for our face, or a frame for our body. An outfit that is tastefully chosen will draw a person to look at your face, to see the beauty of godly character, while an outfit that is inviting lustful glances will draw the eyes to certain body parts. You don't need to wear a sack to be modest, but don't over-sensualize your body.

One time, I had to go through my wardrobe, and say "Lord, help me. What outfits in my closet are more about drawing attention to myself than giving glory to You?" Unfortunately, I found a few clothes that shouldn't have been in my wardrobe. I threw them out. Now, above my closet I have tapped a Bible verse. It reminds me: "But put on the Lord Jesus Christ, and make no provision for the flesh, to fulfill its lusts" (Rom 13:14).

Remember, real beauty comes from spending time in front of the mirror of God's Word, not the mirror on the wall, and not the closet. There's a big difference between dressing attractively and dressing to attract.

Now a quick word about online dating: While I know that many people are spouse surfing online, I highly discourage this practice of courtship. Not only does online dating take away the natural observation possible that you would have when you are getting to know someone in daily life, but it increases the speed and intensity of the romance quite quickly, too fast—often ahead of good common sense. There are a thousand and one reasons why I would say, don't do the online dating thing! It can be like entering a shark tank. And from my experience, it's mostly only the "desperates" who hang out there. Trust me, you do not want to marry a *desperate*, nor do you want to act like *a desperate*. Once in a while, good things can happen, however, I believe there are better ways to start a romance. Give God the pen. He's fully capable of bringing the right person into your life at the right time—in His time.

Also, as you seek to guard your body, and stay pure, guard your mind as well. Unfortunately, extra-marital affairs are all too common, even among believers. As singles, who long for companionship and love, we must always be extra-intentional and on guard to protect the marriages and relationships of those around us. We can never be too careful.

If you work or do ministry with married individuals of the opposite sex, put safeguards in place. If you are a woman, make a point to be friends with both a husband and wife together, rather than just the husband. Put the same safeguards in place if you are a single man working with married women. Don't live in ways that might invite temptation, or that might foster the development of an emotional or physical affair. Never travel alone, or work in a room alone, with a married person of the opposite sex. Make it a habit to always communicate in groups, or in conversations that include the spouse. Don't have lengthy conversations or share deep personal matters of the heart unless talking with a couple together. Don't share physical affection, even playfully. If you find yourself in compromising situations, or you feel a married person making inappropriate advances towards you, run! Cut off all contact. Don't play with fire! Get accountability partners to help you stay focused.

Remember, God sees what others don't. He sees our heart motives. He sees what stirs our soul. Make a commitment to stay morally and spiritually pure, so you can be all that God has called you to be. We can never be too careful, especially when we long for emotional connectedness with those around us. However, if Jesus is our first love, and if we are willing to affair-proof our relationships, He will protect our heart. Often, it's in the process of sacrificial giving and serving others that our own heartaches are healed. It is in sharing the healing power of the gospel with others that we ourselves are made whole.

Last but not least, be respectful towards those of the opposite sex. Even though men and women are very different, there's no excuse for sharing disrespectful or distasteful jokes. Today it's popular to bash men or to tell dumb blonde jokes. Neither are appropriate. Rather we should do all in our power to encourage and lift one another up by our words and our respect. Each man we meet is a son of God, and each woman we interact with is a sister and daughter of the King.

Don't forget, God is after purity of body, mind, heart and soul. He tells us in His Word that He desires "truth in the inward parts" (Ps 51:6). Unless we allow God to put our sexual appetite and desires to sleep during our single years, and our seasons of solitude, the enemy will use these un-restrained passions to put our spiritual appetite to sleep. We cannot indulge what God has not blessed and thrive spiritually. Sexual sin, lust, and spiritual compromise of any kind suffocates the life and breath out of our walk with God. It desensitizes our soul and silences the voice of the Holy Spirit.

Perhaps you no longer have your virginity. Perhaps you've already given away that first kiss, or your thought life has not been pure. Perhaps you struggle with pornography, private sin, or other sins of the flesh. My friend, you can choose right now, today, to begin anew and dedicate your body, mind, and full heart to Jesus once again, until it's *His timing* for you to experience these pleasures within the sacred covenant of marriage.

Remember, no matter our past, we are all *needy sinners* living at the same level at the foot of the cross. Our only claim to God's mercy is our great need.[7] Thankfully, our bridegroom Jesus loves to cover our shame and pain with His white wedding garment of perfect righteousness. He tells us, "Though your sins are like scarlet, they shall be as white as snow" (see Isa 1:18).

It's time to stop letting the sins or shame from your past or present define your life. You don't need to be a victim anymore. Whatever your failures, whatever your scars, throw them at the feet of Jesus. Fall into the arms of His forgiving, unconditional love. He tells us, "The one who comes to Me, I will by no means cast out" (John 6:37).

Trust me, He loves you. He will never turn you away. Not only will He make you pure and clean once again—physically, mentally, emotionally, and spiritually—but He will restore to you the years the locusts have eaten. I'm living proof that at the feet of Jesus a broken heart can become the beautiful gateway to abundant joy.

Steps to Deeper Joy!

(Bible passages, heart questions, and activities for going deeper)

God is love. Rest in His love. If you doubt, look to Calvary and put all doubts away.

> It is God's glory to encircle sinful, repentant human beings in the arms of His love, to bind up their wounds, to cleanse them from sin, and to clothe them with the garments of salvation.[8]

1. What are you to flee, what are you to pursue, and how should you glorify God? Prayerfully read 2 Timothy 2:22; 1 Corinthians 6:18-20; 10:13-14; Romans 12:1-2.
2. If you long to be healed from your scars and wounds from the past, God has some special promises for you. Prayerfully read 1 John 1:9; Psalm 147:3; 30:2; Isaiah 43:19.
3. If you need deliverance from an addiction or stronghold, here are some promises for victory you can claim: Daniel 6:20; Romans 8:31-32, 37; 2 Corinthians 2:14; 10:3-5; Jude 1:24-25.
4. What is the will of God for your life? See 1 Thessalonians 4:3-8; 5:23-24; 2 Peter 1:4; Ephesians 5:8.
5. After reading the above Bible passages, what conviction is the Holy Spirit bringing to your heart? Don't delay obeying what the Holy Spirit is telling you to do!
6. Finally, what fresh reasons for joy do you find in the following passages? Read Micah 7:19; Isaiah 53:5-6.

If you need additional help achieving spiritual victory in some area of your life, read the "Biblical Steps to Freedom in Jesus," Appendix 4 in the back of this book.

As you pray for God to make you pure from the inside out, meditate on the following:

> None are so sinful that they cannot find strength, purity, and righteousness in Jesus, who died for them. He is waiting to strip them of

their garments stained and polluted with sin, and to put upon them the white robes of righteousness; He bids them live and not die.[9]

I encourage you to make a determined choice to pursue Jesus with all your heart. Give Him your thoughts, your choices, your scars, your temptations, and your sins. Fall at His feet in humble surrender and worship. Let Him turn those stones of suffering, sin, and shame into living stones of abundant joy.

CHAPTER 6

"I Will Be Your Husband!"

"My beloved is mine, and I am his . . . and his desire is toward me!"
Song of Solomon 2:16, 7:10

The lake sparkled like a thousand glittering diamonds in the early morning sunshine. I sat back in my hammock at the water's edge, starring with awestruck wonder at the beauty all around me. I was basking in the peace of a quiet scenic hideaway, nestled among the mountains of Montana. The view was simply breathtaking. It was the kind of view you don't want to enjoy alone. Thankfully, I knew that I was not alone.

I looked up into the soft blue sky as I imagined Jesus looking down at me. "What a perfect place to take a get-away together," I whispered to Him with a smile. "This is amazing, like a taste of heaven. I could stay here forever, especially with You!"

I imagined Him smiling back.

It had been a while, far too long since I had taken a real get-away with Jesus. Oh, how desperately I needed it.

I sighed happily, enjoying the sweet moments as the words from Song of Solomon spoke to my heart in a fresh way, "My beloved is mine, and I am his....and his desire is toward me!" (Song 2:16, 7:10)

"I can't believe that Your desire is toward *me!*" I prayed softly.

To be desired by Someone, who loved me so much that He had given up everything for me, had traveled far beyond the moon and back to demonstrate His love, had slain dragons for me, had even laid down His own life for me—all of this was quite unfathomable to my limited, childlike comprehension. And yet, Jesus did all of that and so much more, for me!

How wonderful it was to be treasured and pursued by a Man who knew all my flaws inside and out, and yet still loved me anyway. I could hardly wrap my mind around the beauty of it all. *This must be one of the closest things to heaven I will ever experience!* I thought blissfully to myself.

Again, I spoke out loud, perhaps just wanting the reassurance of His love once more.

"Why do You desire me?" I asked quietly. "Why do You choose to lavish Your love on *me?*"

Of course, Jesus did not speak audibly in response, but I could feel the warmth of His love all around me, holding me tight, as though He would never let me go. I said no more, for there were no words adequate enough to describe the joy bubbling up within my heart. Thankfully, words were not necessary. I knew He could read my thoughts. He knew how much I loved Him, and how I longed to love Him more. I was also learning afresh how much He loved me.

I sat in sacred silence for a long time, enjoying the quiet of my own thoughts. While my Bible was open in my lap to Song of Solomon, my mind was far away, in heavenly places.

Just then two beautiful bald eagles flew overhead—so close that I could see their piercing eyes. *How majestic! How simply breathtaking is their regal bearing,* I thought in awe.

Once again another passage from Song of Solomon came to mind as my gaze followed the eagle pair off into the distant horizon. "He brought me to the banqueting house, and His banner over me was love" (Song 2:4).

Not only had God stretched a loving banner of gorgeous blue across the horizon as far as I could see, but He had filled this banner with beautiful songbirds and majestic eagles to bring my soul delight. At sunset, I knew He would repaint the banner in different hues of purple, red, and gold. When it seemed as though the banner was growing dark and would fade away, He would then splash across it millions of sparkling stars which all testified of His bountiful power and magnificent love. And He did this for me again and again, day after day.

That is my Jesus, always lavishing His love upon me, often in such rich measure that I can scarcely comprehend it.

As I gazed out across the lake once more that morning, I was reminded of the scripture, "Many waters cannot quench love, nor can the floods drown it" (Song 8:7). While many earthly loves had faded, I knew that Jesus' love was here to stay. And no human love can ever compare with the sweet love of Jesus.

My Marriage Vows

It's been over a year since my lakeside getaway in the mountains of Montana, where I first got the inspiration for this book. But I make time for sweet retreats with Jesus whenever possible, whether it's hiking to a scenic Ozark overlook, turning my phone off for 24 hours, or hanging my hammock over a bubbling mountain stream. It's a special habit I've cultivated for nearly three decades now, wherever I've lived, from the jungles of South America to the secluded forests of Norway, from the east coast to the west coast of the United States. It's a habit that helps keep my heavenly romance alive. If you haven't tried this, I encourage you to set-aside some unrushed time in your schedule for such a getaway with Jesus. I promise that it will breathe fresh life into your relationship with Him and fill the longings of your restless heart.

Speaking of loneliness and longings, I must admit that I'm thankful for these emotions that come and go. These very feelings have again and again pushed me deeper into the arms of Jesus. I've learned to find my comfort and strength in solitude with Him. As a result, our love relationship has become *real and vibrant.* I can't get enough of alone time with Jesus. He truly has become my heavenly bridegroom and husband.

I love the promises given in Isaiah 54. I think God put this passage in His Word just for me!

> For your Maker is your husband, The LORD of hosts is His name; And your Redeemer is the Holy One of Israel; He is called the God of the whole earth. For the LORD has called you, like a woman forsaken and grieved in spirit, like a youthful wife when you were refused, says your God. For a mere moment I have forsaken you, but with great mercies I will gather you (Isa 54:5-7).

I still remember the overflowing joy in my heart, many years ago, when I first discovered these beautiful promises. Recognizing that Jesus really should be my husband and first love, I went so far as to write out the marriage vows that are typically spoken at the altar, and I put Jesus' name in the place of "named husband." Our vows were simple and went something like this:

> I, Melody, take you, Jesus, to be my lawfully wedded husband, to have and to hold from this day forward, for better, for worse, for richer, for poorer, in sickness and in health, to love and to cherish, till death do us part, according to God's holy law and purposes.

I signed my vows, "Your loving bride, Melody."

"Lord," I prayed, "I'm taking these vows and these promises from Isaiah 54 literally. I don't have a man in my life right now, so I'm counting on *You* being my man. I'm counting on *You* being my husband. I'm trusting *You* to take care of me, to protect me, and to provide for my needs."

Well, the Lord has done just that. Let me tell you friend, over the last two decades since I first made my marriage vow commitment to Jesus, Jesus has been *more than a husband* to me, and He's taken care of me probably better than any earthly husband ever could have—quite literally.

When I'm traveling the world and feeling weary, I pray, and He gives me strength. When I'm struggling with how to speak to those in need, I ask Him for wisdom, and He gives me the right words to say. When I get in a predicament or things aren't safe, I cry out for help, and He sends someone to rescue me. When I'm struggling to pay my bills, I tell Him, and He gives me the necessary funds. When I need health advice, and I don't know what to do, He sends just the right doctor. When I'm overwhelmed with a huge hospital bill, I ask Him to provide, and He pays the bill. When I'm feeling alone and afraid in the dark, I whisper my fears, and His peace surrounds me. When I cry because I'm feeling needy and insecure, I lean into His presence, and He reminds me that I am His bride, and that I am very loved. When I'm struggling with my thought life, my physical longings, or I'm desiring the things of the world, I pray for deliverance and forgiveness, and He gives me victory. When I'm angry at Him and need to vent, I tell Him exactly what I'm feeling, and He listens to me patiently and still loves me just the same.

The sweet intimacy Jesus and I have shared over the years is quite tangible. The personal and meaningful gifts He gives me often melt my heart with joy. As most of you have probably figured out by now, I'm a complete romantic at heart, and as such, I decided many years ago that if I didn't have a husband to dress up for and give love notes too, I could do this for Jesus. So, every Friday night is our special date night. As I prepare to open the Sabbath, I get the house all clean. I light candles and turn on soft music. Sometimes I even dress up in a special outfit and fix my hair extra pretty before I sit down and enjoy the evening with Jesus. On some occasions I invite company over, but usually it's just Him and me. I write Him love letters, and we sing songs together. It's my favorite night of the week, followed by, of course, the best day of the week. It's wonderful to be Jesus' bride.

I also love to laugh, and I have found that Jesus has a great sense of humor. I remember a funny conversation the two of us had a couple years ago. It was another one of those days where I was feeling especially lonely, and so I cried out to Him once again, "Lord, where is my husband? It seems like he's gotten lost out there somewhere. Does he need directions?"

"I'm not lost," Jesus tenderly replied. Then He sweetly asked His own question. "Am I not better than 10,000 husbands?"

"Yes, Lord!" I giggled joyfully. "But I don't want 10,000 human husbands, I only need *one*!" "Just trust me, my child. I know *exactly* what you need," He winked with a smile.

Many years ago, while I was still in my teens, someone encouraged me to make a list of qualities that were important for me to find in a future husband, so I wouldn't be distracted with guys who didn't hold my values or have the character that I wanted. I made my list and have held on to it for many years now, despite the consternation of some. More than once those, who have seen my list have told me that it will be impossible to find such a man. (I still firmly believe that if God plants a holy desire within your heart, it's because He intends to fulfill that desire.)

One day, over twenty years ago, something special happened. As I was looking back at my prayed-for list, I realized *I had found my man.* What I had been praying for in an earthly husband, Jesus was already offering me *right then* in Himself. Once again, I was awestruck and in love.

So, let me tell you a few more things about my heavenly bridegroom Jesus, the prayers I've prayed all these years, and how He truly is the best husband and most perfect valentine any girl could desire.

My Perfect Valentine

I prayed for a man committed to God. Jesus said, "I and my Father are one" (John 10:30).

I prayed for a man who would be a spiritual leader. Jesus unashamedly declared, "I am the way, the truth, and the life. No one comes to the Father except by Me" (John 14:6).

I prayed for a man of high standards and integrity. Others testified, He "did no sin, neither was guile found in His mouth" (1 Pet 2:22, KJV).

I prayed for a man of the Word. Jesus opened up His arms with love as He whispered, "I am the living Word, and I came to live with you" (John 1:14).

I prayed for a man who knew how to be a servant. Then I heard others whisper with amazement, "Jesus made Himself of no reputation, and took upon Himself the form of a servant, and was made in the likeness of men" (Philm 2:7).

I prayed for a man who was full of spiritual life. He smiled again: "I have come that they might have life, and that they may have it more abundantly" (John 10:10).

I prayed for a man of faith and prayer. Then I watched with amazement as He went out and spent all night under the stars in prayer—for me (Luke 6:12).

I prayed for a man who would provide for my needs. He not only fed the 5,000 long ago, but He also feeds me each and every day today (Mark 6:41; Phil 4:19).

I prayed for a man who would be the head of my home and someone I could look up to and respect. Then I realized that not only had Jesus been knocking on my door, begging to be the Head of my home, but I would have all eternity to learn from Him. "For as the heavens are higher than the earth, so are My ways higher than your ways, and My thoughts than your thoughts" (Isa 55:9). How could I not respect and admire such a man?

I prayed for a man of steel and velvet—someone who could be strong but also tender at the same time. Then I remembered Jesus' words as the nails were driven deep into His hands:

"Father forgive them, for they do not know what they do" (Luke 23:34). I remembered how, when dying upon the cross, some of His last tender thoughts were to make sure His mother would be cared for (John 19:26). I also remembered that when even a little sparrow fell, He noticed and cared (Matt 10:29). His steel resolve and yet tender love even in times of great trial amazed me.

I prayed for a man who knew how to love others, even the unpleasant outcasts. Jesus replied, "In that while you were still sinners, the lowest outcast, I died for you" (Rom 5:8).

I prayed for a man with whom I could share my deepest thoughts and dreams, a man who would walk with me through both joys and sorrows; a man that would not only hold my hand, but would hold my heart. I looked up in awe as He not only began to walk beside me and hold my hand (Isa 41), but also began to share with me the hidden riches and secrets of eternity—a heart companionship and beauty I had never experienced with another (Isa 45:3; Ps 34:8).

I prayed for a man I could stand with, love, and serve for the rest of my life. Then I saw Him standing on Mount Zion with 144,000 behind Him (Rev 14:1), and I prayed, "Lord, help me be one who follows You wherever You go (Rev 14:4), for I want to stand with You, love You, and serve You for the rest of my life!"

"I know this may be frivolous, God, and it's a small thing, but could you also send me a man who is romantic?" I had prayed. *"Could you send me someone who will love me so much, that he'll want me and only me and will be willing to do whatever it takes to win me—even give me flowers and chocolates?"* Jesus, the Rose of Sharon, said nothing as He laid down His heavenly crown to come to earth to win me. Although I doubted His love and resisted His advances at first, He slowly, sweetly, tenderly won my heart and love. Then He led me to His great banqueting house, and the banner He put over me was love (Song 2:4).

"Oh, taste and see that the Lord is good" He tenderly whispered (Ps 34:8). As He looked deep into my heart, I knew that nothing would ever separate us (Rom 8:35- 39), for He had won my heart forever, and His love was much sweeter than the finest chocolate.

Last, but not least, I prayed for a man who would not be afraid of pain or tears. I then realized that it was He, Jesus, who was carrying my cross, and enduring my pain, and making the ultimate sacrifice of love, not just for anyone, but for me (Matt 16:24; Heb 2:9). Tears rolled down my cheeks as I stood in awe. And my heart melted.

No, Jesus is not just any man—He is all this and so, so much more: my Judge, my Lord, my Savior, my Creator, my Redeemer, my Bridegroom, and my King! He is my All In All, the True Love I have yet to fully understand and know. He is my Perfect Valentine, and I am forever *in love.*

St. Augustine of Hippo once said, "To fall in love with God is the greatest romance; to seek Him the greatest adventure; to find Him the greatest human achievement."

I don't know if I will ever walk down the aisle in a white wedding dress. However, the sweet reality is that I continue to discover a fresh love story with Jesus each day as I spend unrushed time with Him in His Word and in prayer. And while the longings for human companionship will probably never go away—after all, God put these desires in my heart—I can honestly say, *Jesus is still enough.* He will always be enough. And if I had to choose between having a human husband or having my Heavenly Husband, I would choose my Heavenly bridegroom any day!

When we are in love, it's natural to pursue the person we love. Did you know that Jesus fell in love and pursued you *first,* my friend? Not because of what you could do, but simply because you are His bride, and you are of infinite value in His eyes. Now, if you are a man reading this, that might sound a bit strange. You don't usually like to think of yourself as a "bride." However, God's church is His bride, and if you are a follower of Jesus, *that includes you.* So, no matter what anyone else has said about your life, you were worth giving up all of heaven to Jesus. He only asks one thing in return—that you love Him back with *all your heart* (Luke 10:27).

Tears of joy come to my eyes as I dream about the future and how wonderful it will be to run into the arms of my heavenly bridegroom and finally see Him face to face. I know that one look from His eyes of love will melt away every heartache and every pain I've ever experienced in this life. All the unanswered questions and difficult circumstances won't matter anymore. It will be worth it all when we see Jesus, for He is far beyond everything we've ever waited for or imagined. Truly He is the Lover of our soul for all eternity.

Steps to Deeper Joy!

(Bible passages, heart questions, and activities for going deeper)

Robert Murray McCheyne once wrote, "Set not your hearts on the flowers of this world. They shall fade and die. Prize the Rose of Sharon and the Lily of the Valley. He changes not."

Will you choose today to intentionally pursue intimacy with Jesus and allow Him to fulfill your deepest heart needs and longings? He wants to be your Best Friend. He wants to be your True Love.

1. What can we learn from Mary's whole-hearted devotion to Jesus? What can we learn from Martha? Read Luke 10:38-42; Psalm 16:11; 36:8-9.
2. How would you describe your current relationship with Jesus? Are you hungry for a deeper walk? Are you willing to invest the time and energy to take your love and intimacy with Him to the next level?
3. Look up the following Bible passages, and ask what God is speaking into your life and heart today. Psalm 36:6-8; 34:8; 46:10; 62:5; Mark 6:31-32; Song of Solomon 2:3-4.
4. Journal your thoughts, prayers, insights, or any additional passages that God gives to you as you open His Word.
5. Start making plans in your schedule for an all-day getaway with Jesus!

You might feel like you don't have the time for an unrushed getaway with Jesus, but the truth is, we always make time for what is important to us. If you'd make time for a special date with a friend or a get-away weekend to grow your marriage, how much more significant is it that you take time to grow your love-relationship with Jesus? I challenge you to start planning today. Once you take this time, trust me, you will wonder why you waited so long. It will jump-start and rejuvenate your walk with Jesus more than you can imagine.

For more ideas on how to spend a full 24-hour retreat with Jesus, see Appendix 3 in the back of this book.

CHAPTER 7

More than Enough

"To them God willed to make known what are the riches of the glory of this mystery among the Gentiles: which is Christ in you, the hope of glory."
Colossians 1:27-28

I have found time and time again, since God set my feet back on His path of life and abundant joy, that Jesus really is enough for all my needs. He truly is an amazing husband, companion, lover, best friend, and so much more. I find great delight and peace in my walk with Him.

However, one of the thoughts that Satan often tries to tempt me with is the feeling that *Maybe I am not enough—maybe I will never be enough, especially for the kind of godly man I have prayed to marry.* You can understand why I might feel this way, after reading my story.

Maybe God is holding back what I've asked for because I am not yet strong enough spiritually, I've wondered to myself. *Or maybe He isn't answering my prayers because He knows I still have too many flaws. Or maybe I'm actually too much—too much of this, or too much of that, too high standards, too quirky, too independent, too tall, too much of a spiritual leader, etc.*

Maybe that is why men aren't interested?

As I get older, the temptations to see myself as "inadequate" and "less than" don't go away—they get magnified unless I keep myself rooted and grounded in God's Word. However, there are a few truths I often speak to my heart, and maybe you need to hear them as well.

First truth: We are enough in Jesus, and He is *more than enough* for us!

Second truth: You and I will never be "too much," and we will never be "not enough," for the right person.

I've often told my friends, "As long as God is leading your relationship, you simply can't ruin things with the right person! If God is in it, your shortcomings, your scars, your failures, your imperfections, your weird quirks, your humanness won't chase the right person away." *(Reality check: If they do get scared and run away, they obviously aren't the right person for you, period stop—and there's no reason to waste your time pining after them.)*

I love how one pastor put it: "One man's 'She's too much for me,' is another man's 'She's everything I hoped and prayed for.'"

Whether you are a man or a woman reading this, remember you will be worth *everything* to the right one—and they will be worth everything to you.

However, if you have already married, and you've discovered you still aren't enough for the person you married, or they aren't enough for you, then what do you do? Well, take heart, because this chapter might still be for you.

The reality is, when two broken people enter a relationship or marry, they are likely to be used by the enemy to break each other even more. That's why we need God to heal the brokenness of our hearts, so we stop breaking others. Of course, we can't heal or fix a spouse, or anyone else for that matter. We can only change ourselves, through the power of the Holy Spirit. So, this chapter isn't about fixing others, but about allowing God to heal our own hearts by finding our identity in Him.

Ephesians 6:12 tells us, "For we do not wrestle against flesh and blood, but against principalities, against powers, against the rulers of the darkness of this age, against spiritual hosts of wickedness in the heavenly places."

Our adversary is set on trying to destroy us mentally, spiritually, and emotionally. Almost every temptation he brings against us starts in the mind. He wants to steal our joy, kill our faith, and destroy our hope of ever becoming who God created us to be. He floods us constantly with his lies—lies to remind us how we don't measure up to the mark. In contrast, Jesus comes to give us life and life more abundant (John 10:10). He comes to speak truth, life, and hope. If we take our every thought captive and grasp the truths of His Word rather than listening to the lies of the enemy, Jesus can and will set us free (John 8:32).

Gabriella's Story

Not long ago, I met a beautiful young woman named Gabriella. She is a wife and mother who attended one of my online women's retreats.

As we began talking and corresponding, I could hear the enemy's lies through every word Gabriella shared. I finally told her, "I want you to write out every negative feeling that you have about yourself, and then we are going to counteract those negative messages with the truth from God's Word, because the enemy is trying to destroy you with his lies."

Gabriella sent me her list. It was brutal. *There is no hope for me. I will never change. I'm full of shame and guilt. I'm not worthy of God's love. I'm broken. I shouldn't be alive. I'm a terrible wife and mother. I want to give up.* The list went on.

Gabriella and I took every negative phrase she had listed and began looking for Bible passages that directly addressed her struggles. Next, I asked her to re-write her list, listing her feelings of failure in small letters, with the hope of God's Word written in large letters, followed by a prayer of thanks. Gabriella's life was transformed as she realized what God's Word had to say about her true worth and value.

Of course, the devil is always looking for new ways to attack. Even to this day, Gabriella still has her good days and her tough days, just as I have mine and you have yours. But when our focus begins to blur, the despair begins to weigh us down, and we feel the stones of condemnation being hurled, it's time to hand those stones back to Jesus and stand on the solid rock of His Word (Luke 6:48). His Word brings healing. Not only will He purify our hearts and turn our stones of condemnation into a beautiful altar and testimony for His glory, but He can and will take what the enemy means for evil and turn it to good (see Gen 50:20). I've seen Jesus do this over and over again. Learning to counteract Satan's attacks with scripture makes all the difference in the world. It is one of the keys to maintaining our peace and joy in Jesus in the midst of challenging times.

I love 2 Corinthians 3:5: "Not that we are sufficient of ourselves to think of anything as being from ourselves, but our sufficiency is from God."

My friend, remember, our identity and worth are not defined by what happens to us or by what others say about us. Our identity and worth are defined by one person—Jesus Christ! Our best efforts will, of course, *always* be woefully inadequate (Isa 64:6). Our righteousness will *always* be just filthy rags (Isa 64:6). But we can take courage. It is not our righteousness or sufficiency that will ever save us. It is His. It is not the strength of our hold on Christ that rescues us. It is the power of His hold on us (John 10:28).

The Bible tells us, "For by one offering He has perfected forever those who are being sanctified" (Heb 10:14). Thankfully, His perfect righteousness covers our entire sanctification journey, all the way to the end of our story.

Perfect and Complete in Christ

God brought me a simple and yet profound healing truth a few years ago, while I attended a weeklong *Call of Elijah*[1] revival event in Tennessee. The leader of the revival, speaking heart to heart, encouraged us to ask God to remove all hindrances from our hearts, including unforgiveness and bitterness, so we could ask for and receive the full baptism of the Holy Spirit.

Bitterness and resentment (another word for unforgiveness) are serious diseases of the soul which pollute and contaminate our entire spiritual journey, if not surrendered to Jesus. In fact, I think nothing hinders the Holy Spirit more, or makes a person more unattractive inside, and out than being bitter. Bitterness sours you. It dries up your soul. It drains all color, beauty, and peace from your life and your face. It's almost impossible to grow in your walk with God while holding on to grudges and bitterness. That's why, I realized later, the revival leader was so in earnest to see us address this significant issue.

"I want you to go home tonight and pray about who you need to write or call and ask forgiveness from or extend your forgiveness to," he challenged us. "Bitterness and unforgiveness are so damaging to our spiritual walk. They rot out the very life of our soul. That's why we need God to give us deliverance from these things. If you don't feel like you can forgive someone, pray, and ask Jesus to give you that forgiveness. He will help you, and you must experience this to go forward."

When the appeal was first given, I didn't realize I had bitterness in my heart toward anyone. I thought I was doing okay. But then, as the revival leader continued speaking, negative emotions began coming to my mind that I hadn't known were there. There *was someone* in my life whom I needed to forgive, someone who had cut me deeply many times with their words and accusations.

That night I went home and wrote an email telling this person that I forgave them and that I loved them. It was tough, but I made myself vulnerable. Then I gave the situation to God as I went to sleep.

I wish I could say that my message of love was well received, and all the pain of the years was instantly wiped away. But that didn't happen. The next day I received a fresh dose of condemnation. I felt deflated. It seemed that no matter what I did, nothing was *good enough* for this person.

That day, the revival meeting leader asked us to do a simple exercise that would radically speak healing to my wounded soul.

"Take out a sheet of paper," he began, "and draw a simple stick-figure picture of yourself.

Put your name at the bottom of the picture."

We all followed his directions.

"Now, across that stick figure in small letters, write out all the bad labels about yourself that you feel, or the lies the enemy has told you, or the hurtful things people have said to you that still affect you. Perhaps you've been told you are a loser, a liar, or something else. Whatever it is, whatever negative labels you feel about yourself or that others have called you, write those labels over your stick figure."

For a few minutes we worked away in silence. It was painful to write out the labels that I felt the enemy was throwing against me. Some had been hidden in my heart and soul for many years. Some were quite fresh. But I wrote out everything that came to my mind.

"Now open your Bible to Colossians 1:27-28," he instructed. Pages rustled as everyone looked for the passage. Then we read together:

> To them God willed to make known what are the riches of the glory of this mystery among the Gentiles: which is *Christ in you*, the hope of glory. Him we preach, warning every man and teaching every man in all wisdom, that we may present every man *perfect in Christ Jesus*.[2]

"Here's the beautiful mystery of the gospel," our leader shared with joy. "The secret of the mystery of the gospel for the Christian is found in this phrase: *Christ in you*!"

"You see," he continued, "the devil speaks many negative labels over our lives, and he uses people to tell you many negative things too, things that wound deeply. But when you accept Jesus, He comes to live in your heart through the power of the Holy Spirit. Because of this, you are no longer defined by what others say or think about you. You are now *perfect* and *complete* in Jesus!"

We all listened attentively.

The leader continued. "Now I want everyone to write across your stick figure in big bold letters, covering up all those negative labels, the phrase 'Perfect in Christ.'"

I still wasn't sure if I was grasping the fullness of what he was sharing, but I read over the passage another time. Then the verses came alive with fresh power. *That's amazing!* I thought to myself, as tears came to my eyes. *It doesn't matter what others say, or what the enemy says, I truly am perfect in Christ!*

Tears rolled down my cheeks as I picked up my pen. In big, bold letters, I wrote "Perfect in Christ" across my "Melody stick figure," covering up all my negative labels. It felt so liberating to write those words. Then, above my stick figure, I wrote in bold letters,

"Daughter of the King."

The leader then invited us to our knees to pray and to give God all our negative labels.

"Always remember," he declared "you are complete and more than enough in Christ!"

It was a simple truth, but it was a truth many of us had waited years to hear. My friend, is this a truth that you've been waiting many years to hear as well?

You may be struggling with your singleness, feeling like you are half a person, like you aren't quite complete until that "other half" comes into your life. Perhaps you are facing a messy divorce, the loss of a child, the loss of a position, health crises, or even the loss of your faith. You can't understand why God has allowed certain things to happen, and you feel like a "less than" in the world in which we live. Perhaps you are struggling with accusations spoken against you. But the beauty of the gospel is, no matter our circumstances, no matter our past or present, we can be complete in Christ.

That means my circumstances don't make me half a person. My singlehood is complete in Jesus. My ministry is complete in Jesus. My peace is complete in Jesus. My purpose is complete in Jesus. *And yours is too!*

When our identity is firmly rooted in Jesus, we don't need to have fear about the future, or being alone, or about finding someone to complete us. We don't need to fear what people might say about us.

We don't need to fear what God might ask us to do. We can go with confidence to far away mission fields, or stand before presidents or kings, because Jesus stands with us and lives inside us. We aren't a greater person in the eyes of heaven because of our accomplishments, nor a lesser person because of our failures. None of these things define us. It is Jesus who defines us—and He already showed us our value, two thousand years ago, at the cross.

Dear one, you are enough in Jesus, and He is more than enough for you. In fact, He's not just enough—He is your EVERYTHING! Rest in this truth with joy. It will change your life!

Steps to Deeper Joy!

(Bible passages, heart questions, and activities for going deeper)

You would never invite a thief into your house. So why would you allow thoughts from the enemy into your heart to steal your joy? Don't allow this evil intruder to rob you of your purpose, calling, and identity in Christ.

1. When it comes to our identity, who should we trust? Who is telling us the truth, Satan or God? See John 8:44; Numbers 23:19; Ephesians 1:3-6; Colossians 2:9-10; 1 Peter 2:9.
2. What do the following Bible passages tell us about God's character and the reliability of His Word? See Romans 5:8; 15:4; 1 John 4:16-19; Hebrews 13:8; 2 Timothy 3:16-17.
3. Do the practical heart activity that was shared in this chapter on pages 99-101.

- Get out a blank piece of paper.
- Draw a stick figure and put your name under it.
- Write over the stick figure, in small letters, all the negative labels you've been carrying in your heart and life.
- Pray that God would help you understand the reality and truth of His unchanging Word.

- Read Colossians 1:27-28 with fresh eyes. Read it two or three times.
- Write "Perfect in Christ" or "Complete in Christ" in big bold letters over your stick figure.
- Pray and surrender all your negative labels to God.

4. If there are other lies that the enemy is speaking over your life, your value, your future, your work or ministry, or your family and relationships, take those lies and counteract them by the truths of God's Word, just like Gabriella did.
5. Take time prayerfully internalizing the Bible passages shared in Appendix 6, "Who You are In Christ," in the back of this book.
6. Every time the enemy tries to remind you of a negative label or of his lies, remind him of God's Word. Claim John 8:32 and 10:10.

As the author Elisabeth Elliot once said, "The secret is Christ in me, not me in a different set of circumstances." So, my friend, look up, away from the darkness of this world—see Jesus!

> When temptations assail you, as they surely will, when care, perplexity, and darkness seem to surround your soul, look to the place where you last saw the light, rest in Christ's love and under His protecting shade; for in His shadow we may find rest and peace. When sin struggles for the mastery in the human heart, when guilt oppresses the soul and burdens the conscience, when unbelief clouds the mind, remember that Christ's grace is sufficient to subdue sin and expel the darkness. Jesus, the sin-pardoning Saviour, is our Advocate in the courts of heaven, and He calls upon us to "arise and shine," because His glory has risen upon us.[3]

As you move forward on the truths of God's Word, keep sharing heaven's joy, because the resources of Christ are inexhaustible. Jesus is enough and so much more! He is everything!

CHAPTER 8

Big Dipper Blessings

"'And try Me now in this,' Says the LORD of hosts, 'If I will not open for you the windows of heaven and pour out for you such blessing that there will not be room enough to receive it.'" Malachi 3:10

One beautiful crisp October evening, a number of years ago, I was headed home after helping lead a large prayer event at Andrews University. My flight was delayed, and I felt exhausted. I'd traveled with our prayer team for over three weeks. We had not only prayed and ministered to hundreds of students daily, we had also worked with church leaders from around the world. I could scarcely believe all the miracles and divine appointments I had witnessed and experienced.

As I sat in the Chicago airport, waiting for my last flight to announce boarding, I felt in awe of God's goodness and leading. "What's next, God?" I prayed as I watched the people around me. "It seems like You've turned my entire world upside down this past year as I've dedicated my life more and more to prayer ministry."

Just then my cell phone rang, interrupting my conversation with God. I was surprised to receive a phone call so late at night, but then I recognized the number. It was a church leader with whom I'd exchanged contact information just a few days before. He was responsible for one of the larger territories in our church. Many members were under this godly man's leadership, and it was obvious God was using him in a mighty way.

"Melody, I'm sorry to be calling so late at night," he apologized. "I've been in committee meetings all day and just now got back to my hotel. I know this is short notice, but God's been convicting me that we need you and your prayer team to come work with us in our division right away. We need more united prayer in our territory. We have important meetings back at our division headquarters next week, and all the leaders of our division and unions will be present. Will you please come and lead us in times of daily prayer?"

My head spun. "Oh, pastor?" I began to protest. "I can't possibly travel overseas *next week*. I've already been on the road for three weeks."

He was not put off with my excuses and continued to share the great needs in their overseas territory. At last, I promised I would pray about his invitation and get back to him the next day.

Not long after I hung up the phone, the gate agent finally announced that it was time to board. As the plane lifted into the sky and left the lights of Chicago behind, I closed my eyes and began to pray again.

"God, I'm overwhelmed. I want to work for You, but I don't feel ready for such a large task! This is a big opportunity that could impact many people. But I feel so small and unqualified. I want to know that this invitation is from You!"

I opened my eyes and looked out the airplane window into the dark night. There, right outside my window, as if sitting on the airplane wings, the Big Dipper constellation filled the night sky. I gasped in childlike wonder and awe, pressing my face against the window, trying to take in the beautiful scene. Just then a shooting star blazed across the sky, shooting straight into the middle of the Big Dipper cup, its tail of light shimmering for a moment before fading away. I felt like I could have reached out the window and touched it.

"Did I really just see that? Was that for me?" I asked myself in amazement.

"Yes, that was for you." I heard God's gentle voice speaking to my heart. "Melody, this invitation is for you, too. I am with you. If you will keep trusting Me, if you will keep walking with Me, abiding in Me, and following where I lead, I will pour out heaven's richest blessings upon you. In fact, you see how massive My Big Dipper cup is—it holds billions of galaxies—yet it cannot begin to contain all the blessings I have in store for you!"

My heart overflowed with joy as I gazed out the airplane window, in awe at the majesty of God. All tiredness left me as I thought about the future. *Could the promise I just heard God speak to my heart really be true?*

As if to answer my thoughts, God reminded me of Isaiah 55:8-9: "For My thoughts are not your thoughts, nor are your ways My ways, says the Lord. For as the heavens are higher than the earth, so are My ways higher than your ways, and My thoughts than your thoughts."

"Lord, I'm willing to go, if this is Your leading," I prayed at last. "But can You please send Your angels with me. *Lots of them.* I can't do this on my own. I need to know You are going with me!"

The three-hour flight home that night felt quite short as I talked with God.

Dear reader, our Heavenly Father longs to overflow our lives with His joy and divine providences. He longs to be our traveling companion and confidant on life's journey. He loves when we talk to Him and pour out our longings, our fears, our questions, and all our needs. He also loves to supply those needs, and to surprise us with fresh pictures of His love. He longs to do in our lives far beyond what we can humanly imagine.

As I'm sure you already guessed, I accepted the leader's last-minute invitation. I took the next several days to pray, prepare my heart, tie up loose ends around the house, wash clothes, and make travel arrangements. Then I quickly repacked my bags, heading off for what would become a series of life-changing trips and ministry adventures on the other side of the globe. It felt like living in a whirlwind. I kept thinking to myself, *Who am I? Why would God call me on such a special errand?* But God had given me peace that I was on the right path, so I knew I should move forward by faith, even though I still felt completely inadequate.

A few days later, I got another phone call. I was just past airport security, headed to my gate, about to embark on 36 long hours of travel.

"Melody, I just saw you!" my friend told me excitedly when I answered the phone.

"What do you mean, you just saw me?" I asked.

"God gave me a vision. I saw you walking through the airport, and then through the airport security checkpoint. *But you weren't alone.* You were surrounded by ten strong angels!"

I stopped walking.

"Kim!" I tried to control my emotions. "Did you know that I'm at the airport *right now,* and I just went through airport security not three minutes ago?"

"I knew you were traveling soon, but I didn't know you were already there," she said.

Goosebumps went up and down my arms. "How do you know the men you saw were angels?" I asked. "What did they look like?"

"I just *know* they were angels," she told me confidently. "They had a regal bearing. I've never seen any men that looked like those men. They were tall and strong and protective. No one would want to mess with those men."

"Did you know that I prayed and asked God, when I was flying home from Chicago last week, to send His angels with me on this overseas trip?" I said, tears coming to my eyes. "I can't believe this! God is good, *so good.*"

We praised the Lord together, and then she hung up the phone as I continued to my gate, rejoicing in the Lord.

God did send His angels with me on that journey, and I felt their presence often. I saw the Holy Spirit move in powerful ways above and beyond my comprehension, as many men and women joined me in prayer at the foot of the cross. This appointment with God's leaders across the ocean started a string of Holy Spirit-led reverberations that continue to impact my life and ministry to this day—one of which is the book you are holding in your hands.

My friend, never be afraid to step out in faith and follow God's leading, for the Fearless One, the Faithful One, and the All-Sufficient One goes before us. He is bigger than all our needs.

The Above and Beyond Miracle Gift

For many years now God has challenged me to ask for *more* in my walk with Him. When the enemy threatens to overwhelm me with my inadequacies, fears, or my past mistakes, God reminds me that I am His, and He is mine. When life's difficult circumstances begin to cloud my vision, or I feel crippled by my lack of energy or resources, God shows me once again that *He* is all I need and so much more.

Time and time again, He brings me back to His special promise, "Now to Him who is able to do exceedingly abundantly above all that we ask or think, according to the power that works in us, to Him be glory in the church by Christ Jesus to all generations, forever and ever. Amen" (Eph 3:20-21).

"Keep daring to ask for more, Melody! Keep believing! Keep praying!" He encourages me. "I still have more in store for you!"

That's why, every time I walk out under the stars, I always look for the Big Dipper. It's God's enduring promise of the inexhaustible blessings He is just waiting to *pour out* through the Holy Spirit. The best thing about the Holy Spirit is that He brings us constant access to Jesus—*Heaven's Greatest Gift.*

> Just think of it!—all heaven has been poured out to you in one gift, Jesus Christ. When God gave His Son, He gave *with Him the richest treasures of heaven.* It is yours, if you will cooperate with Him; He gave all heaven; all heaven He gave in that one gift. All heaven is at our command. All heaven we may claim.[1]

It's hard to imagine that God loves us this much, not only to give us Jesus, but also to send us a Heavenly Helper (John 16:7). This Helper, we are told, brings all other blessings alongside. But something hinders our receiving this gift in all fullness.

> There are many who believe and profess to claim the Lord's promise; they talk *about* Christ and *about* the Holy Spirit, yet receive no benefit. They do not surrender the soul to be guided and controlled by the divine agencies. We cannot use the Holy Spirit. The Spirit is to use us. Through the Spirit God works in His people "to will and to do of His good pleasure." Philippians 2:13. But many will not submit to this. They want to manage themselves. This is why they do not receive the heavenly gift. Only to those who wait humbly upon God, who watch for His guidance and grace, is the Spirit given. The power of God awaits their demand and reception. This promised blessing, claimed by faith, brings all other blessings in its train. It is given according to the riches of the grace of Christ, and He is ready to supply every soul according to the capacity to receive.[2]

Think about the Holy Spirit like this. The Spirit is constantly drawing you to Jesus. If you have the slightest hunger or desire for something better for your life, something better for your singlehood, something to hold onto in the midst of your pain, it's because the Spirit is at work in your heart, *drawing you to God.* He is giving you a distaste for the things of the world and a hunger for the things of heaven.

However, something extra special happens when you choose to repent of your sins, be baptized, and receive Jesus as your Lord and Savior (see John 3:5). Not only do you receive the Living Water, but if you humbly ask, God will start pouring out His Holy Spirit upon you in greater and greater measure.

Luke 11:13 says, "If you then, being evil, know how to give good gifts to your children, how much more will your heavenly Father give the Holy Spirit to those who ask Him!"

Of course, this is only the beginning. God longs to give us a daily baptism of the Holy Spirit, but we must keep asking.

Paul wrote, "Walk in the Spirit, and you shall not fulfill the lust of the flesh" (Gal 5:16). What a timely promise for all of us on the heavenward journey. As we walk and abide with Jesus daily, through unrushed time in prayer, unrushed time in His Word, and obedience to His commands (see Acts 5:32), He continues to fill us until we start to overflow. Jesus says, "whoever drinks of the water that I shall give him will never thirst. But the water that I shall give him will become in him a fountain of water springing up into everlasting life" (John 4:14). This is when we really begin to spill out blessings on others. But we don't want to stop at being a fountain for Jesus. We must keep daring to ask for more!

In John 7:38-39, we catch a true glimpse of what God longs to do in each of us. He tells us, "He who believes in Me, as the Scripture has said, out of his heart will flow *rivers of living water.* But this He spoke concerning the Spirit, whom those believing in Him would receive; for the Holy Spirit was not yet given, because Jesus was not yet glorified."[3]

You see, from *living water,* to *fountains of water,* God wants us to be so filled, so immersed, with the daily baptism of the Holy Spirit, that we become a *mighty river of living water* that the Holy Spirit can flow through. Remember, our own hearts are corrupt. We have nothing good within us. Our righteousness is only filthy rags (Isa 64:6). But when *Jesus dwells within us by faith,* we become a vessel His river of life can constantly flow through, leading others back to the source of all life—back to Him.

If you feel like you're living in a wilderness; if you feel needy or thirsty, and long for His living water to flow through your soul, these words from Isaiah 41:17-18 are for you:

The poor and needy seek water, but there is none,
Their tongues fail for thirst.
I, the LORD, will hear them;
I, the God of Israel, will not forsake them.

I will open rivers in desolate heights,
And fountains in the midst of the valleys;
I will make the wilderness a pool of water,
And the dry land springs of water.

God is waiting to pour out floods of blessing on our thirsty souls. I admit, there's still so much about this Great Gift I don't understand. But one thing I do know—*I want more!* Will you join me in daily asking God for more of this beautiful gift?

Mr. Nice-Looking Shoes

Obeying God's call to share His Word and love others constantly challenges me to step outside of my comfort zone. I have many testimonies I could share. However, sometimes the most challenging witnessing opportunities I've faced have occurred in my own back yard. Sometimes I simply don't want to obey what the Spirit is asking me to do, so I cry and sweat and pray hard, and my heart quakes, and God helps me surrender once more. The beautiful thing is, every time I surrender and step forward in humble obedience, I discover afresh that His Big Dipper cup of blessings always overflows. His cup never runs dry.

I wish I could say that I'm always a bold, cheery witness for Jesus everywhere I go. The reality is I'm still growing in this department—even after all these wonderful years in ministry. I am an introvert, and I don't naturally like to talk to strangers. That's why sometimes God has been forced to give me an extra strong nudge, to help connect me with a divine appointment along the way.

A few weeks ago, heading home on a flight from the West Coast, I felt the Holy Spirit telling me to talk to a young man. He sat across the aisle from me, but he was in the "I'm-way-too-cool-for-you-to-talk-to-me" category and looked barely out of his teens. He was nicely dressed, and I especially noticed his classy pair of shoes.

I watched him for awhile but, despite the conviction I felt, I said nothing. He was wearing headphones and was obviously occupied. When the plane finally landed, all I could think to say was, "Nice looking shoes!" He smiled and walked off the plane, without me sharing any words of encouragement or hope.

However, guess who was sitting in the same aisle of seats with me on my very next flight? You got it right! It was the same young man with those nice-looking shoes. Did I boldly tell him about Jesus? No. For another two hours we flew together across the sky, but I was still too shy to start a conversation. I had a good excuse, though. Another person sat between us.

Finally, as we began our final descent into my home city airport, the young man reached across the person sitting between us and tapped me gently on the arm. I had to pull out my earphones to hear what he wanted to say.

"Hey, ma'am, I have some free drink vouchers, beverage of choice. My travels are over today, and I can't use them. Would you like them?" he offered.

There was no reason for this young man to speak to me, let alone reach out and offer such kindness, except I had smiled at him and complimented him on his shoes. I politely declined his offer, telling him that I was also reaching my final destination. I said nothing more.

He once again got off the plane ahead of me, with no words of encouragement or hope. However, as I began walking towards baggage claim, the Holy Spirit spoke urgently to my heart once more. "Melody, I gave you two opportunities already! You missed them. But I'm going to give you one more chance. Find that young man at baggage claim and give him a book."

A few moments later, I found him. Nervously, I went up and stood in front of him. He looked at me in surprise.

"Hey, I just wanted to say thanks for offering me those drink vouchers on the plane," I told him. "Now, I have a gift for you. God told me to give you this. I think it will change your life!" Pressing the book *God Still Lives* into his hands, I turned and walked away.

That day God was gracious with me. He gave me multiple opportunities. But most of the time, we don't have those second and third chances. Often, we only have *one opportunity,* one chance to touch someone's life for God's Kingdom. We need God to help us be bold and speak when He asks us to speak, trusting that He will give us His words. "But sanctify the Lord God in your hearts: and be ready always to give an answer to every man that asketh you a reason of the hope that is in you with meekness and fear" (1 Pet 3:15, KJV).

Of course, looking back, I should have offered to pray for the young man. I should have shared so much more. After all, God poured out all of heaven to rescue that young man—and to rescue me. But I'm grateful that God takes our feeble offerings of obedience and multiplies them many times for His glory. So, I can leave what *should have happened* in His hands. Maybe what *did happen* was just enough, just what that young man needed. In eternity we will know.

Do You Love Him?

The reality is that we have all been given a divine calling and purpose—the call to be witnesses, to serve Jesus, and to bring as many with us to heaven as possible. This might look slightly different for each one of us, because we all have different gifts, different strengths, and different ways of sharing God's love. We also have different struggles, as well as different stories to tell. But no matter our struggle or our story, *we all have received the same call.*

In *The Desire of Ages* we are told, "Every true disciple is born into the kingdom of God as a missionary. He who drinks of the living water becomes a fountain of life. The receiver becomes a giver. The grace of Christ in the soul is like a spring in the desert, welling up to refresh all, and making those who are ready to perish eager to drink of the water of life."[4]

Did you know there's only one qualification essential for discipleship and service? You don't need an expensive education. You don't need to be talented or highly skilled. You don't need eloquence of words. You don't even need a personality that's naturally bold and assertive. The only question Jesus asks each of us is the same one He asked Peter: "Do you love me?" (see John 21:15-17.)

So my question is: Do you love Him? If you love Him, why not serve Him? Why not ask Him for strength and courage to share?

You may not feel qualified. You may feel weak. You may feel handicapped because of the difficulties and heartaches of life—but look up. See that Big Dipper hanging in the sky? It's God's promise of what's available for you right now in the righteousness of Christ. It is the promise of His overflowing and abundant Holy Spirit.

> "Try Me now in this," Says the LORD of hosts, "If I will not open for you the windows of heaven and pour out for you such blessing that there will not be *room enough* to receive it" (Mal 3:10).

We simply cannot imagine all that God is eager to pour down upon us, and how He wants to use our lives as that river of life, leading others to Him.

I encourage you, prove Him, try Him—trust His Word. Don't settle for living in the wilderness. Keep daring to ask God for more!

Steps to Deeper Joy!

(Bible passages, heart questions, and activities for going deeper)

The missionary C.T. Studd served tirelessly in India and China in his youth. Later, despite poor health and his doctor's warnings about tropical diseases, he left to serve in Africa. To everyone's surprise, he regained his health, and for the next twenty years he won many souls for Christ across the continent. His now famous words live on: "Only one life, 'twill soon be past. Only what's done for Christ will last."

In *The Ministry of Healing*, Ellen White wrote, "By all that has given us advantage over another,—be it education and refinement, nobility of character, Christian training, religious experience,—we are in debt to those less favored; and, so far as lies in our power, we are to minister unto them. If we are strong, we are to stay up the hands of the weak."[5]

Take a few minutes to watch the short, inspirational video on YouTube by Eric Ludy, titled: "Rack of Glory." I also encourage you to watch the seven-minute video, "A Call to Anguish - David Wilkerson." These videos are posted by Ellerslie Discipleship Training and are very moving and so worth watching.

As you pray for Holy Spirit power, to be all that God has called you to be, carefully study through the following Bible passages and heart questions. This study section is more in depth and lengthy than most. Don't rush! What's shared here are just starting points for an amazing adventure with Jesus that could last for the rest of your life.

1. Why is it important to ask for a daily fresh baptism of the Holy Spirit? What will the results of that baptism look like in daily life? See Luke 11:13; Zechariah 10:1; Acts 1:8; 5:32; Galatians 5:22-23.
2. What must happen before God's Spirit will be poured out in Latter Rain power? Read 2 Chronicles 7:14; Joel 2:12-32; Jeremiah 29:13.
3. Are you living your God-given mission, asking for more in your walk with Jesus, or are you trying to work in your own strength? Read Jeremiah 2:13; 32:17; 33:3; Luke 18:27.
4. Why is understanding the sanctuary so significant for our lives today? What does the sanctuary teach us about the gift of the Holy Spirit? See Psalm 77:13; Ezekiel 47:1-12.
5. What is the source of all heaven-sent blessings? What personal invitation is God giving you right now? Read Revelation 22:1-5, 17; Isaiah 44:3.
6. What can we learn from the life of Elijah about rebuilding the broken-down altars of worship? How are we to prepare the way for Jesus' soon coming? Read 1 Kings 18:30; Matthew 3:1-3; Luke 1:16-17.

For additional tips on how to have a vibrant devotional life and walk with Jesus, please see "Back to the Altar: Keys to a Vibrant Devotional Life" in Appendix 1 in the back of this book.

We live in a world of broken-down altars of worship. Many have lost their way. That's why, not long ago, we launched a world-wide, intergenerational revival initiative called *Back to the Altar.* It focuses on removing distractions and repairing broken-down altars of worship, so we can fulfill God's purpose for our lives. This is all about a spiritual revolution from *the inside out.* It's a heart-felt call for believers everywhere, to learn what it means to be disciples and disciple-makers for Jesus.

Following are ten heart questions about your daily life and devotional habits that come from the resource *The Way Back to the Altar.* Answer the questions honestly with either a "Yes" or a "No." You don't need to share or compare your answers with others. This is not about "who's more holy than who." These ten bold heart questions are just meant to help each of us recognize our spiritual need.

Remember, the Bible tells us, "Examine yourselves as to whether you are in the faith. Test yourselves. Do you not know yourselves, that Jesus Christ is in you? — unless indeed you are disqualified" (2 Cor 13:5).

The "Back to the Altar" Discipleship Survey:

- Are you thirsty for something more with Jesus than you currently have? (Yes/No)
- Do you have peace about your salvation by grace through faith? (Yes/No)
- Are you taking *daily, meaningful, unrushed time* alone with God in His written Word? (Yes/No)
- Are you taking *daily, meaningful, unrushed* time in prayer? (Yes/No)
- Do you surrender daily to Jesus as Lord of all you are and all you have, including your attitude and your electronics? (Yes/No)
- Are you daily asking for and receiving a fresh baptism of the Holy Spirit? (Yes/No)
- Do you love your family, friends, and those around you with a sacrificial spirit? (Yes/No)

- Do you have daily worship, with family members or children under your care? (Yes/No)
- Are you free from anything that would make you a slave? (Yes/No)
- Are you discipling or mentoring someone outside your church to trust and follow and share Jesus? (Yes/No)

After you've answered the above questions, read Revelation 3:14-22, asking God what He is saying to you. If you feel a little overwhelmed or discouraged about your spiritual condition, that's okay. Just fall at Jesus' feet. He loves for us to come to Him *just as we are.* Jesus tells us in Mark 2:17, "Those who are well have no need of a physician, but those who are sick. I did not come to call the righteous, but sinners, to repentance." That means He's calling you and me! He will not forsake us in our great need.

If you'd like to go deeper and repair the broken-down altars in your life, I encourage you to study the seven discipleship principles in *The Way Back to the Altar: How to Live Daily as a Disciple of Jesus.* This free resource, that can be used individually, or for a small group Bible study, can be downloaded at www.backtothealtar.org.

Never forget, you are God's joy and song. He sees unlimited possibilities in you. Keep looking for that Big Dipper in the sky, as you continue on your heavenward journey.

CHAPTER 9

Daring to Ask for More, in Relationships

"For we were saved in this hope, but hope that is seen is not hope; for why does one still hope for what he sees? But if we hope for what we do not see, we eagerly wait for it with perseverance." Romans 8:24, 25

Over and over again God has gone far beyond all that I've asked or thought possible, especially when it comes to my relationship with Him and the ministry adventures He has led me on. While life hasn't always been easy, and I've cried my fair share of tears, I wouldn't trade the beautiful years God has given me in my walk with Him for anything. His ways truly are best.

However, as I think back over the incredible ways God has worked during my single journey, a deep conviction has slowly grown in my heart. If God can do abundantly above and beyond all we ask or think in our relationship with Him, and even work miracles, why would He not want to do the same in our choice of a life partner, *if marriage is indeed His plan for our life?* Shouldn't our romance be a heavenly orchestrated love story that's even better than what we hoped or prayed for? Shouldn't every Christian marriage be a vibrant testimony to God's goodness and glory?

A few years ago I heard an amazing testimony that brought me great happiness, and maybe even a little *fresh hope.*

A young woman named K'dee, while waiting for God's best, started a singles group. She and her girlfriends met together each week to study the Bible and pray for one another. They prayed not just that they would *find* the right person to marry, but that they would *be* the right person and know how to embrace their God-given femininity for their future husbands. Somewhere along the line, they also started reading my book, *Daring to Ask for More.*

As they read together, K'dee realized afresh that God's ways are always higher and better. She surrendered her dreams of what a future husband should look like to God. She dared to ask for more, praying that God's will and way would be accomplished.

Not long after, God brought a handsome, on-fire-for-Jesus man named Aron into her life. Aron was a pastor, and different than the type of man K'dee had always imagined herself marrying. However, God made it very clear that Aron was the answer to her prayer. He gave Aron similar confirmations about K'dee. (Incidentally, both of them had been claiming Ephesians 3:20 for their future spouse.) As they moved forward, trusting the Author of Romance, God scripted a beautiful love story between them. They soon realized they were a perfect match in life and ministry.

The Bible tells us, "He who finds a wife finds a good thing, and obtains favor from the Lord" (Prov 18:22).

Last spring I had the great joy of attending Aron and K'dee Crews' wedding. Hearing their love story reminded me anew: Truly God does give His best—even in romance—to those who dare to ask for more and who give their choices to Him.

Unfortunately, most singles today have lost the heavenly vision of true, God-honoring marriages. I see men and women compromising, lowering their personal standards, getting involved in dating relationships that are often less than ideal. Because they have given up hope of ever finding a godly spouse, they sometimes even marry unbelievers. They ignore caution signals and warning signs and go forward thinking that everything will work out okay. But settling usually doesn't bring true happiness. It often brings great heartache. Doing things our way, without God's blessing, never pays.

"You think being single and lonely is bad!" one woman told me, not long ago. "Being married and lonely is a thousand times more heartbreaking."

What a tragic testimony! But this doesn't have to be our story. I still believe in the God who writes beautiful love stories, stories above and beyond all we can ask or think; stories that reflect His character, and that exemplify His love. Give Him the pen of your life. Let Him author your story. Let Him answer your prayers in the way *He* knows best.

Since we serve a heavenly Father who loves to bless His children with *good gifts,* why don't we dare to ask for more in our relationships? Rather than going after just anyone who gives us attention, why don't we put our desires on the heavenly altar and ask God what *He wants* us to look for and pray for? Why don't we also seek to become *the kind of person* that the person we pray to find would want to marry? God's Word tells us, "Ask, and you will receive, that your joy may be full" (John 16:24).

Now, let me digress for a moment. I want to be clear here. God never promised in His Word that *everyone* would get married. Marriage is not a right we can demand from God, any more than any other divine gift. When we read God's Word, it's obvious that marriage is *not* best for everyone (see 1 Cor 7:7-8). While Paul taught about the beauty of sacrificial love between husband and wife, he was also bluntly honest about the distraction and even "trouble in the flesh" having a spouse might bring. Paul was completely focused and "single-minded" (no pun intended). His only aim and life goal was to lift up Christ.

Even today, I know individuals who have intentionally remained single for this same purpose. They believe it is their life calling, and they are content. But others of us have chosen to be content because God has not yet brought a godly partner into our life.

I'll never forget the blunt way my friend Eric Ludy asked his sister about her relationship status one day. "Krissy," he said, "are you called to singleness?"

Obviously, he didn't know that there are *some questions* you just don't ask older single women, even if they do happen to be your sister. But Krissy was not phased or irritated at her younger brother.

"Today I am," she said softly.

While Krissy did eventually marry, her gentle, Holy Spirit-led response to her brother's question, nearly two decades ago, has given me great strength for my own journey over the years. I don't know that singlehood is my calling, but *today* singlehood is the gift God has given me, and for this gift I am grateful.

A Fresh Perspective on Love

Unfortunately, our world has redefined the meaning of love and marriage. While God designed marriage to be a *good thing*, the enemy has turned it into one of the greatest sources of pain and disappointment. One way or another, most of us have felt the devastating effects of *love turned sour*. The woes of failed marriages and broken homes are all around us.

Listen to these sobering words written over a hundred years ago:

> Few have correct views of the marriage relation. Many seem to think that it is the attainment of perfect bliss; but if they could know one quarter of the heartaches of men and women that are bound by the marriage vow in chains that they cannot and dare not break, they would not be surprised that I trace these lines. Marriage, in a majority of cases, is a most galling yoke. There are thousands that are mated but not matched. The books of heaven are burdened with the woes, the wickedness, and the abuse that lie hidden under the marriage mantle . . . The path of married life

may appear beautiful and full of happiness; but why may not you be disappointed as thousands of others have been?[1]

As I reflect on these words of caution, I wonder if part of our problem is that we have allowed the culture to write our guidebook. Let's look at a few cultural norms, and how they contrast with God's Word.[2]

The culture tells us that it's normal to "fall in love." However, when we fall, it's usually an accident, and things that fall almost always break. In contrast, God's Word tells us to "walk in love" (Eph 5:2). When we "walk in love," especially with another, it shows a thoughtful, deliberate, prayerful approach to life, as well as a spiritual alignment of purpose and focus—because you must walk in the same direction.

In other words, before declaring our romantic intentions or desires, we should prayerfully evaluate if our choice is walking in the same direction God is leading us to walk. If God confirms our choice is according to His will, then and only then do we move forward. Of course, it might feel like you are "falling in love," but the difference is that we don't allow ourselves to "fall" until God gives us freedom to do so. It's not just an accident. It's a choice. And that brings us to my next point.

The culture tells us "Love is a feeling." While feelings are a significant part of every romance, and I wouldn't encourage anyone to marry someone for whom they have no feelings, God's Word tells us that love is more importantly a choice. That means feelings will come and go, but true love will choose to hold on and keep giving even when life gets hard, and when there are no warm fuzzy feelings (1 Cor 13:7).[3]

The apostle John wrote, "Beloved, let us love one another, for love is of God; and everyone who loves is born of God and knows God. He who does not love does not know God, for God is love" (1 John 4:7-8).

The reality is, if we don't understand God's love personally, if His love hasn't yet broken our own hearts with wonder and awe, we will be tempted to settle for superficial substitutes of love when it comes to human romance. We also won't know how to give true sacrificial love to another.

The culture tells us, "Marry the person that you love," while God's Word reminds us again and again that it's most important to "love the person that you married" (Gen 24:67, Eph 5:28-29). I once heard it said that the secret to a happy marriage was falling in love over and over again, *always with the same person.*

The culture tells us "Follow your heart." God's Word tells us, "Follow Jesus" (Matt 4:19). The reality is that our hearts are "deceitful above all things and desperately wicked" (Jer 17:9). We can't trust our hearts.

The culture says, "Be true to yourself" or "Believe in yourself." That's another way of saying, "If it feels good, do it. If it feels good, it must be right for you." In other words, if you feel deep in your heart that he/she is the one, they *must be the one* for you. But when we follow our own wisdom, apart from God's wisdom, the Bible tells us we are as "silly children with no understanding" (Jer 4:22). That's why God's Word tells us, "Believe in Jesus" (Acts 16:31). In fact, whoever wants true happiness must "deny himself and take up his cross and follow Him" (Mark 8:34). *Yes, my friend, discipleship and learning to deny oneself is directly related to happiness in romance and marriage.*

Unfortunately, it can be impossible to reason with someone once they have "fallen in love." If you've felt the sense of exhilaration that comes with the "in love" experience, you know that you kind of lose your mind just a little when someone special is in your life. You can hardly think of anything else. You don't want to think of anything else. That's the beauty of being "in love."

God gave us feelings. The joys and euphoria of fresh love are a gift to help a couple bond and work through life's challenges while forming deeper attachments. But strong feelings and unbridled passions can also lead us astray—dreadfully astray. Modern culture tells us, "As long as you are happy, that's all that matters," but the Bible says, "For what shall it profit a man, if he shall gain the whole world, and lose his own soul?" (Mark 8:36).

You see, when God asks for permission to write our life story (or love story), it's because *His way truly is best.* Not only does He want to give us what would bring us the most happiness, but He also wants to give us what would be for our highest eternal good. That's why we must prayerfully surrender our hearts to Jesus and ask Him to choose our spouse for us.

Listen to these additional words of caution:

> It is from the marriage hour that many men and women date their success or failure in this life, and their hopes of the future life . . . Marriage is something that will influence and affect your life both in this world and the world to come. A sincere Christian will not advance his plans in this direction without the knowledge that God approves his course. He will not want to choose for himself, but will feel that God must choose for him. We are not to please ourselves, for Christ pleased not Himself. I would not be understood to mean that anyone is to marry one whom he does not love. This would be sin. But fancy and the emotional nature must not be allowed to lead on to ruin. God requires the whole heart, the supreme affections.[4]

In Psalm 127:1 we read, "Unless the LORD builds the house, They labor in vain who build it; Unless the LORD guards the city, The watchman stays awake in vain." The Bible also tells us, "There is a way that seems right to a man, But its end is the way of death" (Prov 14:12).

If things aren't working out as you hope in the relationship department, or it seems like doors to true love keep closing, perhaps God is simply shielding you from making a big mistake, because He has a more perfect way (Ps 18:30). Don't go desperately banging on closed doors. Don't keep insisting that things must be *your way.* Don't keep monitoring the things that you've left in His hands. Thank Him for saving you for *His best.* Praise Him for those closed doors.

The children of Israel learned a hard lesson when they insisted on having their way. They wanted meat in the wilderness and would not stop complaining until God gave them what they desired. Scripture tells us, "They soon forgot His works; They did not wait for His counsel, but lusted exceedingly in the wilderness, and tested God in the desert. And He gave them their request but sent leanness into their soul" (Ps 106:13-15).

Yes, He gave them the meat they craved, so much that it was coming out their nostrils. But He also gave them *leanness of soul*. The reality is, if we want something bad enough, we can always get it. Anyone can get married. But staying married and being happily married—that's another story. And God alone sees the future that we cannot see.

God Knows How to Tame Wild Broncos

Before I close this chapter, I want to share one more testimony. This story comes from one of my favorite books on the topic of relationships. It's called *Quest for Love* by Elisabeth Elliot. I will share the story here exactly as Elisabeth shared it.

> Before Fred Malir became a Christian he was already engaged—to a Christian. She took him to hear the gospel, and his conversion was followed by a call to missionary work. Here was a whole new direction, not one in which his fiancée was prepared to participate. "I don't want to be the wife of a missionary," she said, and that was that.
>
> "A civil war began in my heart that lasted six months," wrote Fred. He lost his joy in the Lord. He felt he could not possibly give up the girl, and the thought of her marrying someone else drove him crazy—but, as he later learned, "God knows how to tame wild broncos." Patiently He began to soften Fred's heart as he prayed to be made willing to relinquish his beloved.
>
> Toward the end of those miserable six months of conflict the Lord "put some godly backbone in my jellyfish nature and I prayed, 'All right, Heavenly Father, I give her up, totally, absolutely, completely!' . . . I discovered that the best way to understand the Holy Scriptures is OBEDIENCE! As soon as I obeyed the Lord, His omnipotent hand, like an expert surgeon, operated on my heart and removed the passion for that girl that was not His will for me. I was truly set free."
>
> Fred went as a missionary, to Montevideo, Uruguay, where he had grown up, but his desire for marriage did not evaporate. "Twelve

long years went by. Then one day when I was traveling in the U.S. God put me next to a born-again Christian girl on a one-hour drive, and the Presence of the dearest Lord Jesus was so vivid in her that I fell in love with Christ in her."

[Melody's note*:* Notice, Fred didn't just fall in love with her, he fell in love with the Christ he saw in her. This is the way it should be when we fall in love! Now I will let Fred continue his story.]

"For a whole week we were able to see each other often and talk together. We were both conscious that we had fallen in love, but did the Lord want us to be married?"

"Before I was born again, I would kiss a girl first and then would ask myself if I liked her. But now that I was a believer, God made me know that I could not kiss any girl until I was absolutely sure we were going to be married. So, I did not kiss Ann. I expected some kind of supernatural revelation, like a voice from heaven saying as loud as thunder, MARRY THAT GIRL! But I heard nothing. . . ."

"I prayed for a whole week. On a glorious Sunday afternoon, on February 26, 1959, in a way I cannot even explain, I was overwhelmed with the deep assurance from God that He wanted me to marry Ann. I did not hear a thunderous voice from heaven, but somehow, I had the deep assurance that this was His unmistakable will. I knew! But I had a problem: Ann was in Virginia, and I was in Uruguay, as far south of the equator as Atlanta is north of the equator. How could I bridge that gap?"

God knows how to bridge gaps. Fred wrote to Ann, telling her of his week of prayer and the clear answer, then signed his name and—imagine this—added a P.S. with the words, "Will you marry me?"

For three days he held on to the letter, asking for final confirmation from the Lord. Then he mailed it. Knowing it would be two weeks before he could hear from her, he was astonished to receive a letter a few days later, dated February 26. He read: "I suppose I will never know until I will meet my Lord in Glory, why He has laid such a burden upon me to pray for you during all this past week. Then today God gave me the assurance that whatever your need was, He had supplied it."

At last came the reply to his proposal: "On the same day the Lord made His will clear to you, He also spoke to me that we were to be married. God made it so plain to me, that I felt like your wife already!"

"And I hadn't even kissed her yet! When we later checked on the days and even the very hour when these things were happening to us, we were amazed to verify that God made known His will to both of us exactly at the same hour. We were moved to write to each other at the same moment. We both held our letters for three days, then mailed them at the same time. Our letters crossed each other in the middle of the air, and we both received each other's letter simultaneously! What a wonderful God we have, and how minutely intricate and detailed is His high-precision guidance for those who seek to know and do His will."[5]

Fred went on to write how God miraculously made provision for him to travel the 5,300 miles from Uruguay up to the U.S. Ann did not know he was coming and was delightfully surprised when he arrived at her doorstep.

"I had five cents in my pocket, no more," Fred confessed, as they began planning their wedding. "But God gave us a big wedding. Our honeymoon began and now, many years later, it still continues, thanks to God."[6]

Forty some years later, Fred met his first fiancée again. She had married a non-believer, and although she had everything that money could buy, it was obvious she had not lived a happy life. How thankful Fred was that he had waited for a woman who shared his heart for the Lord as well as his passion for missions.

If you are a man looking for that woman of your dreams, be the man God is calling you to be. Hold your hormones in check and prayerfully surrender your dreams to Jesus before you rush wildly ahead. "Many youth mistake strong, uncontrolled passion for strength of character; but the truth is that he who is mastered by his passions is a weak man. The real greatness and nobility of the man is measured by the power of the feelings that he subdues, not by the power of the feelings that subdue him."[7] As you bring your passions and desires under the authority of Jesus Christ, he will reveal the woman of His choice to you. It may take some time, but your wait will be worth it.

If you are a woman praying to find a man after God's own heart, hide yourself in Jesus in such a way that the man of God's choice must be seeking the Lord in order to find you. Pray that such a spirit of heavenly joy will overflow your life that he'll be drawn to not only you, but to the Jesus he sees within you.

It always pays to trust God. "He always answers the cry of the man or the woman who wills (against all wanting) to do His will. It is here that the battle is waged. What do I want? What do I will? which means, what will I do? My will must be baptized with fire—cleansed and purified and consumed as I offer it to God, a living sacrifice. Our God is a consuming fire."[8] And He always gives His best to those who leave the choice to Him.

Keep seeking the Lord and *dare to ask for more* in love!

Steps to Deeper Joy!

(Bible passages, heart questions, and activities for going deeper)

In the book *Our High Calling,* we read the following:

> Our devised plans often fail that God's plans for us may be a complete success. Oh, it is in the future life we shall see the tangles and mysteries of life, that have so annoyed and disappointed our fond hopes, explained. We will see that the prayers and hopes for certain things which have been withheld have been among our greatest blessings. We need not expect all sunshine in this world. Clouds and storms will cluster about us, and we must be prepared to keep our eyes directed where we saw the light last. Its rays may be hidden but they still live, still shine beyond the cloud.

> It is our work to wait, to watch, to pray, and to believe.... It is our privilege to be suppliants, to ask anything and everything of God, submitting our request in submission to His wise purposes and infinite will.[9]

1. Where does all love come from? What can you learn about God's love that you can apply to your relationships, your work, your family, and your current or future romance? See 1 John 4:7-21; 1 Corinthians 13.
2. How are we as believers to walk? What are we to put off and put on? See Ephesians 4:17-24; Romans 13:11-14.
3. What blessings and the cautions do you find in 1 Corinthians 7? (Read the whole chapter!)
4. What special instructions do we receive in Hebrews 13:5, that affect all areas of our life today?
5. How should we wait on the Lord? What beautiful promises can you claim for your own heart's desire? See Psalm 37:3-5; 62:5; Proverbs 10:22.

I love the promise from Joshua 23:14, "Behold, this day I am going the way of all the earth. And you know in all your hearts and in all your souls that not one thing has failed of all the good things which the LORD your God spoke concerning you. All have come to pass for you; not one word of them has failed."

Keep trusting your dreams with Jesus. And don't lower those dreams just to match your current life reality. Instead, increase your faith to match your destiny—God's destiny for your life. Whether married or single, young, or old, in good circumstances or difficult, God loves to restore the dreams we thought were lost. He longs to do for us better than we hoped for. Someday you will thank God that He didn't give you a yes that would have led you away from His best plan.

CHAPTER 10

A Match Made in Heaven

(TO LOVE OR NOT TO LOVE – PART 1)

"As for God, His way is perfect; The word of the LORD is proven; He is a shield to all who trust in Him." Psalm 18:30

I love beautiful love stories. Whenever I meet a couple, no matter their age or profession, if we have any length of time together, one of my questions is always, "How did you two meet? How did you fall in love? Tell me your story."

Just like every human being, each love story is unique, different, and beautiful. No two stories are exactly alike. I think it will be amazing to compare each other's stories in heaven someday—not just the human love stories we've experienced while on earth, but best of all, our love story with Jesus.

Romance wasn't man's creation, by the way—it was God's. God is the Author and King of romance. He came up with the idea in the first place.

In the very beginning of the world, before sin ever came into existence, God created the most perfect and beautiful love story. It was the romance between Adam and Eve, handcrafted by the divine Matchmaker Himself.

When Adam first opened his eyes in Eden, the first face he saw was the face of God. Just imagine—the King of the universe welcoming you to life and introducing you to the glories of your new paradise home.

When Adam began life, he didn't know he was alone. He didn't know he needed a wife. He was perfectly content and happy in his relationship with God.

From the very beginning God gave Adam a mission and a purpose. He didn't wander around aimlessly, like so many today, trying to figure out what to do with himself. His first mission was to take care of the garden (Gen 2:15). Next, he was given the glorious job of naming the animals (Gen 2:21). I'm not sure how he managed to name all the animals, in one day, and get married too, but somehow, with God's help, he accomplished it all.

Notice that it was God's idea, not Adam's, that Adam needed a wife. "And the LORD God said, 'It is not good that man should be alone; I will make a helper comparable to him'" (Gen 2:18). Only then did Adam notice something important was missing. While all the animals had a complimentary partner, he suddenly realized that he had no companion of his own.

Now think of this! God could have created a beautiful flock of women and told Adam, "Here's a selection! Go choose your bride." But God didn't do this. Instead, he put Adam *to sleep*. Then God took a rib from his side and created Eve, the most beautiful companion in all creation.

When Eve first opened her eyes, the first face she saw was her Creator's. The first kiss she received was the kiss of life from her bridegroom King Jesus. Eve didn't know that she needed a man—*Jesus was her Man.* She was also asleep to her desires and needs.

This brings me to a practical heart question.

Are you so in love with Jesus and so asleep to your own personal wants and desires that God can bring you His best in His perfect time? Whether that's helping you find the spouse of His choice, the job of His choice, the opportunity of His choice, the ministry of His choice—whatever you need, will you place your desires on the altar and let God choose for you? Will you give Him your timetable, your expectations, your agenda, your will? Will you truly let Him be *your First Love and your Everything?*

Jeremiah 33:3 says, "Call to Me, and I will answer you, and show you great and mighty things, which you do not know."

I wish I could have seen Adam's face on that introduction day. While the Bible doesn't give us many details, I can only imagine that it was love at first sight.

"And Adam said: 'This is now bone of my bones And flesh of my flesh; She shall be called Woman, Because she was taken out of Man. Therefore a man shall leave his father and mother and be joined to his wife, and they shall become one flesh. And they were both naked, the man and his wife, and were not ashamed" (Gen 2:23-25).

Notice: It was only after Adam and Eve had formed an intimate bond with their Creator that God introduced them. When they fell in love, they were *both* in the presence of God. They were *both* walking in step with their Maker, and they had no shame! However, God didn't bring them together just to spend all their love and attention on each other. As Adam had been given a task and life purpose individually, before beginning his love story with Eve, God gave both of them a task and life purpose *as a couple.* "Be fruitful and multiply," He commanded. "Fill the earth and subdue it; have dominion over the fish of the sea, over the birds of the air, and over every living thing that moves on the earth" (Gen 1:28).

Bearing fruit for God's glory and serving those He's put in our sphere of influence is often forgotten in the bliss of fresh love. However, according to Scripture, the main purpose and mission of all heavenly-ordained marriages is to bear fruit—not just birthing children, though that's often a significant part, but in a much larger sense, the birthing of Holy Spirit fruit, and spiritual children for God's kingdom.

The Bible tells us, "Two are better than one, Because they have a good reward for their labor" (Ecl 4:9).

According to God's original plan, the man and woman were designed to work together in unity, as equals, for His glory, complimenting one another, encouraging one another, and strengthening one another in their heavenly-ordained mission.

In *Patriarchs and Prophets* we read:

> Eve was created from a rib taken from the side of Adam, signifying that she was not to control him as the head, nor to be trampled under his feet as an inferior, but to stand by his side as an equal, to be loved and protected by him. A part of man, bone of his bone, and flesh of his flesh, she was his second self, showing the close union and the affectionate attachment that should exist in this relation. "For no man ever yet hated his own flesh; but nourisheth and cherisheth it" Ephesians 5:29.[1]

What a honeymoon Sabbath that must have been—perfect bliss, in the perfect paradise, with the perfect love story, created by the perfect Author of Romance. Now, if only that perfect love story could have lasted forever . . . we all would be in a much better place today!

Lessons on Love From the Fall

One powerful evidence for the Bible's authenticity is that it does not tell a perfect story about perfect people. It shares the full history of humanity, with all the messy details included. Because of this, we know that we are not alone in our struggles with temptation. If we pay attention, we can learn much from the mistakes and sins of those who lived before us.

Unfortunately, before Adam and Eve even finished their honeymoon together, they got their first heartbreaking lesson on what it means to play with sin and try to do things their own way. Although their love story had been so beautifully written, they let go of their First Love, Jesus.

It all started when Eve wandered away from Adam's side, into the pathway of temptation. Although initially alarmed at finding herself alone next to the forbidden tree, Eve quickly dismissed her fears, thinking she had sufficient wisdom and strength to resist any temptations that came.[2] How often have we done the same, lingering near sin, thinking we won't fall. But the Bible says, "Pride goes before destruction, And a haughty spirit before a fall" (Prov 16:18). It is through the pathway of pride and self-sufficiency that Satan loves to destroy our most treasured relationships, especially our love relationship with God.

When a snake started talking from the forbidden tree, instead of fleeing in alarm, Eve leaned in closer, listening curiously. "Who is this creature? And how does a snake have the magic ability to talk?" she asked herself.

When the serpent started making accusations against God and His character, encouraging Eve to do what God had *specifically* commanded her and Adam not to do, Eve kept listening, and then entered into conversation with her tempter. It is always dangerous to argue with the enemy. His arguments will always outshine our own. Eve was no match for the enemy in disguise. Believing that God was indeed holding back something good, Eve took the fruit and ate and convinced Adam to do the same.

Then came their shame. Instead of running to meet God when He came to the garden, all they wanted to do was hide. Sin always brings shame and spiritual death. It makes us run from the presence of God.

> Adam understood that his companion had transgressed the command of God, disregarded the only prohibition laid upon them as a test of their fidelity and love. There was a terrible struggle in his mind. He mourned that he had permitted Eve to wander from his side. But now the deed was done; he must be separated from her whose society had been his joy. How could he have it thus? Adam had enjoyed the companionship of God and of holy angels. He had looked upon the glory of the Creator. He understood the high destiny opened to the human race should they remain faithful to God.

> Yet all these blessings were lost sight of in the fear of losing that one gift which in his eyes outvalued every other. Love, gratitude, loyalty to the Creator—all were overborne by love to Eve. She was a part of himself, and he could not endure the thought of separation. He did not realize that the same Infinite Power who had from the dust of the earth created him, a living, beautiful form, and had in love given him a companion, could supply her place. He resolved to share her fate; if she must die, he would die with her.[3]

What a tragic turn of events for what could have remained the best love story of all time. That one choice of placing human love above love for God has rippled out and affected millions of lives for over 6,000 long years. If only Eve hadn't taken that first bite. If only Adam had not been willing to follow her lead.

Here is another important lesson when it comes to romance. If anyone, no matter how good looking, beautiful, quick-witted, or amazing, tempts you to doubt God's love, disregard His law, or go against His plain commands in Scripture, that person is not sent by God, but by the enemy himself. *Turn and run away!*

Sadly, even today God's children often linger, drinking in flattering words and allowing themselves to be seduced and led into sin. It never pays to place human loyalty or desire above our allegiance to God. It never pays to trust in our own strength. As Adam and Eve's tragic story reveals, the ending is never good.

However, God is still good, and He still sits on heaven's throne. He can turn around any messed up love story. If two individuals will make Jesus their First Love, and, no matter their past, *pledge to keep Him as their First Love,* their capacity for love and joy in all areas of their life will increase exponentially. Then marriage can truly become a little "taste of heaven" on earth.

The Beauty of Pursuit

I guess it's pretty clear by now that I believe all steps towards a committed love relationship should be *very intentional* and *Holy Spirit-led.* As goes the marriage, so goes the family. As goes the family, so goes the church. As goes the church, so goes our witness to the world. That's why it's so important that we start on the right foot in our pursuit of marriage. If the enemy can mess with our emotions, blur our spiritual focus, or lead us to compromise our standards in the beginning of a relationship, he has a much greater chance of destroying our happiness for the rest of our life journey.

Marriage is probably the most difficult, and yet the most potentially wonderful, relationship we will ever experience this side of heaven. Perhaps parenthood is a close second. I've heard many say that when you choose to marry or start a family, you begin a whole new journey in sanctification. That's why giving Jesus control of the wheel is the best choice we can make. His way is the highway to the Highest way, and He alone can get us (and our families) safely to our heavenly destination.

Now let's talk about "the beauty of pursuit" and what it means to stay in tune with the Holy Spirit.

Obviously, there's no one-size-fits-all approach when it comes to love and romance. However, I believe that no steps towards courtship or marriage should be made *until* both parties have prayerfully sought God's wisdom and leading. This might seem like an unreasonable caution. When we meet someone who seems to be a good fit, the natural inclination is just to let ourselves fall head-over-heels in love, but the statistics for experiencing lasting love in marriage are *not* in our favor.

One author writes, "It is often assumed that Christian marriages are resilient and unlikely to end in divorce, yet recent studies have revealed that the percentage of Christian marriages that end in divorce is surprisingly high."[4] The percentage of Christians who are miserably married, even while determining not to divorce, is probably even higher.

Perhaps that's why the Bible tells us, "Keep your heart with all diligence, For out of it spring the issues of life" (Prov 4:23). We must be so careful and prayerful, as we seek to stay in tune with God's voice and leading.

Psalm 32:8 says, "I will instruct you and teach you in the way you should go; I will guide you with My eye." Another great promise comes from Isaiah 30:21, "Your ears shall hear a word behind you, saying, 'This is the way, walk in it, Whenever you turn to the right hand or whenever you turn to the left.'"

After *much, much, much* prayer, and if God has given the green light "GO," then and only then should a couple move forward. While I know this may seem old-fashioned, as a general rule it is best if the man makes the first move in the pursuit towards romance or marriage. Until then, the woman should wait on the Lord. The Bible says, "We love Him because He *first* loved us"[5] (1 John 4:19).

God designed marriage to be an earthly picture of Christ' love for His bride the church. If we look at the heavenly pattern, it was Christ who took initiative to pursue His bride *first.* He was the one who stepped out of heaven in love *first.* He was the one who took the risk of rejection *first.* He was the one that humbled Himself and lay down His life *first.*

Ephesians 5:21-24 tells husbands and wives, "Submit to one another out of reverence for Christ. Wives, submit yourselves to your own husbands as you do to the Lord. For the husband is head of the wife, as also Christ is head of the church; and He is the Savior of the body. Therefore, just as the church is subject to Christ, so let the wives be to their own husbands in everything."

This passage has often been twisted to excuse abusive, heavy-handed control of husbands over their wives. However, when we read the passage in full context, this couldn't be further from its intended purpose. It is actually a noble appeal for a man to rise up as the godly leader and protector of the heart of his woman—to love his wife sacrificially just as Christ loves His church.

Let's continue reading: "Husbands, love your wives, just as Christ also loved the church and gave Himself for her, that He might sanctify and cleanse her with the washing of water by the word, that He might present her to Himself a glorious church, not having spot or wrinkle or any such thing, but that she should be holy and without blemish. So husbands ought to love their own wives as their own bodies; he who loves his wife loves himself" (Eph 5:25-28).

Ellen White expounds on these thoughts further: "The father who is the 'house band' of the family will bind his children [and his wife] to the throne of God by living faith. Distrusting his own strength, he hangs his helpless soul on Jesus and takes hold of the strength of the Most High."[6]

If anything makes me respect a man, it's seeing a strong, capable godly leader who is humble, and yet who is not afraid to stand courageously for God. One who is incredibly tender and gentle, who will sacrificially love and lead his home, and who will also stand with unwavering strength for truth.

Unfortunately, we live in a world where godly men, husbands, and fathers, who lead in the Spirit and in power and *yet love with the sacrificial love of Christ,* are in short supply. Women often have to step up and fill in the gap. I have met many wives and mothers in the church who are struggling. They are hurting and discouraged by their husbands' lack of godly leadership and tender sacrificial love. The problem usually started long before they married—either because the woman was the one initiating in the beginning of the relationship, or because the man was never a spiritual leader or a tender lover to start with.

The good news is, even if only one is taking spiritual initiative in the home, God can still work. He can sanctify the unbelieving husband through the faithful wife, or the unbelieving wife through the faithful husband (1 Cor 7:14). However, if you are a single woman hoping for a man who will be the godly leader in your future home and marriage, my advice is to encourage his godly leadership now.

Men, stand up! This is your calling. This is your hour. Take the risk! Be a godly leader and initiator in your pursuit of a wife. This is one way you can follow in the steps of Jesus. And when God gives you the "green light," be willing to go fight for your bride.

Of course, this doesn't mean that women can't "rustle some leaves" or show a little "sunshine." Sometimes, when men are on a hunt for something, they can miss the obvious treasure right in front of them. It's okay to be friendly. We should be friendly to everyone who crosses our path. But as a general rule, women should not run ahead, or try to push or manipulate circumstances in the pursuit of romance.

My sisters, wait for God to open the doors. You will never regret waiting! Can you trust God to bring a wonderful man into your life, in His own time and way, who will pursue, woo, protect, and be all that God has called him to be? Can you trust God to speak to the heart of the man He's prepared for you? In the meantime, can you allow Jesus to be your heavenly bridegroom and husband? Yes, you can!

My brothers in the Lord: You don't have to pick every flower in the field to decide which one you want to keep. Save the girls out there some grief. Don't lead a woman on needlessly, especially if you aren't sure you want to marry her. Stay in tune with God. Look to God for direction before you move forward. If marriage is God's will for your future, He can bring the right woman across your path, just like He brought Eve to Adam. Let me remind you again, God is the perfect matchmaker. You will never regret waiting on God's leading, no matter how long it takes.

One author once wrote these timely words: "If we imagine that happiness is to be found by [our] furious pursuit, we will end up in a rage at the unsatisfying results. If, on the other hand, we set ourselves to pursue the wise and loving and holy will of our Heavenly Father, we will find that happiness comes—quietly, in unexpected ways, and, surprisingly often, as the by-product of sacrifice."[7]

True Love Is Worth the Wait!

In *Quest for Love,* Elisabeth Elliot shared a story from a young woman who took her advice seriously:

> I am thirty years old and have been married to a most wonderful man for four years now. I attribute the success and joy of our relationship

> to my early Christian training by my parents, and most of all, to my exposure to [certain] books in my early twenties.
>
> When I met Dale, I was so tempted to chase him—for it seemed he did not notice me for the longest time. For two years I was his friend and never let him know I had any feelings for him. I even had to stand by in silence as he dated my roommate for a few months. But the principles I learned from those books were ingrained in my heart and I determined that I wanted him ONLY if he fell in love with me on his own, with no external prompting. My internal struggle was intense, but I finally gave Dale up on the altar of my heart.
>
> When he did initiate a courtship with me, I was more shocked than anyone. Later he told me that he was attracted to me because of the character, high standards, and self-respect he saw in me. During our courtship we maintained strict rules about physical contact, and the result is a marriage solidly built on trust and mutual respect. We have no regrets, no shame. Our relationship is so joyful![8]

What a beautiful testimony of a godly woman learning to rest and stay surrendered in the arms of Jesus, until He saw fit to awaken her love.

Dear reader, whether you are a single man or a single woman reading this chapter, or anyone who's desperately praying for *something* from the Lord, know that waiting on God always pays—in every area of our life.

The Bible tells us, "The LORD is good to those who wait for Him, To the soul who seeks Him" (Lam 3:25).

If I didn't believe this truth with all my heart, trust me, I wouldn't be writing this book in the first place. Nor would I still be waiting thirty-plus years now to know God's will in this area of my life. I would have married long ago. The truth is I have had several marriage proposals, from good men who I still appreciate and respect. The problem was, God never gave me the green light "Go!" After much prayer, and asking counsel from others, I knew without a doubt that they weren't the one for me. And so, here I am, still waiting. However, I am joyful about the life I have lived. I have no regrets. I know I didn't accidentally miss the boat when it comes to marrying someone sooner. God's ways are best, and I trust His plan.

Give God the pen of your life. Give God the key to your heart. Don't give that key away to anyone, until you know it's His timing and His will. (Not sure how to know God's will? —See Appendix 2, "How to Find and Know God's Will," in the back of this book.)

Of course, again, there is no picture-perfect, cookie-cutter way to go about relationships. Sometimes, even after we have done our very best to honor God, the relationship or marriage still doesn't work out, and our partner still chooses to break our hearts and walk away. God forces no one. He's given each of us freedom of choice. Nonetheless, He can bring any desolate wilderness or broken love story back to life. God is still the miracle worker, and when two people (or even one at first) wholeheartedly pursue Jesus, He can still do the impossible. He can bring beauty out of ashes. Read my friend Cindy Mercer's book *Pray Big: God Can Do So Much More* to hear one such incredible miracle story about a marriage rescued from the brink of divorce. Nothing is impossible with God.

Delays Are Not Denials!

Before I close this chapter, I want to talk about deferred hope and unanswered prayer. The Bible tells us, "Hope deferred makes the heart sick, but when the desire comes, it is a tree of life" (Prov 13:12).

As you will discover, the greatest challenge in receiving great things from God is holding on for the *last half hour*. That's because the hardest ingredient in suffering is often time. As Lettie Cowman wrote, "A short, sharp pang is easily borne, but when a sorrow drags its weary way through long, monotonous years, and day after day returns with the same dull routine of hopeless agony, the heart loses its strength, and without the grace of God, is sure to sink into the very sullenness of despair."[9]

Faith in God includes faith in His timing. Many of God's great men and women throughout history endured great times of waiting, before they saw the prayers they prayed and the promises they longed for fulfilled.

God promised Abraham a son, but he waited 25 long years until Isaac was born. Meanwhile, Abraham got impatient and took things into his own hands.

In *Patriarchs and Prophets* we read, "Abraham had accepted without question the promise of a son, but he did not wait for God to fulfill His Word in His own time and way. A delay was permitted to test his faith in the power of God; but he failed to endure the trial."[10] And thus was born the first Ishmael. Unfortunately, God's people have been birthing "Ishmaels" ever since. So, what is *your* Ishmael? How might you be running ahead of God?

I know waiting is hard. *Trust me, I know!* Delays are frustrating. But God is always at work, even in the delay.

Think of the forty years Moses spent herding the sheep in the wilderness. Think of the additional forty years he spent herding the children of Israel, trying to get them safely into the Promised Land. Think of the fifteen years David fled for his life from King Saul, the thirteen years Joseph served as a slave and prisoner in Egypt, the fourteen years Jacob worked for his love Rachel, the years Hannah spent praying and waiting for a son, and the many quiet years Jesus spent growing as a carpenter in Nazareth. The examples go on and on. While the waiting was not easy, God was always at work in the delay. He's working in your delay, too.

In his book *Rethinking God,* Anil Kanda writes, "When God was in the delay, something immensely greater was being accomplished than what was previously desired. The receiver would in time recognize the better blessing and would have it no other way."

"When God delays, He is not inactive. He is getting ready His instruments; He is ripening our powers; and at the Appointed moment we shall arise equal to our task. Even Jesus of Nazareth was thirty years in privacy, growing in wisdom before He began His work. God is never in a hurry but spends years with those He expects to greatly use. He never thinks the days of preparation too long or too dull."[11]

Just because there is a delay in our love story, just because we haven't yet seen our prayers answered for a child, or for a position in work or ministry, or for deliverance from suffering, it doesn't mean it's an absolute denial. The enemy will always come along and say, "Don't wait for God. He doesn't know what He's doing. There's a better, quicker way to get through this." That's because he wants us to keep birthing Ishmaels. The "son of impatience" will always be at war with the "son of promise." But don't fall for the enemy's temptations. No matter what faith test you are walking through in life, what physical or mental persecution you may be experiencing, or what heartache is bringing agony to your soul, don't run ahead of God. The God of delays is not the God of denials.

Ask God to write the story of your life. Give Him control of the pen. Stop monitoring the things you left in His hands. Whether here or in eternity, I can promise you this: What God has in store for your life and mine will be worth the wait. He makes no mistakes. He is the Alpha and Omega, the Beginning, and the End (Rev 1:8). With Jesus as the Author of our life story, we can be sure it will be *happily ever after,* because we will be with Him.

Steps to Deeper Joy!

(Bible passages, heart questions, and activities for going deeper)

Did you know, "God may interrupt your plans to accomplish His plans. He may shut down something good to give you something better.[12]

As you pray and wait for God's best, be careful not to let your longings for the future slay the appetite of your living in the present. Don't live always thinking about what might be around the next corner. *Live fully in today.* Just because you are still single today doesn't mean you are called to life-long singlehood. Just because you are still waiting for a specific answer to prayer today, doesn't mean the answer will never come. Remember, delays are not denials. But until God opens the doors, until He provides, learn to be content with what He has given today, and embrace joy today.

"Is it possible to trust God so much that I won't be lonely?" one young woman asked.

> The answer is, probably not, at least for most of us, because we need the lessons loneliness brings. It is good for us, for that hidden sanctification. "What about all this impatience I feel, that I don't want?" The answer is the same. Wrestling, loneliness, impatience—for our hidden sanctification. The trial of our faith is a thing more precious than gold. Must we go for the gold? We must. The longing for human love is powerful, but there is a more powerful one. It is for God, although few identify it correctly until they have tried many other springs.[13]

Let's open God's Word and learn what He wants to show us today:

1. What profound lessons on waiting can we learn from the lives of Moses, Abraham, Isaac, Jacob, Joseph, David, Nehemiah, Esther, Elijah, Ruth, and others?
2. What can we learn about "waiting on the Lord" from the following passages? See Isaiah 30:18; Psalm 27:14; Psalm 37:7, 34; 130:5; 147:11 Lamentations 3:25-26; Genesis 18:14; Jeremiah 32:17; Isaiah 40:31.
3. What lessons on love can we learn from the story of Ruth and Boaz? It seems like Ruth led the relationship, however, in what ways did Boaz take initiation and show interest in Ruth, even before she placed herself at his feet? See Ruth chapters 2 and 3. How does Ruth, waiting at Boaz' feet, show a parallel in our submissive relationship to Christ? See Mary's story found in Luke 10:39.
4. What dangerous lessons about lust and passion can we learn from Samson? See Judges 14–16.

Again, what or who is *your* Ishmael? What are you doing in your own way and strength that you should be surrendering and waiting on God to do? Let's not make the same mistake that so many others have by rushing ahead of God. Let's hang all our hopes and desires on God's Word. He will work all things (work opportunities, ministry opportunities, relationships, and much more) out for good in His time. Author Nancy Demoss Wolgemuth writes, "Not only can you trust God to write your story; you can be sure that in the end, He will *right* your story!"[14]

CHAPTER 11

Keys to Finding God's Best in Romance

(TO LOVE OR NOT TO LOVE – PART 2)

"Delight yourself also in the LORD, And He shall give you the desires of your heart. Commit your way to the LORD, Trust also in Him, And He shall bring it to pass." Psalm 37:4-5

Now for the chapter all you "single people" have eagerly waited to read. In the following pages I will share many things to prayerfully consider, as well as important questions to ask yourself, as you look for God's best in the area of romance. Just to warn you, this chapter is a little packed, and may need to be digested in bite size pieces.

When it comes to the type of person we are attracted to, let's admit it: We all have an inner list, even if we don't write it out. We all have a hoped-for ideal. However, there are usually certain things we prefer in a relationship, and certain things we absolutely cannot live without. The question is, are you clear on what those things are? It's important to separate your preference list from your must-have list and not to confuse the two.

For example, you might be tempted to put "good-looking" on your *must-have* list, and "spiritual" on your *preference list.* But the reality is, when you get married, good looks don't go far if your partner isn't on the same page with you spiritually. While you're dating, it's easy to ignore certain issues, like religious beliefs or spiritual depth, but once married, these issues suddenly become everything if you are trying to honor God and your spouse just doesn't get it. Life will become very lonely (if not difficult) when you have to live your faith for God alone. Add children to the picture, and it gets even more complicated. That's why you must prayerfully evaluate your relationship ideals and earnestly seek God's guidance in the area of romance.

Of course, if you are holding out for Mr. or Mrs. Perfect *who is ready for translation*, you will probably be disappointed. We are all a work *in progress*. None of us have arrived. That's why the Bible tells us, "But the path of the just is like the shining sun, that shines ever brighter unto the perfect day" (Prov 4:18).

With this in mind, consider the following questions to ask yourself about a potential spouse: What is the general trend and direction of their life? Is Jesus really first place in their heart? How do you see this practically played out in everyday life? Do they have daily meaningful time in God's Word and in prayer? Do their spiritual beliefs influence their daily choices? Are you really matched? Do you share the same values? Are you on the same page? Are you going to be a team, working together for the same eternal goals?

If your "potential spouse" doesn't meet everything on your preference list, but their life displays an earnest seeking after God with evidence of surrender and distinct heavenward growth, don't write them off. However, if you aren't aligned when it comes to deep, core life issues, then this is a red-flag which means: *Stop! This person may not be God's best for you!*

Remember, God sees what you cannot see. Spend much time in prayer. God will give you clarity and peace if it's His will for you to move forward. If you have questions or doubts about marrying someone, don't make a decision without godly counsel and much prayer. As the Bible says, in the *multitude of counselors* there is safety (Prov 11:14).

> If you are blessed with God-fearing parents, seek counsel of them. Open to them your hopes and plans, learn the lessons which their life experiences have taught, and you will be saved many a heartache. Above all, make Christ your counselor. Study His Word with prayer.[1]

Are you ready to hear some practical keys to a God-written love story? Let's get started.

Practical Things to Consider

Build a Love Life with Jesus First!

If you hope to have a happy love life and marriage in the future, you need to start by developing *a happy love life* now. The most important decision you will ever make in your life is choosing to give your heart unreservedly to Jesus. He must be your love above all others.

Remember, there is no quick-made recipe for a great love story. All great love stories take serious work, and much sacrificial love and prayer. That is why we are told, "It is only in Christ that a marriage alliance can be safely formed. Human love should draw its closest bonds from divine love. Only where Christ reigns can there be deep, true, unselfish affection."[2]

Choosing Jesus as your first love, and then asking Him to help you choose your spouse, doesn't guarantee that you will find romance, of course. But if pleasing God is your highest priority, you will have much better clarity when a potential spouse comes into the picture.

Many years ago, when I was still in high school, a friend gave me a print-out titled "Most Wonderful Love." It was written by an unknown author, and it brought such deep conviction to my heart that I placed it on the back of my bedroom door. It has been there for over thirty years now. Here is what it says:

> Everyone longs to give themselves to someone, to have a deep soul relationship with another, to be loved thoroughly and exclusively. But God to the Christian says, "No, not until you are satisfied,

fulfilled, and content with Me alone—with giving yourself totally unreservedly to Me—to having an intensely personal and unique relationship with Me, that I have so beautifully planned. You will never be totally happily united with another until you are united with Me, exclusive of anyone or anything else, exclusive of any desires or longings.

I want you to stop planning, stop wishing, and allow Me to give you the most thrilling plan existing—one you cannot begin to imagine. I want you to have the best. Please allow Me to bring this to you. You just keep watching Me and expecting the greatest things. Keep experiencing the satisfaction that I am. Keep listening and learning the things I tell you. Just wait, that's all. Don't be anxious. Don't worry! Don't look at the things you think you want, or what others have received. Just keep looking off and away, up to Me, or you will miss what I want to show you.

And then, when you are ready, I will surprise you with a love far more wonderful than any you would dream of. You see, until you are ready, and until the one I have for you is ready (I am working even at this moment to have both of you ready at the same time), until you are both satisfied exclusively with Me and the life that I have prepared for you, you won't be able to experience the pure beautiful love that exemplifies your relationship with Me, and thus is, perfect love.

And dear one, I want you to have this most wonderful love. I want you to see in the flesh a picture of your relationship with Me. I want you to be able to enjoy materially and concretely the everlasting union of beauty, perfection, and pure love that I offer you with Myself. (It is possible!) Know that I love you utterly. Believe it and be satisfied.[3]

Yes, my friend, believe Him, love Him first, and be satisfied!

Wait for Someone Who Will Love God More than They Love You!

Always be cautious of someone who puts you on a pedestal and makes you the most important love in their life. Jesus should be the center of their world, *not you.* Pray for someone who will always love Jesus more than they love you.

Pray for someone who is also quick to obey God's Word. Be cautious of someone who says, "Yes Lord, but . . ." giving all the reasons why they don't want to do what God is telling them. If they love Jesus *most* and are seeking to honor Him as the highest authority in their life, they will be quick to obey His commands, without giving excuses. They will also be able to love you with a sacrificial love and respect rarely seen in these times.

Awhile back I read the following, about the difference between someone who merely professes to be a Christian and someone who is truly a man or woman of God. Prayerfully consider the following:

- A Christian might say that they love you, but a true man or woman of God will love God more than you.
- A Christian might text you Bible verses or have a tattoo of them on their body, but a true man or woman of God will live out those verses in their life and have them written on their heart.
- A Christian might go to church or wear a cross around their neck, but a true man or woman of God will believe that their highest calling is to give Christ glory and lift up the cross.
- A Christian might accidentally compromise your purity, but a true man or woman of God will protect your purity and heart above all else.
- A Christian might be attractive, fun, or charming, but a true man or woman of God will have a beautiful servant's heart that is more concerned with your happiness and joy than their own.
- A Christian might be content to go out with you on a date or buy you nice gifts, but a true man or woman of God will go beyond the superficial and continually hold you up before God in their prayers.
- A Christian might want to marry you and have children with you, but a true man or woman of God will want to prepare for heaven with you and bring others to the kingdom with you.

- A Christian can talk the talk, but a true man or woman of God will walk the walk.

Above all else, you want your future spouse to be genuinely converted and in love with Jesus. Of course, converted people still struggle. They fail at times, and they disappoint. But a converted person won't let their failures ruin their life or their relationships. When they fall, they will repent, confess their sins, and ask forgiveness of all those they have wronged. Then, with the grace of Christ, they will keep walking forward.

Missionary dating—dating with the hope of converting someone—is never wise and doesn't always work out. The non-believing partner usually pulls down the believer, rather than the other way around, and things only get more complicated after marriage. Let someone get settled in their faith before you even consider starting a serious relationship.

Get Healthy—Spiritually, Mentally, and Emotionally.

If you've already read this far in my book, this goes without saying, but repetition deepens impression. If you want to experience true love, you must be healthy enough to give true love. For marriages to thrive, both partners should know themselves well and be healthy spiritually, mentally, and emotionally.

Physical health is important too. Although not everyone is naturally physically strong, we can all do certain things to increase our physical health. Practicing the eight laws of health, as summarized by the acronym NEWSTART,[4] includes eating nutritious food, getting adequate exercise and rest, and living a balanced life. We should do our best to take care of our bodies, not only in honor of God, but in honor of our future spouse.

In *The Ministry of Healing*, we are told, "The choice of a life companion should be such as best to secure physical, mental, and spiritual well-being for parents and for their children—such as will enable both parents and children to bless their fellow men and to honor their Creator."[5]

People who are healthy emotionally and mentally recognize that their core intrinsic value and identity is defined by God Himself, not by what others say or think. They are secure and authentic, and comfortable in their own skin. They don't need to live behind a mask. They also know the world doesn't revolve around them. A healthy person will be other-focused rather than self-focused. They may have scars from their past, but those scars won't control their life or define their identity. They will also have a track record of success in overcoming bad habits or negative thinking patterns. They will be growing and improving daily by the grace of God.

Remember, relationships don't fix you. They don't make you whole. In fact, if a person isn't healthy, jumping into a relationship is like putting a temporary Band-Aid over a bleeding wound. As soon as difficulties arise, the Band-Aid will get ripped off, and the wound will bleed even more than before. Any unhealthy habits that have not been resolved before marriage will be magnified a thousand times in marriage. Get healthy, my friend, as much as possible, before you get married!

Also, don't put previous heartbreaks and failures on your current romantic relationship. We often create scenarios in our mind, based on past hurtful relationships, then act and respond to others according to those imagined scenarios. Trust and think the best of your prospective spouse until you have good reason to doubt their sincerity.

Look for Someone Who has Found Their Life Purpose and Who Knows Where They are Going

Who am I? Where did I come from? Where am I going, and why am I here? We all need answers to these basic questions, and the answers we find will influence the whole course of our life, both now and for eternity. Those who find no answers drift aimlessly.

One of the biggest mistakes you can make is to embark on a lifelong journey with someone who has no life purpose and who's not really going anywhere. If you have no life purpose, it's like taking off on a road trip with no specific destination in mind. While the adventure might be fun along the way, the danger is that you can end up in a ditch just about anywhere. Then you might ask yourself, "How in the world did we get here?" The Bible gives us a simple answer: "Where there is no vision, the people perish" (Prov 29:18, KJV).

God gave Adam and Eve a distinct task and life purpose. They weren't just sitting around playing video games with the monkeys all day, sipping on piña coladas. They had the whole Garden of Eden, and a world full of creatures, to take care of. They were to bear fruit and to multiply for God's glory.

You and I have also been given a task and a specific life purpose. If God leads you to unite your life with another, He will give you a mission and purpose *as a couple.* If you don't yet have clarity on what this mission and purpose is, search God's Word diligently—both individually and as a couple. God will show you (see James 1:5).

Pray, Pray, Pray—Like You've Never Prayed Before

If you prayed a lot before you fell in love, you should pray three and four times as much after. Pray that your vision doesn't become clouded by your feelings, desires, and passions. Pray that God makes His will very plain and that you follow His best plan for your life.

I love the promise in Romans 8:26-27.

> Likewise the Spirit also helps in our weaknesses. For we do not know what we should pray for as we ought, but the Spirit Himself makes intercession for us with groanings which cannot be uttered. Now He who searches the hearts knows what the mind of the Spirit is, because He makes intercession for the saints according to the will of God.

Never move forward without prayer—not if you truly love someone and value your *and their* future happiness.

Pray about Your Personal Relationship Priorities

While you don't want to be unreasonable with your relationship expectations, it's healthy to prayerfully think through what God would have you look for in a spouse. As my daddy often says, "Think long when you may decide but once."

A book I highly recommend is *Finding the Love of Your Life: Ten Principles for Choosing the Right Marriage Partner,* by Neil Clark Warren. While opposites often attract and can result in beautiful marriages, Warren shares that the more you have in common with your spouse, especially in the following ten categories, the easier the adjustments of marriage will be.

As you consider the following, ask yourself: How much am I and my hoped-for marriage partner alike in these areas? How are we different? Which of these areas are most important to me? Which are most important to God? What areas do we still need to address before engagement, so we avoid future surprises?

Again, there aren't necessarily right or wrong answers here, nor are these things shared to create an impossible standard. They are shared simply to help one think and pray objectively. After you've read through the ten categories, I encourage you to re-list them in order of your personal priority.

- **Spirituality.** This will be seen in one's commitment (or lack of commitment) to God; their daily devotional habits; worship styles, and church preference; life mission; how they will teach their children about God; how their beliefs will influence daily lifestyle choices; living by faith; tithing; giving; entertainment choices; music choices; and practically *every other area of life.*
- **Character.** This represents everything about a person, and who they are at the core of their being. Character will be seen in what they stand for, what they fight for, what moves their emotions, and how they live. These things are seen best in regular daily life when there is no one around to impress. Character is also revealed through trials. Godly character is vital to trust in relationships and to the ability to weather life's many storms. (More on character to come!)
- **Personality.** Are they an introvert or an extrovert, or somewhere in between? How do your personalities mesh? How do they relate to others? Are they warm and caring, or distant, aloof, or

reserved? Think of the four personality temperaments often discussed: melancholy, phlegmatic, sanguine, or choleric. Some temperaments blend and mix together easier in marriage than others.

- **Communication.** How well do they communicate? Do they talk only about themselves, or do they also listen to others? Do you feel heard and understood by your partner? Are they able to be verbally intimate? How important is this to you? If two people can communicate in healthy, loving ways, work through conflict and manage anger effectively, and if they can affirm and respect one another, they will be miles ahead of many married couples today. *Good communication is everything!* Of course, even if someone is not the best communicator in the beginning, if they are humble and willing to put in the effort, they can learn. Love is a great motivator.
- **Ambition.** What is their energy level and how does it mesh with your own? What are their life goals or ambitions? Are they making progress towards reaching their goals? Do they complete things they start, or are they always procrastinating or just talking about what they hope to do *someday*? Are they early to appointments, or do they always run late? Do they see what needs to be done, or do they always have to be told? Do they take offense easily? Are they motivated to grow and improve themselves, or are they just going with life's flow? Again, no wrong or right answers here—the point is, can you live with who they are for the long haul?
- **Authenticity.** Do they react and live based on others' expectations and desires of them, or are they able to be genuine and authentic about their feelings and expressions? If they can put away all masks and be true to themselves, they are more likely to be honest and real as they share life with you. Of course, authenticity and vulnerability in relationships requires trust. Are you trustworthy?
- **Intelligence.** While intelligence (IQ) and a solid education are good, they're not everything. Emotional intelligence (EQ) is much more significant. One who has good emotional intelligence knows how to understand and manage their emotions, as well as relate to oth-

ers' emotions effectively. These kind of people are good at not just getting hired for a job but *keeping that job.* When coupled with strong commitment to their spouse, a high level of *emotional intuitiveness* can be a great asset for creating a warm, loving, and emotionally satisfying marriage.

- **Appearance.** It's important to be attracted to the person we marry, to love their smile, to enjoy the sound of their voice, and to find them handsome or beautiful. It's important that we are comfortable with their personal style, their body, and their cleanliness habits. After all, when we marry, we are choosing to sleep beside, awake beside, sit beside, walk beside, eat beside, travel beside, and live beside this *one specific person* for the rest of our life. However, don't put exterior beauty or charm above godly character. It's not so much the physical appearance but the core of who a person is on the inside that will make your journey into marriage either joyful or miserable. Choose someone who brings sunshine into your life, who you can be proud of standing by your side, and who you can love both inside and out.
- **Chemistry.** Do you click? Do you feel warm inside when your partner comes into the room? Do you have increasing desires to be affectionate? Chemistry, sexual attraction, and playful teasing and affection are normal when two people are drawn to one another. That said, while giving and receiving affection has its place, don't let your passions get out of control or lead you ahead of God's will or your level of commitment.
- **Parenting.** If you hope to start a family, address parenting styles and choices prior to marriage. How many children will you and your future spouse have? What type of birth control will you use, or will you go without? What are your parenting styles? How will you raise your children, discipline them, and give them an education? Will one partner stay home to raise the children and teach them, or will you put them in daycare or school? How will you teach your children about God? Do you want your child to grow up to be like the person you are interested in marrying? If the answer is no, you might want to reconsider your choice.

Choosing to spend the rest of your life with someone is a weighty decision. There are so many facets of life to consider. That's why you should get to know your prospective spouse as much as possible, in as many ways as possible, before you get engaged. I always tell my friends, go on a mission trip with the person you want to marry. See how they relate when the going gets rough and patience is tested. Watch how they serve those around them, and how they treat the little people in life—those who can do them no favors. Are they the same person no matter who they are with, or do they change their behavior based on who is around them? Are they just as good "off camera" as they are when the lights are on, and everyone is watching? When a person has nothing to prove, and nothing to lose, you learn a lot about their true self. Do they work hard, or are they lazy? Are they unselfish? Do they think about others? Do they have genuine love for people, or are they just trying to impress you or make a name for themselves? How do they spend money and manage their finances? Are they thoughtful, patient, kind? Are they teachable? What happens when you disagree? Where do they turn when everything is going all wrong? Do they complain all the time, or do they seek to praise God even in tough circumstances? How do others speak of them? *You can never ask too many questions!*

Look for a Person of Character and Be a Person of Character!
As I've heard it said, "Be the type of person that you hope to attract." Unfortunately, we are living in a world where men and women of true godly character, who live according to the principles of God's Word, are few and far between.

The book *Education* describes what makes a man of true character:

> The greatest want of the world is the want of men—men who will not be bought or sold, men who in their inmost souls are true and honest, men who do not fear to call sin by its right name, men whose conscience is as true to duty as the needle to the pole, men who will stand for right though the heavens fall. But such a character is not the result of accident; it is not due to special favors or endowments of Providence. A noble character is the result of self-discipline, of the

> subjection of the lower to the higher nature—the surrender of self for the service of love to God and man.[6]

Whether you are a man or a woman reading this book, will you pray that God will make you a person of such godly character that you cannot be bought or sold—that no matter what you face, you will be able to stand for God, even if you are left standing alone?

I love the following description of a woman of character, compiled by Nancy DeMoss Wolgemuth:

> A true woman [of character] lives a God-centered life. In a self-centered world, she lives for God's glory and pleasure, not her own. She understands that life's not about her—it's all about Him (Ps 86:12). Instead of saying, "What will make me happy?" she asks, "What will please You, Lord?" (Col 1:10) She embraces her created purpose: to join every created thing in heaven and earth in worshiping and glorifying Jesus eternally (John 4:23). She focuses on Jesus in the midst of her problems and sees these challenges in the context of His greatness (Matt 11:28-30). She lives a life of repentance, holiness, and service; but above all, she is enthralled with Christ! (Eph 1:4) A true woman trusts God. While she feels fear at times, she doesn't give in to fear, because she knows that God can be trusted, and He understands everything about her situation. She knows His good and loving plan will not be thwarted (Job 42:2). She leans on Him and depends on Him in times of joy, pain, hardship, uncertainty, and confusion (Deut 33:27). She resists the temptation to worry and manipulate, because she has relinquished control to God (Phil 4:6-7). A true woman says, "Yes, Lord." She believes that God's purposes for creating male and female are good and wise (Gen 2:18). She considers it a privilege and a delight to serve Him as a woman and gratefully embraces His design and roles for her life (Prov 31:10-31). The Word of God is her compass, motivating her to live intentionally and counter-culturally (Ps 25:4-5). She makes personal sacrifices with her time and resources for the kingdom of God (James 1:27).[7]

Remember, a true, set-apart woman does not get between God and His glory. She will also be doing her husband good, *long before* she even meets him. The Bible tells us, "She does him good and not evil *all the days of her life*" (Prov 31:12, emphasis added).

Are you honoring your future marriage partner by your life choices right now? Are you guarding your heart and loving your future spouse by how you treat the men or women in your life, and by how you allow them to treat you?

The following comes from *The Ministry of Healing*:

> Let a young woman accept as a life companion only one who possesses pure, manly traits of character, one who is diligent, aspiring, and honest, one who loves and fears God. Let a young man seek one to stand by his side who is fitted to bear her share of life's burdens, one whose influence will ennoble and refine him, and who will make him happy in her love.[8]

Character, character, character! I can't emphasize it enough. Don't fall in love with someone who doesn't have godly character. Character effects every area of our life.

Look for Someone Who is Humble, Adaptable, and Willing to Grow

One of the most important character traits for the Christian journey, for working through conflicts, and for deeper growth in marriage, is humility. If one is humble, adaptable, teachable, fully committed to God, and willing to grow, there's no limit to what God can do! Unfortunately, pride wrecks so many would-be beautiful marriages. Perhaps that's why God's Word tells us, "By pride comes nothing but strife, but with the well-advised is wisdom" (Prov 13:10).

In the book *Early Writings* we read, "If pride and selfishness [are] laid aside, five minutes [will] remove most difficulties."[9] While this was written in the context of religious conflict, it is also true of personal conflict. Remember, the main goal of all our associations—whether with the person we are dating, our spouse, or a stranger on the street—is to share Jesus' love and grace. Because of this, our lives will look different, and even when we are offended, we will act different, because the Holy Spirit lives in us.

> We cannot afford to let our spirits chafe over any real or supposed wrong done to ourselves. Self is the enemy we most need to fear. No form of vice has a more baleful effect upon the character than has human passion not under the control of the Holy Spirit. No other victory we can gain will be so precious as the victory gained over self. We should not allow our feelings to be easily wounded. *We are to live, not to guard our feelings or our reputation, but to save souls.* As we become interested in the salvation of souls, we cease to mind the little differences that so often arise in our association with one another.[10]

The reality is, if we are humble, we will not take quick offense at what others say or do. The most humble person will be the first to apologize, and the first to serve. When you are humble, you will always look for ways to grow and improve. Remember, a spirit of adaptability and flexibility can patiently work through many differences. As my friend Leslie Ludy once wrote, "What amazing possibilities await when we decrease, and put self and pride aside, that Jesus may increase."[11]

Let Passionate Love Mature to Compassionate Love

Friendship is always the best foundation for any romance. Unfortunately, most people never experience the deep, compassionate love of friendship before they get married. That's one reason there is so much divorce. When the passionate feelings and excitement fades, many believe the relationship is over. But that's when the real relationship is just beginning.

I love the following description of true, compassionate love:

> True love is not a strong, fiery, impetuous passion. On the contrary, it is calm and deep in its nature. It looks beyond mere externals and is attracted by qualities alone. It is wise and discriminating, and its devotion is real and abiding. Love, lifted out of the realm of passion and impulse, becomes spiritualized, and is revealed in words and acts. A Christian must have a sanctified tenderness and

love in which there is no impatience or fretfulness; the rude, harsh manners must be softened by the grace of Christ.[12]

1 Corinthians 13:4-8 gives another picture of love. "Love suffers long and is kind; love does not envy; love does not parade itself, is not puffed up; does not behave rudely, does not seek its own, is not provoked, thinks no evil; does not rejoice in iniquity, but rejoices in the truth; bears all things, believes all things, hopes all things, endures all things. Love never fails."

Compassionate love is unselfish commitment to your partner's happiness. It is the material from which beautiful marriages are built. Author Neil Clark Warren writes, "When you begin to sense that the person you love is becoming more and more aware of the 'real you' and trying to help you get your deepest needs satisfied, you are on the edge of a rich and fulfilling experience. Likewise, when you find that your lover's needs and desires are as important to you as your own, genuine love is being born."[13]

Compassionate love also motivates and empowers couples to enjoy individual interests and freedom, without the need to control or compete. "A good marriage is that in which each appoints the other guardian of his solitude. Once the realization is accepted that even between the closest of human beings' infinite distances continue to exist, a wonderful living side-by-side"[14] relationship can develop and flourish.

Compassionate love is fueled by deep trust. "First, we need to trust our partner to be genuinely interested in us—in our safety and growth and success. Second, we need to trust that our partner will keep promises and avoid compromises that would damage the relationship. And third, becoming trustworthy requires unconditional love. It is this level of trust that makes for generous and genuine love that will withstand the test of time."[15]

Save the Physical Stuff for Marriage!

When it's time for the honeymoon to begin, you want to be able to celebrate your love without shame and with all the God-given joy and passion you have. To help make this possible, make a commitment to yourself, to God, and to each other to maintain self-control, and to guard each other's purity.

Normal loving affection is okay. Affection is what you give to your family—your father, mother, brothers, sisters, grandparents, or to good friends. However, passion is meant only for a spouse. Don't allow your affection to turn into passionate love which exceeds your level or readiness of commitment. Save your sexual passion for marriage.

When we love someone in a romantic way, it's natural to be affectionate. We want to touch them, to hug them, to be close, and to express our love in physical ways. God designed our bodies this way. Loving physical affection and chemistry between a man and a woman is a precious gift, especially when coupled with a deep emotional and spiritual bond. However, the more a couple gets physically intimate, the faster they will lose objectivity and the ability to think rationally about the pros and cons of their relationship. That's why it's wise to guard oneself and not get overly affectionate too fast. Even after engagement, maintain appropriate physical boundaries, and keep the passions at bay. Don't visit each other's bedroom or dark places at night where temptation might be lurking. Save the passionate expressions for your honeymoon and marriage. Rather than spoiling the romance, those who save sex for marriage usually find that married sex only gets better with time.

Again, author Neil Clark Warren writes the following:

> Every expression of sexual passion establishes a new plateau in the relationship. Once you have moved onto that plateau, it is extremely difficult to back off and be satisfied with less. Many couples start off by holding hands, then progress to hugging, kissing, caressing and fondling through the clothing, skin-to-skin contact, hand-to-genital contact, and eventually genital-to-genital contact. With each increase of contact, the physical aspect takes more control of your relationship. Distinctions get blurred, common sense often goes out the window, and individuals get themselves into trouble because they are making a commitment with their bodies that they are not ready to make with their hearts, minds, and souls.

Caught in the throes of sexual passion, many singles get married at a younger age to avoid premarital sexual intercourse, which often creates even more problems, especially if they are not matched [in other life dimensions]."[16]

Don't awaken love until it's time (Song 8:4). When is it time? After you've been to the altar. Some say that just as you need to test drive a car before you buy it, you need to have sex before you marry to make sure you are compatible. This couldn't be further from the truth. Sex is like superglue. You don't need to test superglue to see if it works. It works, and it sticks fast. However, the more partners you are intimate with, the less you will stick.

One of the best ways to know if someone really loves and honors you is if they are willing to wait for sex and passionate love until after you've been to the altar. If they won't honor your desire for purity before marriage, it's quite likely they will not honor you after marriage. Marital affairs happen all the time. Don't think you can play with fire and not be burned.

Red Flags and Danger Signals

I've shared a number of things to prayerfully think about when considering marriage, but there are also danger signs to look out for. Many marriages separate over problems that already existed on the wedding day. Either the man or the woman "were simply terribly naïve, or they willingly pulled the blinders over their eyes and pretended the problems weren't there."[17] Again and again people have told me, with great regret, "I knew on my wedding day that I was making the wrong choice, but I went through with it anyway. Oh, how I wish, I could take that day back."

Take note if people you love and respect are cautioning you not to move forward with a relationship. Your friends and family may see things that you cannot see.

Be wary of someone whose actions and words don't line up, or who continually shows themselves to be untrustworthy, self-centered, or selfish. When conflict arises, does a person fly into a rage and call you names or storm out of the room in anger? Do things get really bad before resolution comes? Do they stonewall, shutting you out, or does your partner often show disrespect or contempt, treating you as if you're beneath them? If so, these are serious red flags. Love and respect are foundational to all good and healthy relationships. Be concerned if you constantly feel put down, less than, inadequate, not enough, or like you just don't quite measure up for your partner. If you struggle with these feelings whenever you are around the one you love, it's a good indication you're not in the right relationship. When you find the one God has for you, you will be *more than enough* to them.

Be cautions of someone who still struggles with ongoing identity issues, unresolved anger or bitterness, depression, or someone who is entrenched in their addictions (like drugs, alcohol, sexual activity, pornography, video gaming, or manipulative self-centered behaviors).

Don't commit to a person who shows signs of controlling or obsessive self-centered love. Remember, there's a difference between genuine love and obsessive love. When someone's love is obsessive, they don't really love you—they only love themselves, and they try to control you because it makes them feel more secure. Someone who is naturally insecure will easily fall prey to this obsessive love because they think, "This is amazing. I am finally wanted. I am desired." But it's not healthy, and after marriage, you will start to feel imprisoned. Obsessive love only gets more deadly with time.

Beware of these six characteristics of obsessive love:

- The individual can't live without you.
- They demand unreasonable amounts of love.
- They ignore others to be with you.
- They show jealousy about your interaction with others.
- They follow you, monitoring and trying to control what you do and where you go.

- They give intense emotion and attention in the relationship that grows to unhealthy possessiveness.

Be wary of someone with a pattern of quickly rebounding from one relationship to another. If you don't want to be part of their trail of heartbreaks, think twice before you get involved. People need time to heal after a relationship ends.

If you have been divorced or are considering marrying someone who has been divorced, make sure there are biblical grounds for divorce (see Matt 5:31-32). Also, be sure there is no chance of reconciliation with their (or your) previous marriage partner before moving forward. Marriage was meant to last for a lifetime, and with God's help, miracles still happen! Impossible situations can be turned around. However, if all doors are closed and you have freedom from God to move forward, take time to work through what went wrong the first time and how the next marriage will be different. Remember, mistakes and failures from previous relationships often keep repeating themselves. The more times one marries and divorces, the more likely they are to divorce again in the future.

If you are considering marrying a widow or a widower, ask yourself if they are emotionally at peace and ready to move on, or if they are using you as a bandage for their grief. Learn as much as you can about their previous marriage. Listen to how they speak about their deceased spouse, and how they process their grief. If they were happily married the first time, it's much more likely that they can be happily married a second time, for they've already learned the keys to building and maintaining a satisfying marriage. I've heard it said that those who've lost someone they loved deeply often have greater capacity to love again deeply, because they understand the fragility of life, and they don't take any relationship for granted.

Whatever the circumstances, no matter how wonderful someone might seem, always keep your eyes wide open. Don't ignore red flags or danger signals! A lifetime of heartache could be the result. If you want to avoid the most common mate-selection errors,[18] consider the following carefully:

- Don't get married too quickly.
- Don't get married too young.
- Don't be too eager to get married.
- Don't marry someone just to please someone else.
- Don't marry someone until you know them in a great variety of ways.
- Don't get married with unrealistic expectations.
- Don't marry someone who has a personality or behavioral problem that you're not willing to live with forever.
- And last, but not least, don't marry someone who is not a believer, and who does not share your core spiritual values.

If you don't have peace from God about marrying someone, or if they have distracted you from your relationship with Christ, rather than pulling you closer to Jesus, don't move forward. Marriage is meant for life and eternity. If someone isn't interested in going to heaven with you, or if they hold you back from your upward journey, it's not worth the sacrifice. It's better to wait for God to bring the right person to you, rather than to wait for God to change the wrong person.

If you have already started things off on the wrong page or messed up royally in the area of romance, perhaps you aren't sure where to go from here. Take heart, my friend! It's never too late to give God the pen and allow Him to turn things around. He is an expert at taking messy love stories, as well as broken life stories, and rewriting them as beautiful testimonies of His grace. The question is, will you surrender all the broken messed up pieces to Him? Will you give God the pen? Whether you are already married and unequally yoked, or simply stuck in a bad dating relationship, will you place the person you love on the altar and say, "God, he/she (name of person) is Yours. Show me how to go forward from here! I'm giving You permission to have Your way in my life from this day forward."

If you can place your dreams on the altar, and pray, "Not my will, but Your will be done in this relationship," then you are on the pathway to restoration. Change is never easy. It takes two to tango, and bad habits and unhealthy relationship patterns die hard. But trust me, you will never regret allowing God to have His way—even in the middle of a messed up story. No circumstance or life is too complicated for Him to turn around. But we have to be willing to lay all on the altar of sacrifice. We have to be willing to give God *our Isaac, our Ishmael,* or whatever else it is that we have been holding on to.

Knowing You've Found The One

Now for the good news! If God is leading in a relationship, and if you truly have found *The One,* there are a few wonderful things you will probably notice.[19]

- **They will have become your very best friend.** Whenever something happens in your life, they will be the first person that you want to tell. You are each other's safe place and priority, second after God. You love doing life together, going on adventures together, being silly together, or doing nothing together. No matter the occasion, you want to be together because you are best friends.
- **There will be peace and trust in your relationship.** Another good indicator you are with the right person is that you feel at peace in their presence, and they feel at peace in yours. When you are with the right person, they have a way of grounding you. There will be deep trust between you, and you will not be caught by sudden unexpected surprises. There will be a sweet consistency and predictability within the relationship. You don't feel restless or wonder if you should move on. *You feel at home in their love, and home is where you want to stay!*
- **They will be at a similar level of readiness as you.** In other words, you won't need to push or drag them along to the next level of commitment. Their emotions and desires will be in harmony with your own. They will be *just as into you* as you are into them. They will be ready and eager to move forward in the relationship.
- **You will be in sync and share similar life vision and values.** The more in sync you are with your partner when it comes to life vision and spiritual values, family perspectives, and even energy

levels, the more satisfying a long-term relationship will be. When a couple is in sync, they work in tandem for the same things. Whether that is working together on finishing a project, cleaning the house, planting a garden, hiking a mountain trail, supporting one another in how they raise the children, or working side by side in ministry, they are a united team. Rather than working against each other in a tug-of-war relationship, they help each other pull in the same direction.

- **They will inspire you to be a better person.** A great sign that you've found the *right one* is that when you're together, you feel like the best version of yourself. You see each other as amazing, and you cherish, nurture, and support one another with all you have. You constantly pour life into each other. You respect, love, and affirm each other often. You love being around each other. You bring out the best in each other. You support each other in fulfilling God-given dreams.
- **They will value and prioritize your needs and wants.** If you've found the right person, they will consistently value what matters to you. They will prioritize you and your needs. No one is going to be perfect. No one will be a superhero all the time. But the point is, if someone consistently does their best to listen, stay in tune, and meet expressed needs, and you do the same for them, you are on the pathway to a truly satisfying, caring, and sacrificial relationship.
- **There will be strong physical attraction.** What separates a friendship from a prospective life partner is chemistry and the desire to express passionate love. Praise God for the attraction you share and for the joys to come—after the altar. Right now, pray for creative ways to bring romance to your love story, and to show your partner that you value them *enough* to wait.
- **They will communicate with love, respect, and kindness.** Good healthy communication doesn't come naturally for everyone. Sometimes it has to be learned. However, when you get to

the point where you can communicate about anything, share both good and bad emotions with love and respect, be kind to one another in all circumstances, and give and receive verbal intimacy, you are probably in a relationship that will be a keeper for the long haul. When you can communicate well, work through conflict, be tender with each other, and your mutual commitment is strong, there's good hope for the future.

- **They will integrate well with your family and social circle, and those closest to you will approve of your choice.** When you marry someone, you don't just marry a person, you marry into their family and their circle of friends. Do they mesh well with your family and social circle? Do you mesh well with theirs?

Does your prospective spouse honor and respect their parents as well as your parents? If you are a woman, does your lover have the maturity to go to your parents and ask permission to marry you? Even at the beginning of an intentional relationship, the blessing given by parents to a young man as he seeks a woman's heart will reap huge benefits. If at all possible, allow your family to be part of your God-written love story.

God's Word reminds us, "Honor your father and your mother, that your days may be long upon the land which the LORD your God is giving you" (Exod 20:12).

If there is conflict or strife between your family and your partner, this doesn't usually get better over time. Perhaps you have a family member who never gets along with anyone. Maybe *your family is the problem* in the equation. However, if your family usually gets along with others, and you have a partner who suddenly brings drama to the normally peaceful family dynamic, then this is a serious reason for concern. A healthy partner should try to build bridges with your loved ones, not push them away—even if he/she doesn't agree with everything they believe or do.

Pay especially close attention to how a man treats and honors his mother. If he loves and tenderly cherishes her and her needs, he will probably do the same for his wife in the future. The same is true for a woman. A woman's real character is often seen by how she respects and honors her father. If she does not have a father figure, observe how she relates to other authority figures in her life. Does she bash or belittle men, or is she respectful and affirming? These attitudes will carry over into marriage. Every woman longs for a tender protector and lover, and every man longs to be his wife's hero. He wants a cheerleader who believes in him, who respects him, and who will support him.

Finally, pay attention to the kinds of friends which surround your prospective spouse. Are they godly? Are they trustworthy? Are they the type of people who will encourage your spouse to be a better person? As they say, "Birds of a feather flock together." Be concerned if someone's closest friends, or those they always hang out with, are not committed believers. Our best friend circle shows the kind of people we are most comfortable being our true self with. It is with our closest friends that we let our hair down. If you don't like the friends of your future spouse, this might be a reason to reconsider.

- **You love and appreciate them as they are right now**. If you love and appreciate someone *as they are right now*—even if they never change—and they feel the same towards you, this is a good sign. While we should always be growing and improving, if there's something you can't stand about your partner and you are already praying earnestly for God to change this person, to make them different in significant ways, then something is not right about the relationship. However, if you genuinely like your partner as they are, if you feel at peace in their presence, and there is deep trust and joy when you are together, these are all good indicators that you may be with the right one.
- **They push you closer to Jesus**. Last, but not least, if the person you want to marry consistently points you to Jesus, and encourages you in your heavenward journey, this is a powerful indication that you are in a God-blessed relationship. If you find that you are even more fruitful in life and ministry, and more in love with Jesus, thanks to their influence, you can rejoice because you might have just found your miracle!

In *Adventist Home*, Ellen White wrote:

> Weigh every sentiment and watch every development of character in the one with whom you think to link your life destiny. The step you are about to take is one of the most important in your life and should not be taken hastily. While you may love, do not love blindly.
>
> Examine carefully to see if your married life would be happy or inharmonious and wretched. Let the questions be raised, Will this union help me heavenward? Will it increase my love for God? And will it enlarge my sphere of usefulness in this life? If these reflections present no drawback, then in the fear of God move forward.[20]

People often ask, "Can I live with this person?" The real question should be, "Can I live without this person?" If the answer is "No," and if God is giving you all the heavenly signs and indicators that His blessing is over your relationship, then go forward with joy. When we follow God's leading, marriage can become a little taste of heaven on earth.

A Green Light for Marriage

In the book *Quest for Love*, Elisabeth Elliot shared a question someone sent her about her husband Jim Elliott. They wrote, "How did [Jim Elliot] know that you were the one for him? How could he know that he would not meet someone that he liked even *better*?"

Don't so many singles struggle with this very question today? While they might have amazing and Godly choices right in front of them, they seem to be always scanning the distant horizon, wondering if they will find someone they like *even more*. This is not to discourage caution or taking time. But at some point, you just need to decide, and not keep dragging things out.

Here's what Elisabeth Elliott had to say about this question:

> More than one man has asked me how Jim Elliot knew that he would not meet someone else that he liked better than me. "I wish I had that kind of confidence," one of them said, "but it looks idealistic, not realistic, to me."

> I think Jim's answer would be quite simple: God had led him to this woman—to me. The search was over. A man could spend the rest of his life (and many do) looking for someone better than the last one. This is where faith and faithfulness come in. Confidence in God. Has He promised to lead? Is He a faithful Shepherd? Will He make it impossibly difficult for His beloved sheep to discern His will, or will He keep His promise to direct your path?
>
> "When does one say O.K., O.K.—this one?" they ask.
>
> Maturity is the acceptance of limitations. Every choice made in life rules out a thousand other possibilities. Love, in the last analysis, is a choice. You marry her because you love her. Then, from the wedding day forward, you learn to love her because you married her.
>
> Circumstances do not change the obligation to fulfill the solemn vow. I am sure that Jim did not make nearly so "big a deal" out of choosing a wife as men seem to today. Must they smell every rose in the world before discovering that the best one is in their own garden? A strong spiritual principle is to pray through things, think about them in the presence of God, and stick with the decision. Did God hear your prayer? Do you believe He wants you to do His will? Then "don't dig up in doubt what you planted in faith."[21]

Of course, every marriage will have its challenges, but if men and women will prayerfully seek God's leading, God will make His will known. He always answers the cry of one who earnestly seeks His will.

Once you've been to the altar, and sealed the deal, don't look back. Don't let the word "divorce" even enter your vocabulary as you build your new life together.

> Though difficulties, perplexities, and discouragements may arise, let neither husband nor wife harbor the thought that their union is a mistake or a disappointment. Determine to be all that it is possible to be to each other. Continue the early attentions. In every way encourage each other in fighting the battles of life. Study to advance the happiness of each other. Let there be mutual love, mutual forbearance. Then marriage, instead of being the end of love, will be as it

were the very beginning of love. The warmth of true friendship, the love that binds heart to heart, is a foretaste of the joys of heaven.[22]

So, there you have it—my suggestions for choosing a spouse or learning to love the one you've already chosen. It's important to remember, "However carefully and wisely marriage may have been entered into, few couples are completely united when the marriage ceremony is performed. The real union of the two in wedlock is the work of the after years."[23]

Make God the first, last, and best in everything. Pray that "in all things He may have the preeminence" (Col 1:18). Ask Him to take the pen. Allow Him to choose for you. He loves to give His best to those who leave the choice to Him. So don't go forward without His blessing. Trust Him with your love life and your heart.

Steps to Deeper Joy!

(Bible passages, heart questions, and activities for going deeper)

In John 4 we find a beautiful love story about the woman who met Jesus at the well. When Jesus asked her for some water, she hesitated because He was a Jew, and the people of Samaria didn't mingle with Jews. It wasn't a likely love relationship. But Jesus loves bringing beauty and sweet surprises out of unusual situations.

"How is it that You, being a Jew, ask a drink from me, a Samaritan woman?" she asked. Jesus answered, "If you knew the gift of God, and who it is who says to you, 'Give Me a drink,' you would have asked Him, and He would have given you living water" (John 4:9-10).

All her life this woman had looked for true love, but she had looked for love in all the wrong places. My friend, have you also been looking for love in all the wrong places?

If you are longing for someone after God's own heart, start by going to the well of salvation. In Isaiah 12:3 we read, "Therefore with joy you will draw water from the wells of salvation."

When we investigate "well encounters" throughout the Bible, we find that special love stories often began beside wells of water. Isaac's bride Rebekah was found faithfully serving others beside a deep well (Gen 24:12-26), Jacob found his wife Rachel beside a well (Gen 29:10), Moses found his wife Zipporah beside a well (Exo 2:15-21), and Jesus found a lonely woman looking to be a bride beside a well too (John 4:7).

If you are a godly man, look for a deep well. If you are a godly woman, make sure the well you've stationed yourself beside has plenty of water, and keep drawing water. Someday, the right man will come along, notice you, cherish you, value you, fight for you, and even start helping you draw water for the thirsty. Then you will discover that true love was indeed worth waiting for.

Again, take courage. Even if you haven't done things in the area of romance as you should, remember tomorrow is always fresh with no mistakes in it. Go to the Well. Jesus is the Living Water. No matter your past or present, God can still turn any love story around and use it for His glory. He can start today and make all things new.

Time to open your Bible and dig a little deeper:

1. Does God want to give you His very best? Is He good to His children? See Proverbs 10:22; Psalm 25:10; 37:4-5; 84:11.
2. What can we learn about finding true love from the story of Isaac and Rebekah? See Genesis 24.
3. What lessons on persevering love can we learn from Jacob? See Genesis 29:20.
4. Is a godly spouse, and even heaven, worth the extra sacrifice you might be required to make along the way? See 1 Corinthians 9:24-27.
5. What are the pros and cons of Internet dating? How might Internet dating bypass some of the significant principles we've talked about in this chapter, when it comes to being able to evaluate a future spouse? Could Internet dating be taking things into our own hands and going after an "Ishmael" relationship?

6. Can we trust God to write our love story? Can we trust that God sees and knows what we cannot see about someone's character and heart? See 1 Samuel 16:7.
7. For some great additional tips, watch the YouTube "11 Signs He's the One for You" with Lana Savchuk.
8. Read chapter 29, titled "Builders of the Home," in *The Ministry of Healing,* by author Ellen White.
9. I also encourage you to read the first few chapters in the book *The Adventist Home,* also by Ellen White. These practical and moving chapters address some topics including The Great Decision, True Love or Infatuation, Common Courtship Practices, Forbidden Marriages, When Counsel is Needed, Compatibility, True Conversion a Requisite, A Happy Successful Partnership, and much more. These chapters are pure gold and can be read for free online at egwwritings.org.

Ellen White writes, "Like every other one of God's good gifts entrusted to the keeping of humanity, marriage has been perverted by sin; but it is the purpose of the gospel to restore its purity and beauty."[24]

To be loved forever by the person that you most love is a God-given miracle, and an experience that cannot be paralleled by any other. Keep giving God your pen and your heart. Every home can become a little heaven on earth when God is the center of the home.

CHAPTER 12

Broken Offerings

"Most assuredly, I say to you, unless a grain of wheat falls into the ground and dies, it remains alone; but if it dies, it produces much grain." John 12:24

We all enjoy reading love stories where the couple sails off into the sunset, into their happily ever after. But sometimes love stories don't work out as we hope. Sometimes, God leads those He loves through the fire.

Janelle had gone straight from nursing school to the Philippines. Enduring the soaking monsoon rains, hiking through dense forests, slipping, and sliding down steep muddy trails, singing praise songs to Jesus, and giving medical care to those in need, was all in a normal day's routine for this young nurse as she shared the love of Jesus high in the mountains of Palawan.

Janelle had been praying about a lifetime career in missions. This came as no surprise to those who knew her. Whether working in the local mission clinic, serving as a pharmacist, or janitor, or working as a flight nurse, Janelle often went above and beyond the call of duty. She even helped villagers in their rice paddies and learned the local language so she could communicate more effectively with the people. Because of this, everyone loved and trusted her, and children flocked around to hear her tell stories.

After a year as a student missionary with Adventist Frontier Missions, Janelle transferred to work as a flight nurse with Philippine Adventist Medical Aviation Services (PAMAS), also based in Palawan. She was a ray of sunshine to everyone she met.

One person who especially appreciated Janelle's joyful heart for the Lord was a young pilot named Andrew. After years of friendship, Janelle and Andrew began to make plans for a life together. They loved working as a pilot-nurse team, and their future looked bright.

On March 1, 2023, the unthinkable happened. On a routine medical flight, Janelle Alder, along with four others, went missing over the Sulu Sea. Her boyfriend Andrew Hosford, tracking the helicopter flight from the airport base, was the first to raise the alarm as he realized that the flight's GPS tracker had stopped working. He gathered rescue supplies and took off in one of the PAMAS airplanes, along with several colleagues. But their search was to no avail.

In the following days and weeks, thousands of hours and thousands of prayers were devoted to the search for the missing helicopter and passengers. Searchers found nothing except a torn pillow belonging to the patient aboard the flight, and Janelle's pair of tennis shoes, floating on the ocean.

What happened is a mystery. But perhaps God allowed these two items to be found as a radical wake-up call to His end time people. Perhaps that lonely, tattered pillow is meant to be a symbol, pleading for all us Laodiceans to arouse from our spiritual slumber. Maybe those empty athletic shoes are waiting to be filled by people like you and me. Maybe they are meant to be a heartfelt appeal for us to put on our hiking shoes and make disciples for God's Kingdom, while there's still time.

As I've heard it said, "We often talk of the Second Coming, but half the world has never heard of the first."[1]

Not long after the tragedy, Andrew wrote the following on Facebook:

"When Janelle and I each accepted our individual call to be missionaries, we understood we were entering a battlefield. It was our job to go behind enemy lines and share how wonderful and loving our God is. While serving, we saw God work in the lives of many. However, fighting enemy fire isn't easy or comfortable. We knew it would be all-out war. We both accepted the risks fully. Each of us were prepared to never come home."

Today, Andrew and the others on the PAMAS team press forward. Despite the pain, and many unanswered questions, they continue to serve, boldly sharing the gospel wherever God opens the door.

"Nearly one out of every three people in the world today know nothing of their Savior and Lord," Andrew reminded an audience recently. "Many more missionaries are needed to go behind enemy lines to rescue those lost in darkness. Janelle's only desire was to see people in Heaven because of her dangerous work behind the enemy lines. Are you willing to continue her passion and legacy, to fill her shoes, to see more souls rescued for the Kingdom?"[2]

The Plow and the Altar

While each testimony is different, I'm reminded of another young couple whose story profoundly impacted my life, especially when it comes to sacrificial ministry.

In 1956, missionaries Jim and Elisabeth Elliot had been married less than three years. While seeking to establish contact with the Huorani people of Ecuador, Jim and four other missionaries were speared to death. To some, their deaths might seem a waste. But that's not how Jim would have seen things. In his journal, Jim had written, "He is no fool who gives what he cannot keep to gain what he cannot lose." Jim and Elisabeth lived out the truth of those words with all their hearts.

I've heard it said, "It is in crisis that character is revealed."[3] The crisis revealed Elisabeth's true character and love for her Lord.

Not long after Jim's death, instead of returning home to the United States, Elisabeth Elliot, along with her two-year-old daughter, went to live among the very people who had killed her husband. As a result, that once unreached tribe came to know Jesus.

Missionary pilot Nate Saint died alongside Jim Elliot, leaving a wife and children behind. "People who do not know the Lord ask why in the world we waste our lives as missionaries," Saint had written before his death. "They forget that they too are expending their lives, and when the bubble has burst, they will have nothing of eternal significance to show for the years they have wasted."

In the years that followed, Saint's sister Rachel, as well as his oldest son Steve, also spent precious time living among and ministering to the Huorani people. Steve grew up to be baptized by a converted Huorani man named Mincaye. Mincaye was the very man who had killed Nate Saint, his father, years earlier.

In John 12:24, Jesus declares, "Most assuredly, I say to you, unless a grain of wheat falls into the ground and dies, it remains alone; but if it dies, it produces much grain."

Will we, like these precious families, surrender our lives to be laid down or given up, however God deems best? Will we use our single years, our difficult years, our barren years, and, most importantly—our fruitful years—as living sacrifices for God's glory?

Ellen White wrote a vivid illustration of what true surrender to the will of God looks like:

> There is a picture representing a bullock standing between a plow and an altar, and with the picture is the inscription, 'Ready for either.' Thus we should be ready to tread the weary furrow or to bleed on the altar of sacrifice. This singleness of purpose, this devotion to duty, is to be expressed in the life of every child of God. This was the position our Saviour occupied while upon the earth; it is the position that every follower of His will occupy.[4]

Charles Spurgeon once said, "The Lord gets his strongest soldiers out of the highlands of afflictions."[5] While I'd like to be a strong soldier for Jesus, I must admit that I really don't relish the hardship and suffering that comes with heavenly soldier training. But God isn't asking us to pretend we are spiritual super heroes. It's okay to hurt. It's okay to cry. After all, most of the Bible writers also had their times of tears and lamentations. They were human, just like you and me, and their life stories and love stories were often shattered. Yet even in the middle of great loss and tragedy, God is always working out a higher plan for His glory.

A woman named Helen Roseveare also has a remarkable testimony. While serving as a missionary doctor, deep in the Congo, in the 1960s, she was taken hostage and brutally raped and beaten by rebel soldiers. The horrific experience lasted almost five months. And yet, throughout the ordeal, Helen's heart was flooded with the sweet peace of Jesus.

"Can you thank Me for trusting you with this experience, even if I never tell you why?" God asked her, early in the experience.

"Yes Lord," she prayed, tears streaming down her face. "My life is Yours. Do with it whatever You will."

Later, as Helen traveled the world sharing about her "Wonderful Jesus" who had sustained her, many asked, "How could a God of love allow you to experience such horror? After all, you were serving Him!"

Helen's answer was profound:

> "For twelve years I tried to share the gospel with the people in the Congo, but they would not listen. They had all been through horrific suffering. Who was I to speak to them? But that all changed. Once I had experienced suffering, even worse than what some of them had been through, they listened, and that's when they started to receive the gospel. It was a privilege to suffer for Jesus. Jesus suffered for me. Why should I not be willing to be beaten and abused for Him? Never forget, someone may touch or abuse or kill our body, but they can never touch our soul—unless we let them. They cannot change who we are in Jesus!"[6]

I love these words of encouragement from Helen. No one can ever touch our soul or change who we are in Jesus—ever! Not unless we let them.

Serving the Lord and making disciples for the Kingdom will always cost us *something.* We may experience loss and heartache in the process. We may even lose someone we deeply love. But God can use even this for His glory, as the ache in our hearts reminds us that this world is not our home. That's why anything that pushes us to our knees and into deeper fellowship with Christ and His sufferings is a blessing in disguise.

I love Oswald Chambers' words, "If through a broken heart, God can bring His purposes to pass in the world, then thank Him for breaking your heart."

Grieving with Hope

Troy Keaton, a pastor and church planter, well known in conservative Christian circles, recently lost his wife Janel to cancer. She was only fifty-six. They had been married for thirty-four wonderful years. It was a devastating loss, both to Troy as well as to the many who loved Janel—including her six little grandchildren. Yet, throughout Janel's long and difficult battle with cancer, this precious couple continued to radiate the joy and peace of Jesus. Their testimony of faith in the midst of great adversity has already inspired many.

Just a few days after Janel's death, Troy wrote the following profound words on his blog. I believe these timely words will help all who grieve, to do so with hope.

> My wife died this week. It was awful to say goodbye to her here on earth and to watch her take her final breath. Nothing can prepare you for this, and we are still reeling from our loss.
>
> I have entered the school of grief. I am not a grief expert but would be better described as a preschooler nervous about their first day. But I've already learned something that I wanted to share.
>
> As I was lying in bed Friday night and wrestling with the reality of Janel's absence, I was praying and seeking the Lord. In those moments, I sensed the Holy Spirit giving me a very simple thought about the days ahead. I share it because I need to publicly state my

intentions in these moments and to encourage us all as we face adversity in our life.

Paul said in 1 Thessalonians 4:13 that as believers we should not "grieve as others do who have no hope." As I am broken over the earthly absence of my bride, I felt the Lord calling me to commit to "grieving with hope" during this unbelievably sad season in our life. What does that mean? I think that it means at least these following 5 simple things.

1. *By God's grace, I will weep:* Paul said we do actually grieve. We just don't grieve like one who has never trusted in Christ. But we weep as did Paul, as did Jesus' mother, as did Mary at the tomb of our Lord, as Jesus Himself wept at Lazarus' death. Janel's absence is so poignant in my life. The sense of her loss is so painful, I won't hold back the tears, tamp the unexpected emotion nor deny the reality of my loss. I am weeping and will continue to grieve.

2. *By God's grace, I will worship:* Every day I must realign my perspective by focusing on the character, the nature, the work, and the promises of God. Through scripture and prayer, I must worship in the midst of my weeping. God is still good. His promises are still true. His Holy Spirit still guides, and His mercies are still new every morning. So, in the midst of loss, I will continue to look up and worship the Lord.

3. *By God's grace, I will be grateful:* While the future looks sad to me right now, and I feel Janel's absence everywhere I turn, I must refuse to get angry or bitter about what I have lost. Instead, I will spend considerable time everyday expressing thanksgiving to God for all that He gave me in Janel's life and companionship. I often told Janel in the past couple of years that our 34 years together were equal to most people's 60 years of marriage. I will give thanks to God every day for the blessings in my life that He has given.

4. *By God's grace, I will be faithful:* I will remain true to all that God has called me to as a Christian, as a father, a grandfather and as a pastor. I will not allow my pain to be an excuse for the indulgence

of attitudes, behaviors or habits of the flesh that could dampen the Spirit's work in me. While devastated, I cannot give in to self-pity or allow Satan to use this pain to harm the work of God in and through me.

5. *By God's grace, I will anticipate:* Believers live with hope. I will look forward to how God is going to use this pain in my life to do something good. I will anticipate the sanctification of this suffering for the glory of God. I will be excited about being back in the pulpit and the day to day ministry in the not too distant future. I will expect God to use this to deepen my intimacy with Him and help me better fulfill the calling He has on my life. And I will look forward to that glorious day that awaits us all when "we who are alive and remain shall be caught up together with them in the clouds to meet the Lord in the air. And thus we shall always be with the Lord" (1 Thess 4:17). I will see Janel again and by God's grace, I will live the rest of my life on earth with Heaven always in view.[7]

I think Troy's words are so profound. What a way to grieve. We all have times in life where we are forced to confront great loss and sometimes even the death of a loved one. However, rather than being swallowed by our sorrow, let us grieve with hope.

From Heartbreak to the Mission Field

I want to share one more story—the ongoing testimony of my friend Gayle Haberkam.

On December 25, 2008, Gayle's world fell apart. On what should have been one of the most joyful days of the year, her husband announced that their 21-year marriage was over. While she'd known things weren't perfect between them, she had figured that whatever he was struggling with would soon pass. She was shocked to discover that he had been unfaithful to her for the past two years.

At the time, her husband was still active in the church, participated in family worship, attended church retreats, and held leadership roles. Their two sons were thirteen and fifteen. Their family lived on a forty-acre farm in Montana, where they gardened, and where Gayle homeschooled the boys. To everyone looking on, their family might have seemed picture perfect.

Stunned, horrified, and overwhelmed with grief, Gayle ran out into the fields behind their home, choking back sobs, trying to digest the ugly words that had just been spoken. What was she to do? Her boys were just barely teens. They needed their father. But the worst of it was recognizing that her husband had chosen the broad path of sin, the path that leads to destruction.

"Where did we go astray, Lord?" Gayle cried. "What did I do wrong, that he would choose to walk away like this?"

Gayle was a nurse, and she knew that the second phase of grief is anger. Immediately she began praying, "Lord, please keep me from being angry or becoming bitter over my husband's choices."

Over the next four months, Gayle fought for her marriage with everything that she had. She clung to many promises in God's Word as she sought to forgive the unforgivable. Although the pain was overwhelming, God heard her prayers. She was able to forgive, and anger and bitterness never took root in her mind. But she still dearly wanted her husband to find victory in Jesus, and she wanted to see their family reunited. She kept praying, yet the adulterous affairs continued, and with each one, a fresh piece of Gayle's heart died. She knew her best attempts were not working. Her husband was not interested in change or reconciliation.

One day, returning from a walk in the fields, Gayle saw her husband walking into the house ahead of her. Just then, like a lightning bolt from heaven, she heard God's voice, louder and clearer than ever before: "Ephraim is joined to idols, Let him alone" (Hos. 4:17).

She stood transfixed. She knew that God had just spoken to her. For months she had sought to forgive. She had followed the advice of counselors. She had longed and prayed for a restored marriage. But in that instant, she realized that God was telling her it was time to let go.

Her mind raced. *Where would she go? What should she do? How was this all going to happen?*

When Gayle shares her story with hurting people, she reminds them that it is exactly in these situations where faith is seen. When all seems dark around you, and you cannot see the way, we should most fully throw ourselves upon our Savior and trust Him even in thick darkness. When He gives us instructions to do something, He won't just walk away, leaving us alone to figure things out. But before He helps us, we must step out in faith, obeying whatever He asks us to do.

C.S. Lewis once said, "God whispers to us in our pleasures, speaks in our conscience, but shouts in our pains: it is his megaphone to rouse a deaf world."[8]

Gayle spent all night praying. She knew it was time to make the 180-degree turn. She had done all she could to salvage her marriage, but God had told her it was time to walk away. She had no idea what to do next. She needed divine wisdom. She cried out to God, as only a broken-hearted woman can do.

Early in the morning the Holy Spirit spoke to her heart, and Gayle began to write a poem. As she wrote, she realized that God's hand held the pen. In the past she had never successfully written a poem, but that day the words flowed without mistakes. She titled her poem, "Oh dear Jesus, take control."

Oh dear Jesus, take control,
Of struggles, fears and doubts.
When life's fierce storms oppress my soul,
And I am tossed about.

Oh dear Jesus, take control,
My life is but a thread.
The skies are dark and billows roll,
And I am filled with dread.

Oh dear Jesus, take control,
I see You through my tears.

Your look of love! You're all-in-all,
Oh please forgive my fears.

Oh dear Jesus, take control,
This long night has an end.
You're always here, You're in control,
On You I will depend!

Oh dear Jesus, my control,
The darkness You erase.
You guide my feet toward the goal!
You whisper: "By My grace!"

Oh dear Jesus, my control,
Through fiery trials You trace.
Your work for good, Your future plan,
To see me face to face!

Oh Lord I love you![9]

From that moment on, Jesus did take control of Gayle's life. The words of the poem He helped her write became the theme and focus of her life going forward. Only three days later she received a call from a friend.

"Gayle," her friend spoke with urgency. "We need you to go to Thailand for three months to relieve some missionaries while they go on furlough. You'd be perfect because you and your boys all have passports, and you're a nurse!"

Gayle's thoughts raced. *No,* she thought to herself. *I am not at all perfect for this assignment, because I am a broken woman. What is my friend thinking? This is the worst time of my life. I am a destitute woman. I am half dead, skinny as a rail and in a huge state of confusion. I'm sure this is the last thing that God would have me do.*

But instead of saying "No" out loud, as she felt like saying, Gayle told her friend that she would pray about the request. And pray she did.

The road around their home was a four-mile block. Gayle often jogged those four miles, and now, she decided to go jogging and pray.

For two miles she prayed, then for two miles she listened. It seemed like God was silent, but right when she got back to her house, she heard God speaking to her heart again. "Ask Me for the money if you're supposed to go!"

Gayle realized that this would be a real miracle. She didn't have any money. Gayle stopped and prayed that if it was indeed God's will for her to go to Thailand, that He would send the money.

The very next day, as she drove in town, her phone rang. It was the same friend as before, now bursting with excitement.

"Gayle, you'll never guess what!" her friend exclaimed, as she tried to catch her breath. "We have the money for you and your boys to go to Thailand. We have enough money for a round trip ticket, as well as enough for your visas and a box of medical supplies!"

Gayle's mouth dropped open in astonishment. She stopped her car beside the road as she exclaimed, "That *was* You, Lord!"

In less than a month Gayle and her boys were on an airplane heading to Thailand.

It's been nearly fifteen years since Gayle walked away from her shattered marriage, as well as her home and all her earthly possessions. She's never looked back. She fell in love with the immigrants from Myanmar who had come to Thailand for refuge and has devoted her life to serving them. She has even chosen to forgo the normal comforts and conveniences afforded missionaries overseas so she can serve in more remote places.

Gayle is seventy years old now, yet, if you ask if all her losses have been too great a sacrifice, she will wholeheartedly say "No!" She daily rejoices that God has taken her shattered heart and given her so much more in exchange. Best of all, He's given her Himself, an intimate love relationship with Jesus such as she had never experienced before. If you ever stumble across Gayle's path, you can't help but feel the warmth that exudes from her life. Her love and joy for Jesus is contagious.

Reflecting on the past fifteen years of mission service with Jesus for Asia, Gayle writes:

In my darkest hour, God filled my hands with work to do for Him. I have pages and pages of God's miraculous leading and provision in my life, and of the tender lessons He has taught me along the way. When I went forward by faith into a strange country which is not my own, and was willing to leave everything behind, He flooded my life with great rewards. Of course, I didn't know the future. I still don't. But step by step God has faithfully upheld, protected, directed, and supplied my needs. I want people to know that we can safely trust our all to Him. It is my prayer that each step we take, no matter our circumstances, will simply help carry out God's Master Plan in reaching the lost. Oh, glory to His name! Let's be faithful, by His grace alone, for He has called and chosen us!

Not one of us is immune to hardship or suffering. And yet we've all been given the same commission, to pour our lives out as a living sacrifice,[10] as disciples and disciple-makers for the Kingdom.

In Matthew 28:18-20, Jesus gives us our mission:

> All authority has been given to Me in heaven and on earth. Go therefore and make disciples of all the nations, baptizing them in the name of the Father and of the Son and of the Holy Spirit, teaching them to observe all things that I have commanded you; and lo, I am with you always, even to the end of the age.

Notice that God's Word doesn't say, "Go make disciples if your life is all in order and if you have money in the bank for emergencies." It doesn't say, "Go be a missionary if you are married and have a husband or wife to go with you." It doesn't say, "Go teach others about Me if your wounds are all healed." It simply says, "I have all power to help you, so GO, and I will be with you!"

Often, when we are spiritually crippled, wounded, struggling in life, or we feel like only half a person, we think, God surely can't have a work for me right now. He surely doesn't expect me to teach others about Him while I am still broken.

It's natural to postpone obedience during life's tough times. But the reality is, serving God will probably never *feel* convenient. We will probably never *feel* completely ready or whole. That's why we come as we are, flawed and broken, and we ask Jesus to be glorified in our weaknesses. We don't need to be all healed to step into the Jordan River by faith. We just need to be obedient and humble enough to lean fully on Him.

I'm thankful for beautiful people like Gayle, Troy, and Andrew, who remind me that even in the darkest times, God still has a purpose and calling for each of us. He will use us, no matter our circumstances, to fulfill His Great Commission, if we are willing.

When suffering a loss, will you grieve with hope? Will you move forward as God leads by the power of the Holy Spirit? Will you answer God's call and become a disciple-maker for the Kingdom today, right now, wherever you are? Will you "Go" or continue to serve the Lord with joy, even if you must do so alone?

Steps to Deeper Joy!

(Bible passages, heart questions, and activities for going deeper)

The nineteenth century missionary David Livingstone once asked, "Why is it that a commission by an earthly king is considered an honor, but a commission by our Heavenly King is considered a sacrifice?"

1. Have you considered God's call "a sacrifice" when He's given it to you as a privilege and honor? Prayerfully read the following as you ask God what He thinks about this question: Mark 16:15; Romans 10:15; 1 Peter 2:9; John 15:16.
2. How can you take part in the Great Commission with joy, even when you feel broken or incomplete? *I will give you a hint: Making disciples was never meant to be about what we have to give, but all about uplifting Jesus and what He offers.* Read 2 Corinthians 1:4-5; 4:5-7, 16-18; Philippians 3:12-14.
3. If you feel like you have nothing to give, what should you do? Read Matthew 11:28-30; Isaiah 55:1-3; Ezekiel 37:5-6; Luke 6:38.

4. What are the steps to running a successful race? Read Hebrews 12:1-2.
5. What is God's promise for your future? Read Joel 2:25-26; 1 Peter 2:9; Deuteronomy 8:7-10.
6. Prayerfully watch the following video: *Called to Serve* https://bit.ly/you-can-serve

What is God asking you to do right now? How might He want to use your current (or past) heartache or trial to help someone else in need? How is He calling you to be a disciple-maker for His Kingdom today?

CHAPTER 13

The Secret Place

"You shall hide them in the secret place of Your presence." Psalm 31:20

I will never forget how the dynamics of my ministry changed forever after a single night of prayer in 2016.

I was speaking at a large university in Romania. It was open house weekend, attended by over 400 young people, along with teachers and staff. I was the only speaker for the entire event, and as such, felt much responsibility for how the weekend went.

After preaching my heart out to the large audience that Friday night, I returned to my room feeling a bit deflated. It wasn't that I hadn't given a powerful message. I had shared many stories and testimonies about God's goodness, how He longs to hear and answer our prayers. I had shared with enthusiasm and joy. But something wasn't clicking. I could tell that the young people, while mildly interested in what I had to share, were for the most part distracted and not really paying attention.

"God, what am I doing wrong?" I prayed as I got ready for bed. "How do I reach the hearts of these young people?"

Before turning out the lights, I got down on my knees, my Bible in front of me. I began looking up different promises in God's Word. Whenever I am faced with a challenge or a difficulty, the Bible is usually the first place I go looking for help or wisdom. It is meeting God in the secret place—the place of His presence—where I find answers, comfort, and peace. That night, I knew once again that there was no other place to go. I needed help, and I needed wisdom that He alone could give. I needed a spiritual breakthrough.

"I'm not going to sleep until You tell me how I'm supposed to reach these young people!" I told God. "This whole weekend will be just another ordinary weekend unless You intervene. You must show me how me how to reach their hearts!"

As it turned out, I didn't go to bed that night. I ended up praying all night long. Finally, as the morning began to dawn, God spoke the answer to my heart that I'd been seeking.

"Melody," He told me patiently, "for the last few years you've traveled the world sharing about My greatness and power, and how I hear and answer your prayers. Your testimony is good. It is challenging people to dare to ask for more. But you need to share with these young people about the nearly 25 years that I've said 'No' to your deepest heart cry. Share with them how your heart has been broken and yet how I have been faithful to you, even in the middle of your long journey as a single woman, even when I haven't answered your prayers the way you hoped."

Fresh tears came to my eyes as I realized what God was asking of me. "Oh no God, I can't do that!" I immediately objected. "My story is too personal. It's not over. I'm still walking this journey. I can't share this story *now.*"

But God spoke to me again through the gentle voice of the Holy Spirit. "Melody, I'm asking you to share your story *today.* You need to be real about the pain, but also be real about how good I've been to you."

I cried harder as I continued to argue with God.

"God, *You have been good to me,* but how can I share something so private? This is so raw, so real. I'm going to bawl in front of everyone if I start talking about this part of my life. Why are You asking me to share this now?"

"Because these young people have heartaches too, and they need to know My goodness, even in the middle of their story, even when it feels like I'm not hearing or answering their prayers as they hope," God answered. "It's okay to cry! Just be real about Who I am to you, and about the beauty of the secret place—*your secret place*—the place of comfort you find again and again in My Presence."

The matter was settled. How could I continue to argue with God? I knew what I had to do. And so, just a few hours later, on that Sabbath morning, I told a story I had never shared before publicly. I titled my testimony, "Growing Above and Beyond Faith, Even When God is Silent."[1]

"I had another prayer message prepared to share with you today," I told my audience. "But last night God told me to share something different. He told me to share about all the years that He's said 'No' to one earnest prayer."

You could have heard a pin drop in the room. All the phones were down, and everyone's eyes were glued on me.

I took a deep breath and began to share the story of my many years of prayers. How God had been good and helped me become strong through my disappointed hopes and broken dreams. As I wiped away tears, the young people began wiping away tears of their own. That morning God moved powerfully on their hearts, such as I never imagined He could do. He gave the spiritual breakthrough that I'd prayed for.

The rest of that weekend those young people, as well as their teachers, listened attentively. Between my talks they pressed around me eagerly, wanting to talk, to connect, to share their own stories of heartache and pain, and to ask for special prayer. That weekend I saw God work many miracles and change many lives—but the biggest life He changed was my own.

A few months later, I traveled to the Philippines and again shared my personal story. Again, I cried, and again the young people pressed around me afterward, wanting to talk or pray. One who came up to me was a 16-year-old young man. He didn't have a lot of words to say, but he pushed a crumpled piece of paper into my hand. When I opened the paper later, I discovered that he had scribbled me a short note.

"Miss Melody," he had written. "Maybe God said 'No' to you so that He could say 'Yes' to us, so you could come teach us how to have a relationship with Jesus."

I wept fresh tears that day as I told God, "If that is why You have said 'No' to my deepest heart's desire all these years, all my years of singlehood will be worth it. In fact, You can keep saying 'No' to my desires for the rest of my life, as long as there are *more souls* in the Kingdom as a result."

My friend, will you testify of God's faithfulness in the middle of your single season, in the middle of that cancer diagnosis, in the middle of your financial setback, in the middle of a painful infertility journey, or while you are still struggling, waiting for your prodigal to come home?

It's great to share testimonies of answered prayers and spiritual victories. It's great to share how God has come through in a powerful way. In fact, if you want to read some life-changing answered prayer stories, I encourage you to read my first book, *Daring to Ask for More.* I also recently had the privilege of helping edit another Holy Spirit-inspired book of testimonies, a little book titled *God Still Lives.* It's available to read freely online, and I highly recommend it, as I've already seen it change many lives.[2]

I love sharing miracle stories that give glory to God, that show we serve the God who still lives and still answers prayer. I love to focus on these type of testimonies. But how powerful is our witness when we can also share about God's faithfulness in the middle of the hard times. About when we don't see the answered prayer or hoped-for outcome, when we can't explain what God is doing. It's when we can testify of God's faithfulness behind the prison bars of suffering that I believe true Christianity shines the brightest.

You know, my story and your story may not be overly dramatic or outstanding, but we all have a story to share. It's the story of what God has done in our own lives and hearts. It's the story of how He continues to walk with us through both our joys and sorrows.

In *The Desire of Ages*, we are told:

> Our confession of His faithfulness is Heaven's chosen agency for revealing Christ to the world. We are to acknowledge His grace as made known through the holy men of old; but that *which will be most effectual is the testimony of our own experience.* We are witnesses for God as we reveal in ourselves the working of a power that is divine. Every individual has a life distinct from all others, and an experience differing essentially from theirs. God desires that our praise shall ascend to Him, marked by our own individuality. These precious acknowledgments to the praise of the glory of His grace, when supported by a Christlike life, have an irresistible power, that works for the salvation of souls.[3]

I think people all around us ache to hear more stories of everyday grace—testimonies of God's faithfulness through the long, quiet solitary seasons, of how we've learned to find strength and comfort in the *Secret Place* with our best friend Jesus.

At Home in the Most Holy Place

Do you have a *secret place* where you run when you need wisdom and peace? Do you have a place of refuge that you can retreat to when life is tough, and you have nowhere to turn? Most everyone does. The problem is that for many, their secret place of refuge is not a place of lasting divine comfort, but only of temporary, earthly relief, like the numbing medicine a dentist gives before they pull out a bad tooth. However, God offers each of us a *secret place* of comfort. His comfort doesn't wear off, no matter what we are going through. We can read about this special *secret place* in Psalm 91.

I think Psalm 91 holds the most power-packed collection of promises in all of Scripture. I memorized this beautiful chapter in my childhood. I still turn to it for comfort today. I would never want to live without these promises.

Reading through the promises of Psalm 91, I think we often skip over its most significant verse: "*He who dwells in the secret place of the Most High* shall abide under the shadow of the Almighty" (Ps 91:1, emphasis added).

The key to everything promised in this chapter revolves around *dwelling in the secret place.* The secret place of the Most High isn't a physical house with roof or walls. It is the sacred place of God's presence. It's God's home. When we dwell in the secret place of continual abiding and constant trust, it's like we make our home in the Most Holy Place. We don't just pop in for occasional visits or come when we have an emergency. No—God's home is our home.

Where are you living today, my friend? Where's your home? Where does your heart dwell? Are you abiding in God's *secret place*? A good litmus test of this is seen by how easily you get ruffled when things go wrong. When we fly off the handle or lose our cool when confronted by obstacles or challenges, it's a wake-up call to return to the *secret place* of the Most High. Remember, God is never stressed. He's on the throne, and when we live with Him, we will share His peace.

As we read through the beautiful protective promises of Psalm 91, it's significant to note that God never said that there would be no terrors by night or arrows by day. He didn't promise that we would be free of all trouble or suffering. But He did promise, "I will be *with you* in trouble" (Ps 91:15).

Some things that happen in this life we simply won't understand this side of heaven. They just don't make sense. They are too brutal, too painful, too full of evil. However, even when our worst nightmare comes true, Jesus never abandons us. While many things that happen to us in this life are not good, He promises to *work all things* (even wicked, horrible things) together for good to those who love Him and who are called according to His purposes (see Rom 8:28).

In *The Ministry of Healing,* we read, "Above the distractions of the earth [God] sits enthroned; all things are open to His divine survey; and from His great and calm eternity He orders that which His providence sees best."[4]

Trusting that God is on the throne and is working all things together for our good, even in the middle of life's storms, is foundational to maintaining peace and joy. It's also foundational to our staying in the secret place, because *He is our Secret Place.* The moment we start doubting His goodness and sovereignty, that's the moment we begin to walk out of that *secret place* of abiding peace and joy.

Perhaps you want to dwell in the *secret place.* You want to believe that God is good and does all things well—but you just don't feel like He's been good to you. You can't find the strength to trust Him in the middle of your difficult and solitary season.

God Does All things Well!

I recently heard a moving testimony about a woman's steadfast trust in God's goodness, despite unimaginable hardship and suffering.

Deborah, as I will call her, was a busy mother and had always been active in the church. She was the lead pianist, and whenever something was happening at church, she was the first to arrive and the last to leave. All seemed to be going well, until one day she suddenly contracted polio spinal meningitis. Her children were only 10 and 12 years old at the time.

Deborah was taken to the hospital, where she barely survived with the aid of an iron lung. The disease twisted her body into painful spasms, and eventually left her paralyzed from the neck down. Her young children didn't see her for two whole years. Every morning, they waited for a phone call from the hospital that would tell them if their mother had survived another night, if she was still alive and fighting, or if she had gone to her rest.

When her children were young, she had taught them to love God. She had also taught them that God is good.

"God can always be trusted," she would often say. "He has done all things well" (Mark 7:37). But her young son struggled as he watched his mother suffer. His understanding of God's goodness didn't make sense with what he saw happening to his mother.

"God, what You are doing?" the young boy often cried, as he lay alone in bed night after night. "My mom is a good person. She loves You. She works hard for the church. Why are You allowing this to happen to her? This isn't fair! This shouldn't be happening to my mom or my family!"

How many times have we said the same to God in the midst of some trial, as if we should be the exception to the sufferings of sin while living in a fallen, broken world?

Finally, one day the children were allowed to visit their mother in the hospital. They were stunned to see how their mother's body had changed over the two years of her illness. The young boy was especially troubled.

"Don't think what you are thinking!" his mother gently reprimanded him, when she saw his expression. "This is not what I ever wanted or planned. But God is doing all things well. And don't you forget it. God is doing all things well."

Six months later, Deborah stabilized enough that she was finally able to come home. It was a day of great celebration, but also a day of deep pain, as the children watched the suffering that their mother continued to endure.

At family worship, that first night Deborah was home, her husband read some Bible passages, then she softly spoke up.

"I'd just like to thank the Lord," she began, "for what He's doing, because He's doing all things well. Now that I'm home again, would you pray with me that God would give me something to do for Him?"

It was wonderful to be together again as a family, even if things were difficult. And once again, they went to church all together, this time pushing their mother in the wheelchair. However, Deborah's condition didn't set well with the rest of the believers. Not long after their pastor came for a visit. It wasn't a good visit.

"The church has voted, and they don't want you to come back. They aren't comfortable with the effects of the polio. Please don't come back," the pastor told Deborah's family.

Everyone sat stunned, but her twelve-year-old son's mind was whirling. *How could the church members say such things? My mother has faithfully served and loved this church for years!*

Deborah appeared unshaken. "I understand, Pastor. We won't come back," she said. "But before you leave, could you do one favor and ask that God would give me something to do for Him?"

"Ma'am," the pastor began. He looked at her hard and long. "You need to understand that God is done with you!"

Deborah's twelve-year-old son boiled with anger. *How dare the pastor talk to my mom that way,* he thought to himself. He jumped up from his chair, as if to go punch the pastor.

"Sit down!" his mother commanded. She had read his thoughts. He sat back down reluctantly, muttering under his breath. His mother turned again to the pastor, who was now looking nervously at the door.

"You're *wrong,* pastor," she declared. "I may be extremely damaged goods, but God loves to use extremely damaged goods. Music was my life, and it's gone. However, God can still use me in some other way!"

After the pastor left, Deborah called her boy to her side. "Son," she said, "God's never done with anybody. If we've got breath, we have something to do for God. I don't know what it is. I don't care what it is. I just want to do something for Him."

Time passed and a new preacher came to town. He dropped by their home for a visit.

"I just wanted to come and introduce myself. I believe that I am called of the Lord to start a new church here in town, and we are just getting going. I heard you all have been through a lot, and I just wanted to come pray with you," he said, smiling.

When Deborah shared about people being afraid of her polio, the pastor assured her and the family, "I don't know anything about polio, but I know a little bit about God. Why don't you come? You can sit on the front row with me!"

"Thank you for the invitation," she replied. "Pastor, can you pray that God would give me something to do for Him?"

The pastor knelt down and began to pray earnestly. Her son had never seen anyone pray like this before. He wasn't sure what to think, but something about the pastor made him feel at peace.

"This lady loves You, dear Lord," the pastor began. "She has testified to me that You are doing all things well, but she wants to do something for You. God, please don't leave her wondering what she should do. Please show us what You want her to do..."

Suddenly the pastor stopped praying and jumped up to his feet. "God just told me what you can do. How would you like to lead our new children's program? We don't have any children yet, but you can start, and if you bring your two children, we will have our first program!"

After the pastor left, Deborah grinned from ear to ear as she told her family: "See, God is doing all things well!"

Strapped in her wheelchair, she began to teach week after week. She couldn't do anything for herself. She couldn't feed herself, or move her arms, but she could tell stories and speak of the love and goodness of Jesus. Whether only her own children attended, or twenty children sat before her, she poured her heart into everything she did. The children all loved her.

Soon word spread around the city about the woman in the wheelchair teaching children at church each week. The class grew. But Deborah wasn't content, and as the years passed, she prayed that God would bring even more.

"Son," she called to her now teenage boy one day. "God has given me an idea. We need a bus to go through the city and pick up kids and bring them to worship each week. Let's go to the big bus company downtown and ask them to give us a bus!"

"Mom!" he objected. "I don't think they give away their buses!"

But Deborah spoke up again. "Don't you understand, son? Ask and you shall receive. I can't get them to give me a bus, and you can't get them to give me a bus, but God can!"

Not long after, they visited the bus company. The vice president laughed that a wheelchair-bound woman would make such an audacious request and tried to dismiss her. But when he admitted that he wasn't the owner of even one of the buses, Deborah insisted on meeting the owner. Again, she explained her need. The president of the company nodded slowly, his heart clearly being moved, but he also hesitated.

"Lady," he said, "I have a question. If I gave you a bus, so you could get kids from around the city to come to church each week, *who* would drive it?"

Deborah sighed. "I never thought about that. I guess I need you to give me a bus and a bus driver."

The man shook his head. "Lady, something is tearing me up inside. This seems so crazy, but I'm going to give you one bus, and one driver, for one day. Just once!"

Deborah spoke up again. "There are actually two sides to this city, and I was too fearful to ask, but I really need two buses and two drivers."

The teenage boy stared at his mother in disbelief, then looked back to the bus company owner.

The owner spoke again. "Okay, lady, two buses, and two drivers. For one day only. But you must promise me that God knows about this, and that He is really The One leading this!"

"Oh, He knows. He told me to ask you!"

"I don't believe this," Deborah's son told her later as they headed home. "You got two buses and two drivers. This is amazing!"

"I didn't do that!" his mother reminded him. "The God I serve did that! I can't feed myself, but I have a God who does all things well, and He is in control."

True to his word, the owner of the company gave Deborah two buses and two drivers only for that first weekend. But the next weekend, he gave her three buses. Within less than two years he was giving Deborah 35 buses and 35 drivers every weekend, so that kids from all over the city could attend church. Over the next five years, attendance in the children's program grew to over 5,000 a week. But that wasn't all. The bus company owner and his entire family, as well as many of his bus drivers, came to know the Lord because of Deborah's witness. God used a paralyzed woman, though only damaged goods in one person's eyes, to touch thousands of lives for His Kingdom.

My friend, if you don't feel qualified to work for Jesus, never forget that God loves to use damaged goods for His glory. God can use anyone that has breath as a missionary for the Kingdom. Life is often messy, and sometimes it's easy to wonder what God is up to, especially when everything seems to be going all wrong. But rather than complaining, rather than cursing God, run to the secret place of God's presence and rest in His love.

In *Acts of the Apostles*, we are told:

> Patience as well as courage has its victories. By meekness under trial, no less than by boldness in enterprise, souls may be won to Christ. The Christian who manifests patience and cheerfulness under bereavement and suffering, who meets even death itself with the peace and calmness of an unwavering faith, may accomplish for the gospel more than he could have effected by a long life of faithful labor. Often when the servant of God is withdrawn from active duty, the mysterious providence which our shortsighted vision would lament is designed by God to accomplish a work that otherwise would never have been done. Let not the follower of

> Christ think, when he is no longer able to labor openly and actively for God and His truth, that he has no service to render, no reward to secure. Christ's true witnesses are never laid aside. In health and sickness, in life and death, God uses them still.[5]

What a privilege we've been given to carry the good news of salvation to the hurting. What a privilege to suffer, just a little, for the sake of Christ. If God must say "No" to our deepest heart's desire and longings so that more souls can join the Kingdom, let us rejoice, for He is worthy, and He truly does all things well.

Steps to Deeper Joy!

(Bible passages, heart questions, and activities for going deeper)

We may be living in the winter of earth's history, but a better day is soon to come!

> This earth is the place of preparation for heaven. The time spent here is the Christian's winter. Here the chilly winds of affliction blow upon us, and the waves of trouble roll against us. But in the near future, when Christ comes, sorrow and sighing will be forever ended. Then will be the Christian's summer. All trials will be over, and there will be no more sickness or death. "God shall wipe away all tears from their eyes, and there shall be no more death, neither shall there be any more pain; for the former things have passed away." [Revelation 21:4.][6]

1. Have you ever been tempted to wonder why those in "the world" seem to have everything they desire, why they find marriage partners quickly, why they have great temporal or material success, while you as a believer struggle with temptation, with singlehood, with paying your bills, or with unexplained trials? You're not the only one who's had these questions. Read Psalm 73, and ask yourself, "Who truly comes out best in the end?"
2. Where is the best hiding place? Psalm 31:19-20; 91:1-2; 119:114; Colossians 3:2-3.

3. If you hunger to dwell in the secret place, prayerfully read the following: Psalm 5:7; 15:1-2; John 14:6; Jeremiah 29:13; Matthew 6:33; Hebrews 11:6.
4. Ask the Holy Spirit to speak to your heart as you reflect on what it means to dwell in the secret place: Psalm 16:11; 17:15; 26:8; 27:4-5; 36:8; 84:10.
5. What will your future look like when you make the *secret place* of God's presence your continual dwelling place? Read Psalm 23:6; 92:13-15.

Have you ever tried to imagine what God has prepared for you? It's actually not humanly possible to wrap your mind around all that God has in store.

1 Corinthians 2:9-10 tells us, "Eye has not seen, nor ear heard, nor have entered into the heart of man the things which God has prepared for those who love Him. But God has revealed them to us through His Spirit. For the Spirit searches all things, yes, the deep things of God."

Praise God for the gift of the Holy Spirit, who searches out and gives deep revelations of the love of God. No matter what we're going through, God's love never changes. He is our safe place, our secret place, throughout life's storms.

CHAPTER 14

Our Joy Cannot Be Cancelled!

"And the ransomed of the LORD shall return, and come to Zion with singing, with everlasting joy on their heads. They shall obtain joy and gladness, and sorrow and sighing shall flee away." Isaiah 35:10

If anyone in the New Testament understood the reality of ongoing suffering and tribulation, I believe it was the Apostle Paul. If it wasn't persecution from the enemies of Christ, it was persecution from the believers of Christ.

Again and again we find Paul encouraging weary travelers struggling on the heavenward way. It's like he was reminding them all, "Don't lose heart, my friends! Things may not look good now. You might not feel like you can endure another moment. I understand. I feel that way too. But we can't look at the outward things. We must look at the eternal, invisible things. God is doing something amazing. He's doing something special inside each of you—and that's what matters most right now."[1]

Paul went on to write, "For our light affliction, which is but for a moment, is working for us a far more exceeding and eternal weight of glory" (2 Cor 4:17).

In 2 Corinthians 11 Paul described the challenges and hardships he faced in his ministry:

> Are they ministers of Christ?—I speak as a fool—I am more: in labors more abundant, in stripes above measure, in prisons more frequently, in deaths often. From the Jews five times I received forty stripes minus one. Three times I was beaten with rods; once I was stoned; three times I was shipwrecked; a night and a day I have been in the deep; in journeys often, in perils of waters, in perils of robbers, in perils of my own countrymen, in perils of the Gentiles, in perils in the city, in perils in the wilderness, in perils in the sea, in perils among false brethren; in weariness and toil, in sleeplessness often, in hunger and thirst, in fastings often, in cold and nakedness—besides the other things, what comes upon me daily: my deep concern for all the churches. Who is weak, and I am not weak? Who is made to stumble, and I do not burn with indignation? If I must boast, I will boast in the things which concern my infirmity (2 Cor 11:23-30).

Despite all Paul had endured, what held first place in his thoughts? His concern for the churches, for the hearts of believers, for those struggling with temptation.

Paul also experienced what he called "thorns" in his life, thorns that didn't go away. Although Paul kept asking God for deliverance, for some reason, God didn't remove those thorns. Instead, God told Paul: "My grace is sufficient for you, for my strength is made perfect in weakness" (2 Cor 12:9).

Paul could have cursed and complained, but he accepted the Lord's will. He told the believers of Corinth, "Therefore most gladly I will rather boast in my infirmities that the power of Christ may rest upon me. Therefore, I take pleasure in infirmities, in reproaches, in needs, in persecution, in distresses, for Christ's sake. For when I am weak, then I am strong" (2 Cor 12:9-10).

Have you ever felt tempted to give up on life or ministry because of the thorns or trials you've faced? Nothing would make the enemy happier than if we let those "thorns of life" pull us away from our relationship with Jesus, from being the joyful witnesses God called us to be. The reality is, we're all dealing with thorns in some shape or fashion. Even Jesus had a crown of thorns pushed into his head. Thorns aren't fun. They hurt! *But God is still with us, and His grace is still sufficient, even through the thorns.*

As Paul prepared to leave for Jerusalem, he testified to the elders of Ephesus, "chains and tribulations await me, but *none of these things move me*;[2] nor do I count my life dear to myself, so that I may finish my race with joy" (Acts 20:24).

Paul knew that he was likely on his way to arrest and martyrdom, yet he was not to be moved. He was determined that no matter what happened, no matter what thorny experiences lay ahead, he would finish his race with joy!

How about you, my friend? Will you finish your race with joy?

Trusting God in the Midst of Suffering

Not long after I began writing this book, devastating news hit my family. We found out that, once again, my mother had multiple cancerous tumors growing in her lungs.

Overwhelmed with grief, I sat down at my piano and started to play. I sang and praised God for several hours that day, as I kept wiping the tears from my eyes. I wasn't rejoicing over the diagnosis we had just received, but I was praising God that He's still in control, and that nothing catches Him by surprise. I also praised God for the seven additional wonderful years of life that He had already given my mom.

Seven years earlier, my mom was diagnosed with stage IV lung cancer for the first time. It was the result of chemicals burning her lungs in the workplace. At the time, she already had difficulty breathing, and should have died. But God intervened. Through much prayer and a heavy regime of natural alternative therapies,[3] that lung cancer diagnosis was reversed. And the past six years, my mom has been completely cancer-free.

Over these last few miracle years, my parents have been blessed to welcome eight grandchildren into the world—grandchildren my mom might not have otherwise ever known or gotten to love. God has also opened new doors of ministry for her and my father, mentoring and discipling people in our community. Their lives have been, and continue to be, an encouragement to many.

My mom has experienced multiple health challenges her entire adult life. I remember fearing that she might die when I was only nine or ten years old. At one point her weight dropped to 79 pounds, and she looked like a walking skeleton. After multiple surgeries, doctors still couldn't find the cause of her digestive disorders. And yet she survived, basically living on air and a few simple foods that her body could tolerate. While her mysterious symptoms continued to baffle doctors, and pain was often her closest companion, my mom continued to press forward, joyfully loving and serving everyone in her sphere of influence.

My parents also continued to grow and thrive in their love for one another. "When we got married, we always prayed that our hardships in life would never come from each other," they often told me. "God has been so good. He heard and answered those prayers."

Now, at 73, my mother is still one of the most giving and unselfish people I know. Time and again she and my father bend over backwards to help me, my brothers, or someone else in need. Once my parents opened up their home for a single mother with seven young children. These precious people were part of our family for three years before the single mother remarried and moved on. Years later, some of those grown-up children still come back to visit and call our place *home.*

Despite my mom's health struggles and her personal pain, she has never turned away anyone in need. Sometimes she bemoans the fact that she hasn't had the health to do ministry overseas like others have done, but I know that my mom's influence, love, prayers, and sacrificial giving have touched lives around the globe.

Now her body is getting tired, and lung cancer may eventually have its way, but she continues to praise Jesus and do all that she can to point others to Him. She is at peace because she's found the beauty of abiding in that heavenly *secret place.*

Staying in that secret place of quiet rest, trusting God in the midst of suffering, doesn't happen without intentional prayer and determination. The Bible tells us, "You will keep him in perfect peace, whose mind is stayed on You, because he trusts in You" (Isa 26:3). If we don't keep our focus on Jesus, if we stop trusting Him and start focusing on all that's going wrong around us, we will leave that secret place.

I wish I could say that I always stay in the secret place, that my courage and faith never waver. But when the rubber meets the road, I must admit that sometimes it's a battle to maintain my peace in Christ.

Another Night of Wrestling Prayers

One evening, not long after learning of my mom's fresh cancer diagnosis, I found myself overwhelmed with fears about the future. I didn't feel ready to lose her. (When are you ever ready to lose someone you dearly love?) Thinking of what might lie ahead, I started to panic.

Pushing my fears aside, I tried to sleep, but I simply could not relax. I tried to pray, but my prayers felt like they were just bouncing against the ceiling.

How timely of the enemy! I thought, as I tossed and turned. *Here I am just starting to write a book on finding peace and purpose in life's difficult and solitary seasons, and now we discover that my mom's cancer is back.*

My anxiety grew as the minutes ticked by. I knew that I couldn't stay in bed any longer. Turning on the light, I got up, dressed, and put on my shoes. Grabbing my flashlight, I stepped outside, under the stars, hoping to regain my peace with Jesus.

What will the days ahead be like without my mom? I worried. *Will she suffer a lot in dying? I wonder how long we have left, or if she can beat this cancer again? What will I do when both my parents are gone? Will I be single forever? Will I have to go through the time of trouble alone?*

Dark thoughts continued to whirl around my mind, as the blackness of the night pressed upon me.

"Lord," I prayed, looking up into the sky. "I'm exhausted, but I can't sleep. My heart is racing, and I am afraid. Please help me, please restore my peace!"

The cool night air felt refreshing. Crickets chirped all around, and in the distance, I heard the soft call of a whippoorwill.

"How will I survive anything in the time of trouble if I am so overwhelmed with fear right now? Please help me, God!" I pleaded. "I need to know that You are with me!"

I thought of calling one of my best friends to ask for prayer support. I have a circle of precious friends I love dearly, and whom I also know love me. Anytime I reach out in need, they will be there. But somehow, I knew this spiritual battle wouldn't be solved by the help of praying friends. I needed to wrestle it out with God on my own, alone. *He* had to deliver me! *He* had to be my peace. *He* had to bring me back to *His* secret place.

For two hours I paced back and forth under the stars, praying. I fought off my fears with the promises of God's Word. I claimed the words of Jacob as he wrestled with God: "I will not let You go Lord, except You bless me!"

I wasn't praying that God would heal my mother. All around us people are dying from sickness and disease. Who are we to think that we should be exempt from such suffering in this sinful world? No. I simply prayed that God would restore my peace and give me strength for whatever lay ahead.

As I thought about my mother, and the great joy that has always overflowed her life despite physical pain, I felt shame for all the times I've complained about my own hardships, my loneliness, my trials.

"My suffering will never compare to Jesus' suffering," my mom had often told me. "I am at peace because Jesus promises to hold my hand all the way. My only prayer is that I finish strong, and that all my family and loved ones are with me in the Kingdom."

"I know that Mom is right," I prayed. "Nothing compares to Your suffering, Lord. And someday it will be worth it all. I know heaven will be cheap enough. But we aren't in heaven yet," I cried. "I need help *now.* I don't want to see my mom suffer. Please deliver me from my fears!"

I continued to pace in the darkness. Finally, at long last, peace settled in my heart. Jesus had heard my prayer. He had brought me back into His secret place, and I knew that whatever tomorrow held, it would be okay, because He was already there.

Exhausted, but filled with fresh joy, I went back inside my house, crawled in bed, and soon fell asleep. It was almost midnight.

Joy Has Not Been Cancelled!

As I write, it's been nearly eight months since the horrible news of the cancer's return, but we praise God that my mother is still with us. While she tires easily and spends much time resting, her life continues to shine for Jesus. She also keeps loving those around her with everything she has.

I'm grateful that ever since that night of wrestling prayer, my heart has been at peace, and I've not struggled with fear or anxiety about losing my mom. When the day comes, I know it will be hard. I dread losing my parents, and I can't imagine life without either one of them. But even when they are gone, I will still bless the Lord for His goodness (Job 1:20-21), and for the fact that our separation will be short, as heaven is soon to come.

As I look back over the past few years, I see many signs pointing to the fact that Jesus is soon to return. While there are still many to reach, the gospel is going far and wide via satellite, television, Internet, and radio as never before. We also see Matthew 24 *literally* being fulfilled before our very eyes. The world is in upheaval. Societies are falling apart politically, socially, economically, and spiritually, as religious persecution grows worldwide. Wars and rumors of wars, natural disasters, and emergent diseases are all around us.

I will never forget how Covid-19 brought the globe to a grinding halt. Chaos and fear filled the hearts of people everywhere. It felt like we were all living a bad dream. Everyone was affected. Everyone lost someone, or knew someone who had lost someone, to the dreaded virus.

The day I tested positive for Covid, my fever soared. I could barely muster enough strength to get up to the restroom. Every bone in my body felt like it was on fire. My head throbbed. I felt like the life had been sucked out of me. I was away from home on a ministry trip and found myself quarantined in a tiny room on an academy campus. And yet, into that tiny room, God sent an angel of mercy to help me. A lifelong friend, fearless of the risks she was taking, broke into my prison of suffering to bring me medicine, to rub my head and shoulders, and to comfort me.

"Aren't you afraid of getting sick?" I asked her. "I feel like a leper. You shouldn't be here, much less touching me." "I'm not afraid," my missionary friend replied with sweet peace. "God will take care of me." *And God did take care of her.* To this day my friend Fawna Sutton has never gotten Covid.[4]

I think it's time we stop indulging in self-pity. It's time we stop wallowing in our miseries, our singleness, our heartaches, and our fears. If we think we have a tough life, there's always someone else who is struggling more. It's time we put away bitterness and selfishness and start being "angels of mercy" to the dying world around us. It's time we learn to serve and be the hands and feet of Jesus to those in need—whether we receive a paycheck or whether we don't. It's time we practice living by faith, even when all our emotions are screaming that we can't trust God anymore, that He has forsaken us.

What about when we are really persecuted for our faith? Will we stand tall when we are falsely accused, when we are betrayed, when we are put in prison because we are trying to live by God's Word? Will we be faithful even when threatened with death? It's sobering to talk of these things, but the Bible tells us that God's people will experience this kind of treatment in the very near future (see Matt 24:4-14).

> The season of distress and anguish before us will require a faith that can endure weariness, delay, and hunger,—a faith that will not faint, though severely tried. The period of probation is granted to all to prepare for that time. Jacob prevailed because he was persevering and determined. His victory is an evidence of the power of importunate prayer. All who will lay hold of God's promises, as he did, and be as earnest and persevering as he was, will succeed as he succeeded. Those who are unwilling to deny self, to agonize before God, to pray long and earnestly for his blessing, will not obtain it. Wrestling with God—how few know what it is! How few have ever had their souls drawn out after God with intensity of desire until every power is on the stretch. When waves of despair which no language can express sweep over the suppliant, how few cling with unyielding faith to the promises of God.[5]

As I reflect on the past few years and on what happened during the Covid crisis, I see how fast our world can be turned upside down. I also remember a lot of things that got cancelled. Travel was cancelled, meetings were cancelled, work was cancelled, school was cancelled, weddings were cancelled, worship services were cancelled, certain ministries were cancelled, politically incorrect opinions were cancelled, and even family fellowships were cancelled. But what I found most troubling was seeing expressions of joy and faith in God cancelled.

Somewhere in the midst of all the craziness, singer and concert pianist, Kim Collingsworth wrote a beautiful song which she titled: "Joy is Not Cancelled!" The lyrics couldn't be more appropriate for the times in which we live, nor for the times that I believe are soon to come.

The lyrics go like this:

> When life is put on hold, all our plans have cancelled, things have changed. Nothing feels the same. Disappointments, fear, and doubt go hand in hand and waves of worry threaten me. Everywhere uncertainty. But in the midst of chaos, in the midst of fear. There is something to remember, yes there is something we all need to hear.
>
> Joy is not cancelled. Peace still remains. God's goodness, kindness, His grace isn't running low. And He has not changed. His power is still abundant. His mercies are still new. God's plans have not been cancelled. He's still in control, and everything that matters still remains.
>
> So, when the trials and test they come, darkness only hides the sun, and you can't seem to find Your way, no light of day. There are some things we know for sure, they never change, they will endure, no matter what things look like all around us. So, in the midst of chaos, in the midst of all your fears, there is something you should remember. Yes, there is something we all need to hear.
>
> Joy is not cancelled. Peace still remains. God's goodness, kindness, His grace isn't running low. And He has not changed. His power is still abundant. His promises, they're all still new. God's plans have not been cancelled. He's fully in control, and everything that matters still remains. Yes, everything that matters still remains.[6]

What a timely song and message. I encourage you to listen to the song on YouTube if you haven't yet heard it. As you listen, remind yourself that though the enemy might try to cancel your joy, although he might even eventually get *you cancelled* because of your faith, God promises, "I will never leave you nor forsake you" (Heb 13:5). And His joy can't ever be taken away.

This side of heaven, we can't explain away the difficult seasons of life or the suffering we are forced to endure. Nonetheless, we are told:

> God never leads His children otherwise than they would choose to be led, if they could see the end from the beginning, and discern

> the glory of the purpose which they are fulfilling as co-workers with Him. Not Enoch, who was translated to heaven, not Elijah, who ascended in a chariot of fire, was greater or more honored than John the Baptist, who perished alone in the dungeon. 'Unto you it is given in the behalf of Christ, not only to believe on Him, but also to suffer for His sake.' Philippians 1:29. And of all the gifts that Heaven can bestow upon men, fellowship with Christ in His sufferings is the most weighty trust and the highest honor.[7]

Just imagine when we get to heaven, running into Jesus' arms. Imagine gathering with millions around God's throne in joyful praise and worship. Imagine no more disappointments, no more crushed hopes. Imagine no more loneliness, no more long, dark nights, no more heartbreaks, no more tears, no more temptations. Imagine no more broken relationships, no more health struggles, no more cancer, no more growing old and dying, no more pain.

In heaven God will make all things new! "And the ransomed of the LORD shall return, and come to Zion with singing, with everlasting joy on their heads. They shall obtain joy and gladness, and sorrow and sighing shall flee away" (Isa 35:10).

> Eternal life is ours, if we endure the trial of our faith. Is it not enough? Will any complain of the roughness of the way?—Would you enter heaven if you could without suffering, and dwell in the presence of that Jesus, who suffered so much for us, whose loveliness and glory is unspeakable? He for your sins, was once the meek slain lamb, wounded, bruised, smitten and afflicted. O, it would be no place for you. Any other place would be far preferable. You would feel that you had no right there. Let us, then, cheerfully suffer something for Jesus' sake, crucify self daily, be a partaker of Christ's sufferings here, that we may be made partakers with Him of His glory, and be crowned with glory, honor, immortality and eternal life.[8]

Jesus saw the joy. Hebrews 12:2 declares that He "endured the cross" motivated by "the joy that was set before Him." His joy was *you*! Can we not endure a little hardship in this life for Him?

Remember, true joy is not the absence of trials or difficulties or stressful circumstances. Heaven's joy is living in gratefulness for Jesus every moment, resting in His peace, being content with what He provides, having quiet assurance that He loves you, saves you, walks with you, and sings with you in the rain![9]

True joy cannot be cancelled, because *Jesus is our joy!*

"Whom having not seen you love. Though now you do not see Him, yet believing, you rejoice with joy inexpressible and full of glory" (1 Pet 1:8).

Steps to Deeper Joy!

(Bible passages, heart questions, and activities for going deeper)

The prophet Habakkuk served during the "death throes" of the nation of Judah. Again and again, God used him to call the nation to repentance, but the people stubbornly refused. As a result, God revealed to Habakkuk the terrible punishment about to come on the nation. Habakkuk fell to his knees, trembling, acknowledging the sovereignty of God. Yet, in the midst of great sorrow, he finished his prayer with the following words of praise.

> Though the fig tree may not blossom, nor fruit be on the vines; Though the labor of the olive tree may fail, and the fields yield no food; Though the flock may be cut off from the fold, and there be no herd in the stalls— *Yet I will rejoice in the Lord, I will joy in the God of my salvation.* The Lord God is my strength; He will make my feel like the deer's feet. And He will make me walk on my high hills (Hab 3:17-18).

Yes, though all hell was about to break lose, Habakkuk knew where true joy was found—and He was determined to trust God and stay true to God, no matter the outcome. God is asking us to do the same.

1. Will you choose to serve the Lord? Will you choose, starting today, to store up treasure in heaven? Prayerfully read Joshua 24:15 and Matthew 6:19-21, 33. Tell God your answer.

2. What promises can you cling to in the face of death or great loss? See 1 Thessalonians 4:13-18; Isaiah 57:1; 1 Peter 1:3-9.
3. What additional words of hope and comfort do you find in the following passages? See Psalm 126:5; Isaiah 52:9; 61:7; 65:19; 1 Peter 4:13.
4. What does God long to do in your life, and how does He want to use you in the lives of others? See 2 Corinthians 1:3-4; 5:18-20; John 17:3; Mark 3:14-15; Isaiah 61:1-3.
5. As this book comes to an end, what has spoken to your heart most deeply? How are you going to embrace joy and live the principles shared in your own life going forward?

While you've come to the end of *My Single Joy!*, your journey with discovering true joy has only just begun. Would you consider taking the "Thirty Days of Joy" daily heart challenge as you pray that God would teach you even more from His Word regarding true joy? (See Appendix 7.)

If We Could See

If we could see beyond today as God can see,
If all the clouds should roll away, the shadows flee;
O'er present griefs we would not fret,
Each sorrow we would soon forget,
For many joys are waiting yet, for you and me.

If we could know beyond today as God doth know,
Why dearest treasures pass away, and tears must flow;
And why the darkness leads to light,
Why dreary days will soon grow bright,
Someday life's wrongs will be made right, faith tells us so.

If we could see, if we could know, we often say,
But God in love a vail doeth throw across our way.
We cannot see what lies before,
And so we cling to Him the more,
He leads us till this life is o'er, trust and obey.

Written by Norman J. Clayton

APPENDIX 1

Back to the Altar

(Keys to a Vibrant Devotional Life)

"Then I will go to the altar of God, to God my exceeding joy; And on the harp I will praise You, O God, my God." Psalm 43:4

George Müller once wrote, "The first great and primary business to which I ought to attend every day is to have my soul happy in the Lord." Profound words of wisdom.

What is keeping us from this "happy soul" in the Lord experience? Not surprisingly, the biggest excuse for those who don't experience a vibrant devotional life is usually, "I simply don't have enough time!" Yet the reality is, we always make time for what is truly *important* to us. Perhaps a realignment of "spiritual priorities" is what we most need.

God's Word tells us, "But seek first the kingdom of God and His righteousness, and all these things shall be added to you" (Matt 6:33).

The following tips are not a magic formula, but if followed with a sincere heart and desire to know Jesus, they will help breathe fresh life into your daily devotional experience. Remember, the Holy Spirit is the best teacher of how to grow your walk with Jesus, so listen for His voice.

1. **First, go to bed at a reasonable hour each night**, so you aren't too tired to wake up when God calls in the morning. As I've heard it said, "Early to bed, early to rise, makes one healthy, wealthy, and

wise"—especially when it comes to the things of heaven. See Isaiah 26:9; Psalm 63:1; Proverbs 15:6.

2. **Ask God to be your alarm clock and wake you up each morning whenever He's ready to meet with you.** God loves to awaken His children (Isa 50:4). Even though it might be earlier than expected, get up when He calls. You'll be surprised how much He will share with you when you give Him plenty of unrushed time. See Psalm 63:1; Isaiah 26:9; Mark 1:35.

3. **When you get up, don't get distracted!** Remember the motto, "Word before World." Before you check your phone, your email, your social media, the news, and before you get interrupted by others, spend time with Jesus. Let His face be the first face you look for each morning. Let His kisses of love be the first you seek as you start each day. See Psalm 5:3; Job 23:12; Song of Solomon 1:2-4.

4. **Come to Jesus as you are.** No matter how spiritual or unspiritual you feel, your life struggles, or where you are in your faith journey, Jesus loves you, and He can handle you. You don't have to be in a "perfect spiritual mindset" to have devotions. Come as you are and allow Him to change you from the inside out. He will never turn you away. See John 6:37; Matthew 11:28-30.

5. **Confess your sins, remove spiritual breaches**. Put away anything that is between you and God or that could be breaking down your altar of worship. Don't let this time of daily repentance and confession turn into a dry routine. Ask God to search your heart. He will! See Psalm 139:23-24; Psalm 51:1-12. (For a comprehensive study on removing spiritual breaches, see chapter 13, "Looking for Spiritual Breaches," in my book *Daring to Ask for More.*)

6. **Worship Jesus with praise and thanksgiving.** Murmuring and complaining separates the soul from God and brings darkness (Deut 28:45-47), but worship and songs of praise draw us heavenward. Even if life is difficult and ugly, there are still reasons to worship and praise God. Praise God for His character (who He is), then thank Him for the gift of salvation, and other good things

He does. Keep a journal of "Remembrance" where you chronicle the blessings He sends your way. Journal and record answered prayers. Pray the Psalms if you aren't sure where to begin! See Psalm 95:1-6; Psalm 96:1-13; Psalm 98:1-9; Psalm 100:1-4.

7. **Take unrushed time in the Word and in Prayer.** This is so significant. You need to eat, drink, and breathe fresh air to survive. The same is true spiritually. The Bible is God's bread and water, and prayer is the breath of the soul. We need meaningful, consistent, unrushed time with Jesus daily to keep our love relationship thriving and strong. See Matthew 5:6; 2 Timothy 2:15; Psalm 40:1.

8. **Look for Jesus in the Word.** The Word is a treasure chest, and Jesus is the Living Treasure (Luke 24:27). There are pictures and symbols of Jesus everywhere. The more you look for Jesus, the more pictures of Jesus you will see. Here are some examples: Genesis 1:1; Revelation 1:8; Genesis 37:23; Proverbs 12:12; Matthew 13:44; John 6:51; John 8:12; John 10:11; John 14:6; Revelation 5:5, Revelation 22:17.

9. **Pray the Word.** Look up Bible promises and pray them back to God in your own words. God's Word is forever settled in heaven (Ps 119:89). His Word does not return to Him void (Isa 55:11). He cannot lie (Num 23:19). Praying the Word will revolutionize your prayer life. "The honor of His throne is staked for the fulfillment of His Word to us" (*Christ Object Lessons*, p. 148). I have put together over a 100 "Prayer Promise" cards to teach people how to pray the Word. Just click on the QR code with your smart phone camera.

10. **Ask for a daily baptism of the Holy Spirit**. Don't take this gift for granted—this is the key to all other spiritual gifts we receive. It is the key to all spiritual power. (See Luke 11:13; Acts 1:8.) Want to take things deeper and revolutionize your spiritual perspective? Do a study on all the times the "Holy Spirit" is mentioned in the Bible, and how God's prophets and followers responded to the leading of the Spirit.

11. **Listen to the convictions of the Holy Spirit.** As we study God's Word, His Spirit speaks to our hearts, prompting us to make life changes. Making time with God each day is futile if it doesn't change our life. Ask God to help you honor Him with your life choices and to obey what He teaches you in His Word, no matter what it costs—it will always cost something. While obedience does not save us (only Jesus saves, Eph 2:8-9), obedience gives visible evidence of our salvation. In genuine full-hearted obedience to God's Word and the convicting voice of the Holy Spirit, we show our love and devotion. See James 1:22; 1 John 2:6; John 14:21-23; Acts 5:32; Rev 2:10.

"If you will seek the Lord and be converted every day; if you will of your own spiritual choice be free and joyous in God; if with gladsome consent of heart to His gracious call you come wearing the yoke of Christ,—the yoke of obedience and service,—all your murmurings will be stilled, all your difficulties will be removed, all the perplexing problems that now confront you will be solved" (*Mount of Blessings,* p. 101).

12. **Journal what God teaches you.** I love journaling because it's a way to remember the special things God teaches me each day. We are told to write God's Word on the tablet of our heart (Mal 3:16; Prov 3:3)—it doesn't hurt to write His Word down on paper, either. This helps us not forget His goodness. "We have nothing to fear for the future, except as we shall forget the way the Lord has led us, and His teaching in our past history" (*Last Day Events,* p. 72).

13. **Share what God teaches you with others.** When you find great heavenly treasure, you simply cannot keep it to yourself. Be a witness, pray for divine appointments, and look for opportunities to share what you are learning with others. See Mark 5:19; 1 Peter 3:15; Acts 5:32.

14. **Live at the Altar and abide with Jesus as you go through each day.** Jesus wants to walk with you, to dwell with you through His Holy Spirit, and to live through you. As He dwells in our hearts,

His fruit will blossom and bloom in our life. (See 1 Cor 6:19-20; John 15:4-11; Gal 5:22-23; Eph 2:19-22.)

One of my favorite Bible passages comes from Psalm 27:4. "One thing I have desired of the LORD, That will I seek: That I may dwell in the house of the LORD All the days of my life, To behold the beauty of the LORD, And to inquire in His temple."

What is the "one thing" you desire? When Jesus becomes your one desire and you live daily in His presence, you cannot help but be full of joy as you surrender your life to Him. That's why we are encouraged again and again, "Lay all upon the altar, a living, consuming sacrifice. Bind it with cords, if you cannot keep it there. Give yourselves to prayer. Live at the altar. Strengthen your purposes by the promises of God" (*Testimonies,* vol 1, p. 169).

I pray these devotional keys are a blessing. To go deeper in what it means to live daily as a disciple of Jesus, download the booklet called *The Way Back to the Altar: How to Live Daily as a Disciple of Jesus* at: www.backtothealtar.org.

APPENDIX 2

How to Find and Know God's Will

"The humble He guides in justice, and the humble He teaches His way."
Psalm 25:9

Everyone wants to know the will of God, especially when it comes to making big life decisions—decisions like where to go to school, what to do as a career, which job to take, who to marry, how to reach unsaved loved ones, and where to serve in the mission field.

"Wouldn't it be nice if God would just write His will in the sky?" I've often heard people say.

If only things were that simple.

However, God has given us His Word, and some pretty helpful guidelines to discovering His will. We don't have to live completely clueless. I pray the following steps[1] are helpful, as you prayerfully seek God's will and leading in your life.

Step 1 - Die to your own will. The first step in finding and knowing God's will is that we must be willing to die to our own will. When we can hold our hands up before the Lord and say, "God, I surrender my choice to You, not my will but Your will be done," then we are at a place where we can hear what He wants to tell us, even if His answer doesn't fit our agenda or expectations. Even Jesus had to die to His own will (see Matt 26:39).

> Consecrate yourself to God in the morning; make this your very first work. Let your prayer be, 'Take me, O Lord, as wholly Thine. I lay all my plans at Thy feet. Use me today in Thy service. Abide with me, and let all my work be wrought in Thee.' This is a daily matter. Each morning consecrate yourself to God for that day. Surrender all your plans to Him, to be carried out or given up as His providence shall indicate. Thus day by day you may be giving your life into the hands of God, and thus your life will be molded more and more after the life of Christ" *(Steps to Christ*, p. 70).

Jesus tells us, "All authority has been given to Me in heaven and on earth" (Matt 28:18). Surrender all your will and choices to that authority daily. Remember, Jesus is our advocate in heavenly places. He is standing on our behalf (Eph 1:20-22).

Step 2 – Repent of any known sin or spiritual compromise. The second step in seeking the will of God is to make sure nothing is compromising our faithfulness to Jesus. We should repent of anything the Holy Spirit brings to mind, and trust in the blood of Jesus as we seek to keep the heavenly channels of communication open.

Isaiah 59:1-2 tells us, "Behold, the LORD's hand is not shortened, that it cannot save; Nor His ear heavy, that it cannot hear. But your iniquities have separated you from your God; And your sins have hidden His face from you, so that He will not hear."

Step 3 – Believe that God is good and wants what's best for you. God is good, and He truly does have good desires towards His children. The Bible tells us, "For I know the thoughts that I think toward you, says the LORD, thoughts of peace and not of evil, to give you a future and a hope" (Jer 29:11).

Here are two more powerful promises to claim:

"For the LORD God is a sun and shield; The LORD will give grace and glory; No good thing will He withhold from those who walk uprightly" (Ps 84:11).

"The LORD takes pleasure in those who fear Him, in those who hope in His mercy" (Ps 147:11).

Step 4 – Humbly ask God for wisdom. James 1:5 promises, "If any of you lacks wisdom, let him ask of God, who gives to all liberally and without reproach, and it will be given to him." Keep asking until God gives you the wisdom you need.

We have another powerful promise in Proverbs 3:5-7. "Trust in the LORD with all your heart, And lean not on your own understanding; In all your ways acknowledge Him, And He shall direct your paths. Do not be wise in your own eyes; Fear the LORD and depart from evil."

In *Christ Object Lessons,* we read, "To those who in humility of heart seek for divine guidance, the angels of God draw near" (*Christ Object Lessons,* p. 59).

Step 5 – Pray earnestly and claim God's promises. Reflect on the promises of 2 Peter 1:3-4 and Ephesians 6:10-12 as you pray in the authoritative name of Jesus. Every decision we make, that is for God's glory, the enemy is trying to counteract and overrule. We need divine help, protection, and wisdom to know the way to walk. We also need to pray in the authority of Jesus' name (Phil 2:10).

Step 6 – Wait on the Lord. Don't rush ahead of God's leading. I can't emphasize this step enough. "Be still and know that He is God" (Ps 46:10). Claim the promises of Psalm 25:5 and Jeremiah 33:3 as you wait in God's presence for Him to reveal His wisdom to you. *Wait with expectation.* He delights to honor the sincere believer who wills against all wanting to honor Him.

If you don't receive the answer right away, keep waiting. Sometimes we need to step aside from everything and just fast and pray. However, God doesn't always reveal His will in certain areas immediately. Sometimes, just like in the case of Abraham, Joseph, Moses, and others, the answers take days, weeks, months, or even years to be revealed. Be patient and keep seeking the Lord. Don't move forward on a significant decision, or take things into your own hands, without clarity that God is leading.

Step 7 – Evaluate all conclusions or decisions in the light of God's Word. The Bible tells us, "To the law and to the testimony! If they do not speak according to this word, it is because there is no light in them" (Isa 8:20).

Always test your conclusions with the written Word of God. When you feel like you have an answer, ask God, "Is there anything in Your Word that affirms *or challenges* my conclusions?" Claim the promise of 1 John 5:14.

God's Word has wisdom for every situation: "All Scripture is given by inspiration of God, and is profitable for doctrine, for reproof, for correction, for instruction in righteousness, that the man of God may be complete, thoroughly equipped for every good work" (2 Tim 3:16-17).

Step 8 – Seek godly counsel and watch for indications of divine providence. Find godly parents, mentors, loved ones, or friends who love God's Word and who you trust. Sometimes it's also good to seek counsel from unbiased sources, and people who have nothing to gain or lose by the decision you are praying about.

Scripture tells us, "Where there is no counsel, the people fall; But in the multitude of counselors there is safety" (Prov 11:14).

Do you have peace that God is opening or closing a specific door? Has He given special divine providences or signs that He is leading?

Perceived divine providences, signs, miracles, and wonders are *not always* indicators of God's approval or will. *Be careful with signs.* After all the devil knows how to plant signs and miracles too. And He knows just what we are looking for. However, if providential indicators and signs compliment and agree with what is already being spoken to us through the Word, and through godly counsel, these things should be considered as confirmations of God's leading.

In the book *Education,* Ellen White wrote, "We need to follow more closely God's plan of life. To do our best in the work that lies nearest, to commit our ways to God, and to watch for the indications of His providence—these are rules that ensure safe guidance in the choice of an occupation" (*Education*, p. 267).

Step 9 – Above all, pray that God will be glorified. You can never go wrong praying this prayer. No matter the path taken, or the choices made, our highest desire should always be for the glory of God. "Not unto us, O LORD, not unto us, But to Your name give glory, Because of Your mercy, Because of Your truth" (Ps 115:1).

Step 10 – Finally, live the will God has already revealed. If we truly desire to know God's will for our lives, we should follow, to the best of our ability, the will He's already revealed to us. If we aren't living in obedience to what He's revealed, then we shouldn't be surprised when His voice is silent, and no further light is given. See Isaiah 8:20; John 7:17; John 9:31.

Let's pause a moment and talk about the revealed will of God. Scripture shares the following:

- First, the Bible tells us it is God's will that we be saved (2 Pet 3:9). Have you confessed and repented of your sins, and are you currently living in a saving relationship with Jesus? Are you allowing Jesus to be Savior *and* LORD of your life? *If your answer is "Yes," you are living according to the revealed will of God in this area.*
- The Bible tells us that it is God's will that we be filled with the Spirit (Eph 5:18). When one is filled with the Spirit, they are controlled by the Spirit. The fruit of the Spirit is evident in their life (Gal 5:22-23). They are also listening and in tune with God's still small voice. They seek to honor and obey God's Word. Are you asking for the daily baptism of the Holy Spirit? Are you seeking to honor God and His Word to the best of your ability? *If your answer is "Yes," you are living according to the revealed will of God in this area.*
- The Bible tells us that it is God's will that we be sanctified (1 Thess 4:3-4). This doesn't mean we suddenly become perfect, mature believers who never sin or make any mistakes, but we should be daily growing. As professed followers of Jesus, the general trend

of our life should be headed heavenward, and there should be a decided difference between where we were (without Christ) and where we are now (in Christ). When we sin or fail, which we will do, we repent, get back up, and surrender to God again (Prov 4:18-23). *If you are surrendering to the sanctification process, and daily seeking to become more like Jesus, you are living according to the revealed will of God in this area.*

- The Bible tells us that it is God's will that we be submissive (1 Pet 2:13-16). It's hard to hear direction from God when we are dishonoring our parents, our family members, our teachers, our boss at work, or governmental authorities. It's especially difficult to hear God's voice when we are dishonoring God Himself. *If you are living with a submissive, humble spirit towards those in authority, and especially toward God as the highest authority, you are living according to His revealed will.* (Note: If someone ever asks us to do something that conflicts with God's Word, God's Word always has the final say—see Acts 5:29.)
- Last but not least, the Bible tells us that it is God's will we live up to the light He has revealed. In other words, if He's asked us to do something, and we refuse to do it, or we are living in sin, we can't expect Him to give us further directions until we follow the ones He's already given (see James 4:17; 1 Pet 4:17).

Let me share a very practical example when it comes to relationships and romance—an example that unfortunately happens all too often.

A Tragic Tale of Misguided Will

Let's say that a woman named Joanne has grown up in a Christian home. She's had a Christian education, and she knows God's Word. She has been taught all her life that Christians are only to marry fellow believers, and that sex is to be saved until marriage.

One day, a tall, good-looking Prince Charming named Jarod comes along on his white horse and sweeps her off her feet. While Joanne knows she probably shouldn't date Jarod, as she can't marry him (according to biblical principles), she agrees to date anyway because she's lonely, and after all, he's wonderful.

While she remembers that the Bible says, "Do not be unequally yoked together with unbelievers. For what fellowship has righteousness with lawlessness? And what communion has light with darkness?" (2 Cor 6:14), she disregards this clear warning.

As time goes on, the couple grows closer. While Jarod is not a believer, and holds no profession of faith, Joanne continues to rationalize this red flag and others away because of the many other positive qualities she sees. Jarod is kind, he has a job, he doesn't drink or smoke, he's attractive, and they both love doing outdoor activities together. While Jarod doesn't want to go to church with her, and isn't really interested in God, he seems to be respectful of her beliefs, so Joanne allows herself to fall more and more in love. (Remember, things that fall usually break!) Loved ones try to warn her that this relationship isn't according to God's plan, but she ignores their counsel.

A few months into their relationship, when Jarod asks Joanne to marry him, she says an enthusiastic yes. Before long they are sleeping together, which she knows also goes against God's Word. However, since they are already planning their wedding, Joanne again rationalizes her concerns away as she tells herself, "It's okay. After all, we are going to get married anyway, and God wants me to be happy. I'm sure He understands."

Then a difficult decision faces them. While Jarod starts stressing about the future, Joanne turns to her faith.

"Dear God," she prays, "Please show us which direction we should go with this difficult situation. I don't know what to do!"

But God doesn't seem to be giving any clear answers. He is silent, and the young bride-to-be is in despair, as she thinks to herself, *What is wrong? Why won't God tell me His will? Why won't He show us what to do?*

Of course, the above is all just a made-up, imaginary story, but I'm afraid that this very scenario has too often been the reality for many.

Ellen White wrote some sobering words. "When God is not thought of and reverenced, when He is not chosen as their counselor and their strong tower of defense, how soon secular thoughts and wicked unbelief come in, and vain confidence and philosophy take the place of humble, trusting faith. Often temptations are cherished as the voice of the True Shepherd because men [and women] have separated themselves from Jesus" (*Testimonies*, vol. 5, p. 426).

Here's the take-away summary thought:

If we desire to find and know God's will, we should follow, to the best of our ability, the will He's already revealed to us through His Word. When we live up to the light we have, He always gives us more light.

If you are struggling to know the will of God about a situation in your life, perhaps a special 24-hour retreat away with Jesus would be a good idea for you. See Appendix 3.

APPENDIX 3

A Personal Retreat – 24 hours Alone with God

By Don MacLafferty

"Be still, and know that I am God; I will be exalted among the nations, I will be exalted in the earth!" Psalm 46:10

Why would you want to go on a personal retreat with God?

- To jumpstart and refresh your spiritual focus
- To experience more of God and find out what is on His heart
- To come apart from your busy life and enjoy spiritual peace and rest
- To review how God has provided for you in the past
- To pray for wisdom, guidance, and clarity for the future
- To receive fresh, God-given perspective on your life's roles
- To discover God's agenda for your current circumstances
- To enjoy unrushed communion in prayer and time in the Word

- To engage in Holy Spirit-led planning for life or ministry

Often we make plans and then ask God to bless them, when we should seek God's agenda and His heart first, *then* ask His blessing on our plans.

What Can You Do to Prepare?

- **Environment.** Choose a distraction-free environment that is safe and quiet, and out in nature. If budget allows, rent a motel room or cabin near a state park, or stay in someone's vacant guest house. If you are a man, perhaps you might even want to camp. Before you set out, notify loved ones where you are going and let them know your phone will be off, but you will check in with them at designated times. Plan to be away for two parts of a day with a night in between, if possible.

  Note: If you are a single women with safety concerns, it might be best to have a buddy system, and go with another female friend for this 24-hour getaway. Meet with God separately and guard each other's personal time (so it doesn't just turn into a "girlfriend gab session"). Have regular check-ins while you are out in nature. Don't be too far apart and carry a whistle, and maybe even pepper spray, in case of emergency.

- **Prayer Partners.** Ask the treasured people in your life to intercede for you during your retreat. You may want to pick a prayer partner whom you can get together with afterward to debrief your experience. Choose someone of your same gender who is faithful to God and knows God's Word. Get their honest feedback on your experience.

- **Food.** Bring your food and water with you. Do not go out to eat in a restaurant. Free yourself of all distractions. Eat simply. Avoid excessive sweets and oils. Eat basic fruits, nuts, grains, and vegetables. Maybe even consider fasting during this time.

- **Media.** It's especially helpful to fast from all media. Turn off the noise. Even recorded music can distract. Let your focus be on God and Him alone. This retreat is a time for you to get away from all outside influences, clutter, and distractions, and hear what's on God's heart. It's also time for Him to hear what is on yours.

- **Materials.** A Bible and a journal. If you keep a prayer journal, bring it to reflect on what God is doing in your life. If you do not keep a journal, take one to record your reflections and the ideas that God brings to your mind. Also bring some pens, pencils, and Bible highlighters.
- **Additional Items.** A camping chair, a hammock, or a blanket. Appropriate clothes to stay warm or avoid sunburn. Tissue, bug spray, pepper spray, a whistle. Most of all, make sure you bring an open and expectant heart.

How Can You Make this Retreat Meaningful?

- **Be still.** Slow down from your busy pace. Hike. Take time to just be still in His presence. This may take an hour or two. If you have a long drive to your destination, that may be your slow down time. Let go of business and pressures. Make yourself available to God. Tell Him you are available. Ask Him, "What's on your heart? What do you want to tell me during this time together?" (See Ps 46:10.)
- **Praise.** Spend time praising God for Who He is and celebrate what He's presently doing in your life. Note the times over the past year(s) that God has provided for you, blessed you, and encouraged you. Sing your praise to God. You do not need a great voice. God enjoys hearing the voice He gave you! (See Ps 92:1, 2.)
- **Confess.** Make things right with God. Surrender your attitude, desires, and heart to Him. You may need to make a quick call to someone you have wronged to clear the slate. If this is needed, do so. Then, go into the rest of the retreat feeling good and restful in spirit. Rejoice in the fact that God has forgiven you. (See Zeph 3:17.)
- **Feed your mind.** After you've made things right with God, spend time in the Bible. This is God's Word to you. Read His promises

and personalize them by adding your name. Reflect on stories of Bible characters of great faith. Here are a few options for promises and stories to study and reflect on in God's Word.

- Ephesians 3:20-21
- Jeremiah 33:3
- Philippians 4:13, 19
- James 1:5; James 4:2
- 2 Corinthians 9:6-11; Luke 6:38
- Ecclesiastes 11:1
- Romans 8; Psalm 91; 1 Corinthians 13
- Noah – Fearless end-time prophet who took God at His Word
- Joseph – Fierce loyalty to God in the midst of darkness and injustice
- Job – Faithful during great adversity and loss
- Ruth – Devotion, investing in relationships, love story
- Nehemiah – Building what others said could not be built
- Esther – One who seized the day for God
- Daniel – Integrity, strategic influence for God's purposes
- Elijah – Faced a showdown with God's strength
- Elisha – Surrounded by a great army of heavenly chariots
- Paul – Bold pioneer for the Good News of Christ
- Philip – Following the Holy Spirit to "barren" places

Reflect on Life Roles and Relationship Priorities

- List your life roles. (Examples: disciple of Christ, son, daughter, spouse, parent, grandparent, uncle, aunt, neighborhood friend, leader, coach, etc.)
- Concentrate on your top 4-8 roles.

- Review your roles with God and what is happening in these roles right now.
- Ask God what you can celebrate.
- Ask God what He thinks needs to change.
- Ask God which one or two things you need to change or do in each role to be faithful to what He has entrusted to you. God has a vision for the roles He has entrusted to you, so ask Him.

Listen, Plan, Pray

- Take breaks to hike, to listen for the Holy Spirit's voice, and to pray.
- Jot down reflections on what God brings to your mind. Sleep on it.
- Spread out your reflections and convictions before God. Ask God: "This is what I am seeing - am I understanding what You want me to see?"
- Review and add to what you have. Let God's wisdom on your life roles impact the way you accept or reject the opportunities before you. Perhaps you need to say "No" to some good things in your life, so you can say "Yes" to the best things in life—the things God is asking you to prioritize and focus on.
- Are the life decisions you are making helping you be more or less faithful to the roles God has entrusted to you? How should these decisions change? Always test the insights you receive with the written Word of God.
- **Claim God's promises to accomplish His will.** Thank Him. (See Prov 2:6-7.)
- **Debrief with one of the prayer partners who prayed for you while you were on your retreat**. Share how God blessed you. Share what God is asking of you in your life roles for the coming year. Invite honest feedback. Ask him/her to pray that you will follow through with God's leading in your life.

APPENDIX 4

Biblical Steps to Freedom in Jesus

"What then shall we say to these things? If God is for us, who can be against us?... Yet in all these things we are more than conquerors through Him who loved us." Romans 8:31, 37

Do you long to have spiritual victory in your life? Are you discouraged because you keep failing? Take heart! God's Word tells us, "The things which are impossible with men are possible with God" (Luke 18:27).

My favorite Christian author once said, "The very first work for us to do individually is to put ourselves into the Lord's hands, giving ourselves to Him as willing and ready to do anything He sets before us, not in our way, or according to our plans, but in His way."

Then Jesus said to his disciples, "If anyone desires to come after Me, let him deny himself, and take up his cross, and follow Me" (Matt 16:24).

Prayerfully follow these Biblical steps, as you ask God for freedom and victory in Jesus.

1. **Receive Jesus' unconditional love.** No matter where you are, no matter your failures or sins, remember that God chose you, He loves you, and He was willing to empty all heaven on your behalf. You are of infinite value in His eyes. Ask Him to overwhelm your heart with His great love. Read Romans 5:8; Deuteronomy 7:6-7; Romans 8:38-39; Ephesians 1:4.

2. **Humbly tell God about your specific sin and ask His forgiveness.** Yes, He already knows, but speaking it is like saying, "God, I finally get it! I agree with You! This is wrong!" (Ps 51 gives an excellent model of a prayer you can pray as you seek cleansing and forgiveness.) It's only when we acknowledge the sin and ask Him to wash us clean, based on the merits of His shed blood, that the cleansing can really take place. Accept the forgiveness He freely offers, claiming 1 John 1:9.

3. **Turn and walk a new way.** Don't play with sin anymore. Make a complete about face! Surrender your will to God (it's a daily choice), and through the power of the Holy Spirit, walk a new direction, away from sin. "He who covers his sins will not prosper, but whoever confesses and forsakes them will have mercy" (Prov 28:13).

4. **Obey what God leads you to do.** Don't delay! As I've heard Elisabeth Elliot say, "A whole lot of what we call 'struggling' is just a nice word for 'postponed obedience.'"

5. **Avoid presumption and triggers like the plague.** If you flirt with sin, you are sure to fall. You may think, "Yeah, I know that this (circumstance, these people, this situation, this place, this action) has been a problem with me in the past, but it is no big deal now. I can handle it." Don't play with fire or place yourself in temptation's pathway. Close the door to triggers for temptation as much as possible. Also, don't confuse faith and presumption. God responds to the prayers of faith for deliverance when you are unintentionally placed in places of temptation. However, when you place yourself into temptation, don't expect God to always save you. Ellen White wrote, "By watchfulness and prayer, [we] may so guard [our] weakest points that they will become [our] strongest points. Through the grace of Christ, [we] may acquire moral stamina, strength of will, and stability of purpose . . . to arise above the alluring, infatuating temptations of Satan, and to become loyal, devoted Christians" (*Gospel Workers*, p. 126).

6. **Live like a child of the King.** Even though you have blown it many times in the past, remember that you are still God's Son/Daughter whom Jesus died for. Live like a child of the King! Satan will try to make you doubt this precious truth. Don't listen to His lies. "For you did not receive the spirit of bondage again to fear, but you received the Spirit of adoption by whom we cry out, 'Abba, Father.' The Spirit Himself bears witness with our spirit that we are children of God, and if children, then heirs—heirs of God and joint heirs with Christ, if indeed we suffer with Him, that we may also be glorified together" (Rom 8:15-17).

7. **Ask Jesus to face your temptations for you.** Don't open the door or attempt to face temptation in your own strength. Jesus lives inside of you, via faith. Send Jesus to answer temptation's door. Allow Him to be your victory. "To them God willed to make known what are the riches of the glory of this mystery among the Gentiles: which is Christ in you, the hope of glory. Him we preach, warning every man and teaching every man in all wisdom, that we may present every man perfect in Christ Jesus" (Col 1:27-28).

8. **When you fall, run back to Jesus.** When you slip up or fall into sin again, the tempter will taunt you, reminding you that you are a guilty sinner, and urging that you just give up and stop trying. But the Spirit of God says, "Keep running back to Jesus. Claim His forgiveness and move forward again by His power." Remember, He came into this world not to save the righteous, but to save sinners like you and me. See 1 Timothy 1:15; Mark 2:17; 1 John 3:20; Ephesians 5:8; 2 Corinthians 4:6-9.

9. **Live by the power of the Word.** Ask God to fulfill His promises and give you victory. Jesus conquered His enemy by the words, "It is written." We can too! Claim the promises of Ezekiel 36:24-36, until you have complete victory. Declare, like Jacob when wrestling with the angel, "I will not let You go, Lord, except you bless me!" Remember, overcoming is not a matter of self-discipline, self-control, will-power or grit. If you depend on these alone, you will always fail. Jesus alone is your victory.

10. **Start thanking God before you see the fulfillment of His promise.** This is one of the most important things you can do. Praise and thank God before you even see His blessing! "But thanks be to God, who gives us the victory through our Lord Jesus Christ" (1 Cor 15:57).

> "For the pardon of sin, for the Holy Spirit, for a Christlike temper, for wisdom and strength to do His work, for any gift He has promised, we may ask; then we are to believe that we receive and return thanks to God that we have received. We need look for no outward evidence of the blessing. The gift is in the promise, and we may go about our work assured that what God has promised He is able to perform, and that the gift, which we already possess, will be realized when we need it most" (*Education*, p. 258).

Important note: These steps are not just done once, but every time you face a temptation or feel like you are losing control, go through the steps again. God promises deliverance. (See Jude 1:24.)

As you praise God for giving you victory, and a renewed heart and mind, consider the following thoughts. There is power in God's Word!

> "The prince of this world cometh," said Jesus, "and hath nothing in Me." John 14:30. There was in Him nothing that responded to Satan's sophistry. He did not consent to sin. Not even by a thought did He yield to temptation. So it may be with us. Christ's humanity was united with divinity; He was fitted for the conflict by the indwelling of the Holy Spirit. And He came to make us partakers of the divine nature . . . By what means did [Jesus] overcome in the conflict with Satan? By the word of God. Only by the word could He resist temptation. "It is written," He said. And unto us are given "exceeding great and precious promises: that by these ye might be partakers of the divine nature, having escaped the corruption that is in the world through lust." 2 Peter 1:4. Every promise in God's Word is ours. "By every word that proceedeth out of the mouth of God" are we to live. When assailed by temptation, look not to circumstances or to the weakness of self, but to the power of the word. All its strength

> is yours. "Thy word," says the psalmist, "have I hid in mine heart, that I might not sin against Thee." "By the word of Thy lips I have kept me from the paths of the destroyer." Psalm 119:11; 17:4 (*Desire of Ages*, p. 123).

No matter what you are struggling with, remember, Jesus wants to give you newness of life, and He will. Praise Him with joy for what He's about to do.

"Therefore we were buried with Him through baptism into death, that just as Christ was raised from the dead by the glory of the Father, even so we also should walk in newness of life" (Rom 6:4).

APPENDIX 5

Reading Recommendations and Songs for the Night

(As you go deeper and prepare for love)

"Finally, brethren, whatever things are true, whatever things are noble, whatever things are just, whatever things are pure, whatever things are lovely, whatever things are of good report, if there is any virtue and if there is anything praiseworthy, meditate on these things" Philippians 4:8.

I've heard it said that the person you will be in five years depends largely on the books you read, the people you spend time with, the things you watch, the music you listen to, the food you eat, the habits you adopt, and the conversations you engage in today. Choose wisely!

I'm a big reader and lover of books. I also love having and cultivating quality relationships. *I don't just want mediocre.* That's why I prayerfully recommend the following resources. These aren't just good reading suggestions—these are life-changing books. If you take time to read any of these, you will be blessed.

Books about Trusting God in Suffering

- *A Fresh Look at Fear: Encountering Jesus in our Weakness* – Dan Baumann

- *Be Still My Soul* – Elisabeth Elliot
- *Count it All Joy* – Helen Roseveare
- *Heaven Rules* – Nancy DeMoss Wolgemuth
- *Suffering Is Never for Nothing* – Elisabeth Elliot
- *Suffering: Gospel Hope When Life Doesn't Make Sense* – Paul Tripp
- *Streams in the Desert* – L.B. Cowman
- *The Scars That Have Shaped Me* – Vaneeth Rendall Risner
- *When God Doesn't Fix It* – Laura Story
- *With God in Solitary Confinement* – Richard Wurmbrand
- *You Can Trust God to Write Your Story* – Nancy DeMoss Wolgemuth

Books on Going Deeper with God

- *31 Days to Trusting God* – Jerry Bridges
- *Continuous Revival: The Secret to Victorious Living* – Norman Grubb
- *Daring to Ask for More* – Melody Mason
- *Daring to Live by Every Word* – Melody Mason
- *Discipline: The Glad Surrender* – Elisabeth Elliot
- *From Pigpen to Salvation* – Frank Fournier
- *God Still Lives* – Don MacLafferty
- *Heart Lift: Experiencing God's Freedom* – Jill Morikone
- *Home at Last* – Walton J. Brown
- *Humility: The Beauty of Holiness* – Andrew Murray
- *Hudson Taylor's Spiritual Secret* – Dr. & Mrs. Howard Taylor
- *Incomparable: 50 Days with Jesus* – Nancy DeMoss Wolgemuth
- *In the Spirit and in Power* – Pavel Goia

- *Kept for the Master's Use* – Frances Ridley Havergal
- *Live Like Elijah* – Don MacLafferty
- *Living the Life of Enoch* – Ellen White
- *Steps to Christ* – Ellen White
- *The Coming of the Comforter* – LeRoy Froom
- *The Desire of Ages* – Ellen White
- *The Only Hope* – Feliz A. Lorenz
- *They Found the Secret* – V. Raymond Edman

Books for Preparing for an Amazing Love Story

- *101 Questions to Ask Before You Get Engaged* – H. Norman Wright
- *And the Bride Wore White: Seven Secrets to Sexual Purity* – Dannah Gresh
- *Did I Kiss Marriage Goodbye* – by Carolyn McCulley
- *Finding the Love of Your Life: Ten Principles for Choosing the Right Marriage Partner* – Neil Clark Warren
- *Lady in Waiting* – Debbie Jones and Jackie Kendall
- *Letters to Young Lovers* – Ellen White
- *Passion and Purity* – Elisabeth Elliot
- *Preparing for Marriage* – John Piper
- *Quest for Love* – Elisabeth Elliot
- *Sacred Singleness* – Leslie Ludy
- *Singled Out for Him* – Nancy DeMoss Wolgemuth
- *The Lost Art of True Beauty* – Leslie Ludy
- *The Mark of a Man: Following Christ's Example of Masculinity* – Elisabeth Elliot

- *When Dreams Come True* – Eric and Leslie Ludy
- *When God Writes Your Love Story* – Eric and Leslie Ludy

Books for Breathing Fresh Life and Hope into Your Marriage

- *Come Home* – Don MacLafferty
- *Courtship After Marriage* – Zig Ziglar
- *His Needs/Her Needs* – Willard Harley
- *Love and Respect* – Emerson Eggerichs
- *Married Friends, Married Lovers* – Steve and Annie Chapman
- *Marriage on the Rock* – Jimmy Evans
- *Pray Big: God Can Do So Much More* – Cindy Mercer
- *The First Ninety Days of Marriage* – Eric and Leslie Ludy
- *The Five Love Languages* – Gary Chapman
- *The Power of a Praying Wife* – Stormie Omartian

Songs for the Night Seasons

The following songs come from a variety of musical artists and talent. Some are from albums you can purchase on iTunes and others are from YouTube videos. Whatever your musical taste, I pray the heartfelt messages in these songs will point you to Jesus and be a blessing as they have been to me.

- "All Along" – Sung by Marleta Fong
- "All Things" – Sung by Buddy Houghtaling
- "Always Good" – Sung by Andrew Peterson
- "Amazing Grace" – Sung by *Maranatha* (2012 Edition)
- "Be Still My Soul" – Sung by *Libera* or *Selah*
- "Bend Your Knee" – Sung by Laura Williams

- "Blessings" – Sung by Laura Story
- "Bow the Knee" - Sung by Chris Machen
- "Create in Me a Pure Heart" – Sung by Vonda Beerman
- "Consider the Lillies" – Sung by Charlotte Ritchie
- "Crown Him" – Sung by the Nebblett Family
- "Family Reunion" – Sung by Buddy Houghtaling
- "Far Beyond" – Sung by Eric & Leslie Ludy
- "Give Me Jesus" – Sung by Marleta Fong
- "Gratitude" – Sung by the Nebblett Family
- "God Alone" – Sung by the Nebblett Family
- "Goodness of God" – Sung by *The Asidors*
- "He Already Sees the Rainbow" – Sung by the Collingsworth Family
- "He Giveth More Grace" – Sung by the *Living Stones Quartet*
- "He Is Exalted" – Sung by *Sounds Like Reign*
- "Here I Am, Lord" – Sung by Collin Raye
- "His Strength is Perfect" – Sung by Ingrid DuMosch
- "How Deep the Father's Love" – Sung by the Nebblett Family
- "I Believe" – Arranged by Sara Lyn Baril
- "I Look to You" – Sung by Marletta Fong
- "I Love Living in Love with Jesus" – Sung by the Collingsworth Family
- "I Surrender" – Sung by Leslie Ludy
- "I Will Wait" – Sung by Katie M. Peters
- "I Want Jesus in Your Heart" – Sung by Dianne Wedge Wirtz
- "If He Hung the Moon" – Sung by the Collingsworth Family

- "In Christ Alone" – Sung by Keith & Kristyn Getty
- "In the Lord's Time" – Arranged by Sara Lyn Baril
- "Is He Worthy?" – Sung by Andrew Peterson
- "It Matters to the Master" – Sung by the Collingsworth Family
- "Jesus King of Angels" – Sung by Fernando Ortega
- "Joy Is Not Cancelled" – Sung by Kim Collingsworth
- "Learning to Lean" – Sung by Marleta Fong
- "Least I Can Do" – Sung by *The Ball Brothers*
- "Let Me Introduce You to Jesus" – Sung by *3 Heath Brothers*
- "Lord Keep Me in Your Will" – Sung by Marletta Fong
- "Middle of the Storm" – Sung by the Clark Family
- "Miracles for Me" – Arranged by Sara Lyn Baril
- "My Redeemer is Faithful and True" – Sung by the Nebblett Family
- "No More Night" – Sung by David Phelps
- "Nothing is Impossible" – Sung by the *Living Stones Quartet*
- "O Come, All You Unfaithful" – Sung by *Sovereign Grace Music*
- "Praise You in This Storm" – Sung by Melody Joy Williams
- "Press On" – Sung by *Selah*
- "Press On" – Sung by Keith & Kristyn Getty
- "Redeemer of the Rain" – Sung by Sharlenae Collingsworth
- "River of Joy" – Sung by the Nebblett Family
- "Songs of Suffering" – Songs and message by Joni Eareckson Tada
- "Sometimes He Calms the Storm" – sung by *The Ball Brothers*
- "Stand" – Sung by the Clark Family
- "Stand Still" – Sung by *Pictures of Grace*

- "The Final Call/I Will Hold Your Hand" – Sung by Noah, Deanna & Thea Mañez
- "The Healing Hand" – Arranged by Sara Lyn Baril
- "The Midnight Cry" – Sung by the Neblett Family
- "Turn Your Eyes Upon Jesus" – Sung by the Wissmann Family
- "Two Or Three" – Sung by the Collingsworth Family
- "When I Wake Up in the Morning" – Sung by the Nebblett Family
- "Will You Love Jesus More" – Sung by Vonda Beerman
- "With All My Heart" – Sung by Babbie Mason
- "Worthy is the Lamb that was Slain" – Sung by the Nebblett Family
- "Yes, I Believe" – Sung by the Clark Family
- "Your Grace Still Amazes Me" – Sung by *Champion Baptist College*
- "Your Ways Are Higher than Mine" – Sung by the Collingsworth Family

As you listen to the songs above, consider the following profound words about the love of God and what we are called to share with the world. May His love comfort our hearts, transform us, and give us fresh joy to share with others.

Ellen White wrote:

> "It is the darkness of misapprehension of God that is enshrouding the world. Men are losing their knowledge of His character. It has been misunderstood and misinterpreted. At this time a message from God is to be proclaimed, a message illuminating in its influence and saving in its power. His character is to be made known. Into the darkness of the world is to be shed the light of His glory, the light of His goodness, mercy, and truth...
>
> "Those who wait for the Bridegroom's coming are to say to the people, 'Behold your God.' The last rays of merciful light, the last message of mercy to be given to the world, is a revelation of His character of love. The children of God are to manifest His glo-

ry. In their own life and character, they are to reveal what the grace of God has done for them.

"But no man can impart that which he himself has not received. In the work of God, humanity can originate nothing. No man can by his own effort make himself a light bearer for God. It was the golden oil emptied by the heavenly messengers into the golden tubes, to be conducted from the golden bowl into the lamps of the sanctuary, that produced a continuous bright and shining light. It is the love of God continually transferred to man that enables him to impart light. Into the hearts of all who are united to God by faith the golden oil of love flows freely, to shine out again in good works, in real, heartfelt service for God . . .

"In the great and measureless gift of the Holy Spirit are contained all of heaven's resources. It is not because of any restriction on the part of God that the riches of His grace do not flow earthward to men. If all were willing to receive, all would become filled with His Spirit. It is the privilege of every soul to be a living channel through which God can communicate to the world the treasures of His grace, the unsearchable riches of Christ. There is nothing that Christ desires so much as agents who will represent to the world His Spirit and character. There is nothing that the world needs so much as the manifestation through humanity of the Saviour's love. All heaven is waiting for channels through which can be poured the holy oil to be a joy and blessing to human hearts" (*Christ Object Lessons*, pp. 415-419).

"No one has seen God at any time. If we love one another, God abides in us, and His love has been perfected in us. By this we know that we abide in Him, and He in us, because He has given us of His Spirit" 1 John 4:12-13.

APPENDIX 6

Who You Are in Christ!

(Remember, you are worth all heaven to Jesus. He couldn't live without you! Let Him give you your identity. You are more than enough in Him!)

You are known!	Jeremiah 1:5
You are loved!	Jeremiah 31:3
You are chosen!	Ephesians 1:4
You are God's child!	1 John 3:1
You are the apple of God's eye!	Zechariah 2:8
You have been bought with a price!	1 Corinthians 6:20
You have been saved by grace!	Ephesians 2:8-9
You have been redeemed!	Psalm 71:23
You are free from condemnation and sin!	Romans 8:1, 2
You are forgiven!	Ephesians 1:7
You are healed!	1 Peter 2:24
You are washed clean!	Isaiah 1:18
You are free from your past!	Galatians 5:1

You are rejoiced over!	Zephaniah 3:17
You are a masterpiece!	Ephesians 2:10
You are fearfully and wonderfully made!	Psalm 139:14
You are a crown of glory in God's hand!	Isaiah 62:3
You are adopted into God's family!	Romans 8:15
You have direct access to God through the Spirit!	Ephesians 2:18
You are a habitation of God through the Spirit!	Ephesians 2:22
You are a new creature in Christ!	2 Corinthians 5:17
You are made righteous in Christ!	2 Corinthians 5:21
You are complete in Christ!	Colossians 2:10
You are perfect in Christ!	Colossians 1:28
You are a bride of Christ!	Isaiah 54:5
You are sanctified!	1 Corinthians 6:11
You are chosen and set apart!	1 Peter 2:9
You are a friend of Christ!	John 15:15
You are an ambassador of Christ!	2 Corinthians 5:20
You are a co-laborer with Christ!	1 Corinthians 3:9
You are a co-heir with Christ!	Romans 8:17
You can do all things through Christ!	Philippians 4:13
You are a minister of reconciliation!	2 Corinthians 5:17-20
You are a branch of the True Vine!	John 15:1, 5
You are enabled to bear fruit!	John 15:16
You have a secure future!	Jeremiah 29:11
You have grace and mercy in time of need!	Hebrews 4:16
You have been given all that you need!	Philippians 4:19
You are a citizen of heaven!	Philippians 3:20
Nothing can separate you from God's love!	Romans 8:35

APPENDIX 7

Thirty Days of Joy

(A Continuing Devotional Journey)

"Therefore with joy you will draw water from the wells of salvation" Isaiah 12:3.

Did you know that more than 150 verses in Scripture mention joy? Here are several of my favorites summarized:

In His presence there is fullness of JOY! (Ps 16:11) God is my exceeding JOY! (Ps 43:4) He makes me to hear JOY and gladness, and He promises that the bones He's broken will yet re-JOY-ce! (Ps 51:8) We might sow in tears, but we will someday reap in JOY! (Ps 126:5) He promises He will make my wilderness like Eden and my dry desert spots like a Garden of the Lord where JOY and gladness will be heard, as well as thanksgiving and the voice of melody. (Isa 51:3) One day, everlasting JOY will be upon our heads (Isa 51:11), and He will re-JOY-ce over you and me with singing! (Zeph 3:17)

For the next thirty days (and beyond), ask God to help the Bible come alive as you spend un-rushed time seeking to understand the true meaning of joy. To make this study most meaningful, cultivate the daily "Back to the Altar" devotional habits shared in Appendix 1. Then meditate on the selected passage on joy as you pray each day,

"Jesus, please help me to find fresh JOY in Your presence today. Help me also find fresh JOY in Your Word."

The following are a few simple tips on how to mediate on a single passage in Scripture.

1. After praying for the Holy Spirit to teach you, read the daily passage.
2. Read it a second time more slowly, highlighting key words or phrases that jump out to you.
3. Ask God what He wants to tell you through the specific passage on joy.
4. Read the passage a third time.
5. Write out the passage in your journal, one word or phrase at a time, with the practical meaning of each word in parenthesis. Focus on making the passage personal to you. See the example below for what it might look like to meditate/reflect/journal/pray over a passage.

Today's passage on joy: Psalm 16:11 – "You will show me the path of life; In Your presence is fullness of joy; At Your right hand are pleasures forevermore."

You – The Lord

will – That's a promise, not a "maybe" or a "might," but a promise—You will

show – Reveal, make clear

me – That's personal. This promise is for ME!

the path – This is a distinct place to walk. It's not off in the brambles, or down in the ditch

of life – This is key to living spiritually, and I want to live spiritually. I don't want to walk the path of death. I want to stay on the path of life.

In – Not outside, not away from, not above or below or beside, but *in* means *in.* I want to be on the inside with You!

Your Presence – Whose presence? Jesus' presence!

is – Not was, but is right now.

fullness – Not partial filling, not just a superficial filling, but fullness

of joy – Pleasure, gladness, deep joy, nothing better, transcends even difficult circumstances

At Your right hand – The right hand and right arm often symbolizes strength and power, so thank You, Jesus, for giving me Your best and strongest gifts and blessings.

are – Not were, but present tense

pleasures – Delightful, beautiful, lovely, tasty

forevermore – They are perpetual, they don't go away. They will last forever!

Example of a journal prayer:

Wow. Thank You Lord, for this amazing promise. If I take time to learn and listen and watch You, You will show me the path to life—not just how to live, but how to thrive with fullness of joy. As I reflect on this passage, I'm reminded that joy does not depend on my circumstances or on anything that is happening to me or around me. Joy depends on staying IN YOUR PRESENCE. When I stay in Your presence, there's always pleasure and joy in my heart, not because life is always going well, but because I serve the King who rules above all and who is the giver of life and life more abundant. Thank you for giving me Your best, deep, abiding joy, from Your strong right hand. Most of all, thank You for giving me Yourself! Help me learn what it means to stay and live in Your presence.

6. Next, follow the "Making it Real" heart challenge, and go wherever God takes you, in the remainder of your time with Him. Bask in His presence. Don't hurry! When you finish your devotions, ask God to help you live what He has shown you today, and every day. Don't forget to share. As they say, "Joy shared is joy multiplied."

Thirty Days of Joy

(The Daily Challenge for a Healthy Joyful Heart)

Day 1 – His joy gives strength

- **The Word:** Nehemiah 8:10
- **Meditate/Reflect/Journal/Pray** over what God shows you.
- **Making it real:** Whose joy is your strength? Jesus' joy is your strength! Thank Him for *His joy* that He gives you. Thank Jesus for being *your Joy*. Thank Him for what makes His joy so much above and beyond what we usually call happiness.

Day 2 – The power of joyful song

- **The Word:** Job 29:13
- **Meditate/Reflect/Journal/Pray** over what God shows you.
- **Making it real:** Singing songs of praise can be an expression of joy! Sing your favorite praise songs to Jesus as part of your worship today.

Day 3 – Finding peace in joy

- **The Word:** Isaiah 55:12
- **Meditate/Reflect/Journal/Pray** over what God shows you.
- **Making it real:** Do you see joy and peace always going together? Why or why not? Which one of these do you have more of? Share your observations about your own joy and peace with Jesus.

Day 4 – Joy chases away sighing and crying

- **The Word:** Isaiah 35:10
- **Meditate/Reflect/Journal/Pray** over what God shows you.

- **Making it real:** What life experiences the past few months have made you sigh or cry? Pour out your heart to Jesus as you give these things to Him in prayer. Leave these things with Him.

Day 5 – Finding joy in gratitude

- **The Word:** Isaiah 51:3
- **Meditate/Reflect/Journal/Pray** over what God shows you.
- **Making it real:** Being thankful leads to joy and joy leads to being thankful! The two go together. Tell God in three minutes what you are thankful for. Find a melody of thanksgiving and go sing to a family member or friend.

Day 6 – A joy that continues for generations

- **The Word:** Isaiah 60:15
- **Meditate/Reflect/Journal/Pray** over what God shows you.
- **Making it real:** How will your joy influence generations that come after you? Tell God what you think about this. Tell Him specific ways you hope the joy you have in Jesus will influence others in the future. Ask Him what is on His heart, and how today you can start leaving a legacy of joy for generations to come. Do you have children in your life? Even nieces, nephews, grandchildren? Take a moment to share with each of them how they bring you joy.

Day 7 – Everlasting joy

- **The Word:** Isaiah 61:7
- **Meditate/Reflect/Journal/Pray** over what God shows you.
- **Making it real:** How can God promise you everlasting joy? Search God's Word for other passages that would support this promise. Claim all the promises you find in prayer.

Day 8 – Joy in the Word

- **The Word:** Jeremiah 15:16
- **Meditate/Reflect/Journal/Pray** over what God shows you.
- **Making it real:** At this time in your life, how much does the Word of God influence your joy? Little? Much? Search God's Word for some good news about God the Father that will fill you with joy. Don't stop searching until you find something sweet to your taste. Tell God what you discovered, then ask Him to make His Word part of your daily diet.

Day 9 – The joy of salvation

- **The Word:** Habakkuk 3:18
- **Meditate/Reflect/Journal/Pray** over what God shows you.
- **Making it real:** Do you have peace about your salvation? Please read the following: Romans 5:8; Revelation 3:20; 1 John 1:9; Ephesians 2:8-9; 1 John 5:13. Ask Jesus to live in your heart as your Lord and Savior. Thank Him for the joy of His personal gift of salvation for you. Rest in His love! Nothing can separate you from His love.

Day 10 – Reasons to have exceeding joy

- **The Word:** Matthew 2:10
- **Meditate/Reflect/Journal/Pray** over what God shows you.
- **Making it real:** The wise men saw the star as the fulfillment of the prophesied Messiah and rejoiced. Search for another prophecy about Jesus that has also been fulfilled. Rejoice with your Father God for the Gift of Jesus!

Day 11 – The joy of discovered treasure

- **The Word:** Matthew 13:44
- **Meditate/Reflect/Journal/Pray** over what God shows you.

- **Making it real:** Read Psalm 119:162; Proverbs 15:6; Isaiah 33:6; and Matthew 6:21. Jesus Christ is your greatest Treasure. List the specific and personal ways He is your Treasure, then find someone to share what you discovered with. Ask God to help you find more treasures of Jesus in His Word that you can share with others!

Day 12 – The joy of serving an awesome God

- **The Word:** Matthew 28:8
- **Meditate/Reflect/Journal/Pray** over what God shows you.
- **Making it real:** The fear mentioned here is more like "AWE." What have you seen God do that fills you with awe for how awesome He is? Tell Him about these things and why this makes you joyful!

Day 13 – The joy of good news.

- **The Word:** Luke 2:10
- **Meditate/Reflect/Journal/Pray** over what God shows you.
- **Making it real:** The good news of Jesus is for ALL people. List categories of people on this planet that may not know the joy of Jesus. Present them to God in prayer and thank Him for offering the joy of Jesus to everyone! Then ask God who He wants you to reach out to today, to share some extra joy. Do a kind deed for a neighbor or find a stranger who needs prayer. Share the good news.

Day 14 – There is joy in heaven

- **The Word:** Luke 15:7
- **Meditate/Reflect/Journal/Pray** over what God shows you.
- **Making it real:** There is a direct relationship between repentance and joy. Ask God what compromises your full commitment to Jesus as Lord. Ask for His grace and power to turn away from

all spiritual compromise and to fully repent. Make the angels of heaven sing for joy. Now rejoice in your God-given freedom, and don't let the enemy rob you of this new-found joy.

Day 15 – The joy that remains

- **The Word:** John 15:11
- **Meditate/Reflect/Journal/Pray** over what God shows you.
- **Making it real:** Make a list of activities that make you happy. How long do each of these activities last? Do you feel sad when they are finished? Ask God for the full joy of Jesus. Thank Him for joy that lasts forever. Carry His joy with you as you go through your day.

Day 16 – The joy no one can take away

- **The Word:** John 16:22
- **Meditate/Reflect/Journal/Pray** over what God shows you.
- **Making it real:** God wants you to have permanent joy in Jesus. Read Hebrews 13:8 and tell God how this promise impacts your joy in Jesus now and for always. The next time the enemy whispers that God has forgotten you, remember Hebrews 13:8. His love does not change!

Day 17 – The joy of asking and receiving

- **The Word:** John 16:24
- **Meditate/Reflect/Journal/Pray** over what God shows you.
- **Making it real:** Read Jeremiah 33:3. How much are you presently asking of God? Ask Him what He longs for you to ask for and receive by faith so that your joy may be full. Then ask and receive!

Day 18 – The joy found in His presence

- **The Word:** Acts 2:28
- **Meditate/Reflect/Journal/Pray** over what God shows you.

- **Making it real:** Read Psalm 16:11 and Matthew 28:20. What is special to you about the presence of Jesus? Tell God your answer.

Day 19 – The joy of the Holy Spirit

- **The Word:** Acts 13:52
- **Meditate/Reflect/Journal/Pray** over what God shows you.
- **Making it real:** You shouldn't be surprised that joy and the Holy Spirit go together! Read Galatians 5:22, 23. How do the other fruits of the Spirit positively impact your joy? Ask God to grow His fruit in you by the power of the Holy Spirit. Thank God for the fruits of the Spirit that He has given you already. Ask Him for the fruits you need.

Day 20 – Joy is more than food

- **The Word:** Romans 14:17
- **Meditate/Reflect/Journal/Pray** over what God shows you.
- **Making it real:** Set aside a meal today and fast. Praise God during the time you would have eaten. Do meals have too much influence over your day? Praise God for WHO HE IS during this fast and thank Him for fulfilling Philippians 4:19 in your life.

Day 21 – The joy of trials

- **The Word:** 2 Corinthians 8:2
- **Meditate/Reflect/Journal/Pray** over what God shows you.
- **Making it real:** What trial or difficulty are you facing right now? Write it on a slip of paper. Write out Luke 1:37 and Philippians 4:13 in big bold letters over your difficulty. Thank God in prayer for Jesus and the strength you find in Him during trials.

Day 22 – The joy of hope

- **The Word:** Romans 15:13
- **Meditate/Reflect/Journal/Pray** over what God shows you.

- **Making it real:** What kind of things are you hoping for? Who is your hope? Ask God what truth in His Word, when you fully believe it, would bring you greater joy, peace, and hope than you've yet experienced. Thank God for this truth. Thank Him again for the Holy Spirit.

Day 23 – The joy of His name

- **The Word:** Psalm 5:11
- **Meditate/Reflect/Journal/Pray** over what God shows you.
- **Making it real:** How has Jesus been your defender? What are some of the different names of Jesus that you love? Watch: *He Is (The Names of God)* by Eric Ludy on YouTube. Read Proverbs 15:23. How can you share one of His names with someone today?

Day 24 – The joy of Holy Spirit baptism

- **The Word:** 1 Thessalonians 1:6
- **Meditate/Reflect/Journal/Pray** over what God shows you.
- **Making it real:** What do you think fills the Holy Spirit with joy? Look for a Bible story where a person's character is transformed by the Holy Spirit. Thank God for the joy of the Holy Spirit and ask for a fresh baptism of the Holy Spirit every day, from this day forward.

Day 25 – The joy that brings purpose in suffering

- **The Word:** Hebrews 12:2
- **Meditate/Reflect/Journal/Pray** over what God shows you.
- **Making it real:** Read Philippians 2:5-11. Ask God to give you the attitude of Christ so that you may have joy in Him, even when you are suffering. List some of the most difficult times in your life. Thank God for how He has been with you through those times. If you can't think of anything, ask Him to show you.

Day 26 – The joy of growth

- **The Word:** James 1:2-4
- **Meditate/Reflect/Journal/Pray** over what God shows you.
- **Making it real:** Read Acts 16:22-25. Find a hymn to sing to God for His faithfulness in the darkest days of your life. Sing it to Him now. Pray right now that God will bring this hymn back to your memory when you are facing your next challenge of faith.

Day 27 – The joy of the unseen glories to come

- **The Word:** 1 Peter 1:8
- **Meditate/Reflect/Journal/Pray** over what God shows you.
- **Making it real:** Read I Thessalonians 4:13-18. Are you weary with the trials of life? Have you lost a loved one to death? Close your eyes and tell Jesus that you believe in Him and in His soon coming. Get down on your knees and worship Him and praise Him for being Faithful and True! Praise Him that He is the Author and Finisher of your faith.

Day 28 – The joy of Eden Restored

- **The Word:** Isaiah 35:1-2
- **Meditate/Reflect/Journal/Pray** over what God shows you.
- **Making it real:** Have you spent too much time living in a desolate, barren wilderness? Read Ezekiel 36:33-36. What does God tell us He can do with a wilderness? How does this bring you joy? Read Isaiah 44:3. Are you thirsty for a deeper walk with Jesus that will continue for the rest of your life?

Day 29 – The joy of walking in truth

- **The Word:** 3 John 1:4
- **Meditate/Reflect/Journal/Pray** over what God shows you.

- **Making it real:** Know that your faith walk brings great joy to the heart of God! Read I John 3:1. Thank God that He calls YOU one of His children. Call up a friend, read them I John 3:1, and remind them that God calls them one of His children too!

Day 30 – The joy of victory in Jesus.

- **The Word:** Jude 24
- **Meditate/Reflect/Journal/Pray** over what God shows you.
- **Making it real:** As you read Jude 24, put your own name in the passage. Then read Titus 3:5-7, again putting your own name in the passage. Praise Jesus for His perfect righteousness that covers your sins. Do you worry about what temptations will come tomorrow? Claim 1 Corinthians 10:13. To learn this passage in song, point your phone's camera at the QR code. Then stand to your feet and sing with joy, as you thank God for His power to bring you victory through Jesus Christ. Rejoice in your Savior, your faultless Righteousness! He loves you, and He's coming soon to take you home!

May this be only the beginning, not the end, of your journey of joy!

ENDNOTES

Introduction

1 Quote by Nancy DeMoss Wolgemuth.

Chapter 1

1 One thing I found particularly helpful in my recovery from depression was Dr. Neil Nedley's Depression and Anxiety Recovery Program. You can learn more here: https://www.nedleyhealth.com/recovery-programs/residential-depression-recovery

2 Ellen G. White, *Testimonies*, vol. 9, p. 286.

3 Grant Colfax Tullar (1869-1950).

4 Ellen G. White, *Thoughts from the Mount of Blessing*, p. 101.

Chapter 2

1 Elisabeth Elliott, *Suffering is Never for Nothing*, p. 9.

2 Quote by Nancy Guthrie on Instagram.

3 Ellen G. White, *The Ministry of Healing*, pp. 473, 474.

Chapter 3

1 For more of Shelly Powell's writing and inspiration, visit: https://www.mounting-withwings.com.

2 Ellen G. White, *Testimonies*, vol. 7, p. 269

3 Ellen G. White, *Gospel Workers*, p. 258

4 Ellen G. White, *Desire of Ages*, p. 301

5 Ellen G. White, *Gospel Workers*, p. 516

Chapter 4

1 Quote by Douglas A. Kamstra in *The Praying Church Idea Book*, p. 16.

2 I'm so thankful for Jerry and Yvonne Eller, Brent and Brenda Palmer, Brian and Karen Holland, and Jerry and Janet Page, who have loved me and believed in me for many years, in some cases even from childhood.

3 The Christian hymn "Be Still, My Soul," was written in German ("Stille meine Wille, dein Jesus hilft siegen") in 1752 by the Lutheran hymnwriter Catharina von Schlegel (1697–1768), and translated into English in 1855 by Jane Laurie Borthwick (1813–1897).

4 To read a precious miracle story of how

God used "Be Still, My Soul" to encourage my journey, read chapter five in my book *Daring to Live by Every Word.*
5 *Singled Out for Him,* pp. 11-12 by Nancy DeMoss Wolgemuth.
6 Read my book *Daring to Ask for More: Divine Keys to Answered Prayer* for the full testimony.
7 Lyrics by Babbie Mason, written 1990. My friend Marisa Ferreira, also a single on her own journey with Jesus, recorded and shared the song with me a few years ago. Her rendition of it is one of my favorites.
8 I had a few days free between speaking appointments in Europe and went to see my dear friend Raluca Ril in Germany. "We are going on a road trip to Switzerland!" she informed me. She took me, without knowing my desires, to the exact places I've always wanted to visit and hike. Only God could have arranged this gift! I will forever cherish this memory. (See photos on book cover!)
9 Quote by Lisa Harper from Instagram.
10 Ellen G. White, *Mind, Character, and Personality,* vol. 2, p. 650.
11 Ellen G. White, *The Ministry of Healing,* p. 472.
12 Ellen G. White, 9LtMs, Lt 65a, 1894, par. 13.
13 Quote by Jon Bloom, Instagram.

Chapter 5

1 Many New Testament scholars believe that Mary Magdalene and Mary of Bethany are the same Mary. Neither was married, both had money, both had the same name, and both were devoted followers of Jesus, but their names are not ever mentioned together.
2 Thank you to Doug Batchelor for the inspiration behind the story of Mary Magdalene.
3 Story based on John 8:1-11.
4 See Matthew 5:28.
5 These lyrics, from the song, "Clear the Stage," were written by Christian songwriter Ross King, who recorded the song in 2002.
6 Inspired by a message given by Pastor Vladimir Savchuk, unknown date. I'm grateful for his messages on purity, which have influenced my life.
7 Ellen G. White, *The Ministry of Healing,* p. 161.
8 Ellen G. White, *Prophets and Kings,* p. 668.
9 Ellen G. White, *Steps to Christ,* p. 52.

Chapter 7

1 To read *Live Like Elijah* or learn more about this Holy Spirit-led ministry, visit: https://indiscipleship.org
2 Emphasis added.
3 Ellen G. White, "The Source of Strength," *Signs of the Times,* October 22, 1896, p. 5

Chapter 8

1 Ellen G. White, *Faith I Live By,* p. 45. (Emphasis added.)
2 Ellen G. White, *The Desire of Ages,* p. 672.
3 Emphasis added.
4 Ellen G. White, *The Desire of Ages,* p. 195.
5 Ellen G. White, *The Ministry of Healing,* p. 105.

Chapter 9

1 Ellen G. White, *The Adventist Home,* p. 44.
2 I thank Pastor Vlad Savchuk for the inspiration behind this section. His insights have been profound and have helped me as I write.
3 Important note: There are times it's not wise to hold on or stay in a relationship, or even a marriage. There are times it's best to move on and let go. I'm not delving into those deeper topics in this book, or to the biblical or unbiblical reasons for separation or divorce. I'm just referring to the shallowness with which the modern culture often views the meaning of "true love."
4 Ellen G. White, *The Adventist Home,* p. 43.
5 Elisabeth Elliot, *Quest for Love,* pp. 28-30.
6 Elisabeth Elliot, *Quest for Love,* p. 32.
7 Ellen G. White, *Counsels for the Church,* p. 198.
8 Elisabeth Elliot, *Quest for Love,* p. 35.
9 Ellen G. White, *Our High Calling,* p. 318.

Chapter 10

1 Ellen G. White, *Patriarchs and Prophets,* p. 46.
2 Ellen G. White, *Patriarchs and Prophets,* p. 53.
3 Ellen G. White, *Patriarchs and Prophets,* p. 56.
4 https://www.myhoustondivorce.lawyer/christian-divorce/rates/Accessed February 24, 2024.
5 Emphasis added.
6 Ellen G. White, *Testimonies,* vol. 4, p. 616.
7 Elisabeth Elliot, *Quest for Love,* p. 147.
8 Elisabeth Elliot, *Quest for Love,* p. 82.
9 Lettie Coeman, *Streams in the Desert,* p. 91.
10 Ellen G. White, *Patriarchs and Prophets,* p. 145.
11 Quote by Dr. Jowett, source unknown.
12 Quote by Mark Finley.
13 Elisabeth Elliot, *Quest for Love,* p. 168.
14 Quote by Nancy Wolgemuth.

Chapter 11

1 Ellen G. White, *The Ministry of Healing,* p. 359.
2 Ellen G. White, *The Ministry of Healing,* p. 358.
3 Author unknown.
4 NEWSTART is an acronym developed by Weimar University. The word stands for Nutrition, Exercise, Water, Sunshine, Temperance, Air, Rest, and Trust in Divine Power. When these eight health principles are combined, they help us live a balanced, healthy lifestyle.
5 Ellen G. White, *The Ministry of Healing,* p. 357.
6 Ellen G. White, *Education,* p. 57.
7 Taken from Nancy DeMoss Wolgemuth's "The Marks of a True Woman." Adapted slightly and used with permission. Copyright *Revive Our Hearts,* www.ReviveOurHearts.com.
8 Ellen G. White, *The Ministry of Healing,* p. 359.
9 Ellen G. White, *Early Writings,* p. 119.
10 Ellen G. White, *Gospel Workers,* p. 475. Emphasis added.
11 For a deeper picture on what it means to be truly humble, read Appendix 1—The Humility "Heart Challenge," in the back of my second book, *Daring to Live by Every Word.*
12 Ellen G. White, *The Adventist Home,* p. 51.
13 Neil Clark Warren, *Finding the Love of Your Life,* p. 97.
14 Neil Clark Warren, *Finding the Love of Your Life,* p. 98.
15 Neil Clark Warren, *Finding the Love of Your Life,* p. 99.
16 Neil Clark Warren, *Falling in Love For All the Right Reasons,* p. 140.
17 Neil Clark Warren, *Falling in Love For All the Right Reasons,* p. 53.
18 This first seven in this list was inspired by Neil Clark Warren, from *Finding the Love of Your Life,* p. 161. I have adapted and added to his suggestions.
19 I thank YouTube blogger Mat Boggs for some of the inspiration behind this section.
20 Ellen G. White, *The Adventist Home,* pp. 43-45.
21 Elisabeth Elliot, *Quest for Love,* p. 141.
22 Ellen G. White, *The Ministry of Healing,* p. 360.
23 Ellen G. White, *The Ministry of Healing,* p. 359.
24 Ellen G. White, *Thoughts from the Mount of Blessing,* p. 64.

Chapter 12

1 Quote by Oswald J. Smith.
2 This testimony was compiled from various Facebook posts, as well as an Adventist Frontier Missions testimony by Leonda George.
3 Ellen G. White, *Christ's Object Lessons*, p. 412.
4 Ellen G. White, Lt 244, 1908, par. 3.
5 Quote by Charles Spurgeon.
6 Hear Helen Roseveare's full testimony on YouTube. Look for "Where's God in suffering? - Helen Roseveare's story."
7 https://pastortroyequips.wordpress.com/2024/04/28/grieving-with-hope/ accessed May 1, 2024.
8 C.S. Lewis, *The Problem of Pain*, p. 91.
9 I'm grateful to Gayle for sharing her testimony and poem with me personally so I could share it in this chapter. I believe her story will encourage many. Even when our hearts have been broken, God can still bring beauty out of ashes.
10 See Romans 12:1.

Chapter 13

1 My testimony "Growing Above and Beyond Faith, Even When God is Silent" can be seen multiple places on YouTube or listened to on AudioVerse. However, this book contains the most up-to-date and complete testimony as of 2024.
2 *God Still Lives* by Don MacLafferty is available for free download at: https://www.backtothealtar.org/archives/resource/god-still-lives-ebook
3 Ellen G. White, *The Desire of Ages*, p. 347, italics added for emphasis.
4 Ellen G. White, *The Ministry of Healing*, p. 417.
5 Ellen G. White, *Acts of the Apostles*, p. 465.
6 Ellen G. White, *4LtMs*, Ms 28, 1886, par. 13.

Chapter 14

1 My personal paraphrase of 2 Corinthians 4:16.
2 Emphasis added.
3 We took my mom to Hope4Cancer in Cancun, Mexico. We could never have afforded such treatment, but many who have been touched by my parent's lives sacrificially donated funds to help. It was God's miracle. Hope4Cancer, as well as time at Eden Valley, helped my mom experience remission for six years. We are forever grateful for all who have been part of blessing us during her cancer journey.
4 Thank you, Fawna Eller Sutton, for not being afraid to be the hands and feet of Jesus during my Covid crisis. Thank you for not being afraid to touch me with His love. Thank you for all you and Jeff and your entire Sutton and Eller family continue to do, to share Jesus with the world in need. I love you all!
5 Ellen G. White, *The Great Controversy*, p. 621.
6 Lyrics written by Kim Collingsworth and shared with permission. To hear the song and watch the story behind the song, visit this link: https://youtu.be/YUUQjAj9b6o
7 Ellen G. White, *The Desire of Ages*, p. 224.
8 Ellen G. White, "To the Saints scattered abroad," *Review and Herald*, February 17, 1853, p. 156.
9 I am thankful to Pastor Don MacLafferty for his help with this beautiful definition of joy.